PERSPECTIVES ON MORALITY
Essays by William K. Frankena

Perspectives
on Morality
Essays by William K. Frankena

EDITED BY

K. E. Goodpaster

UNIVERSITY OF NOTRE DAME PRESS
NOTRE DAME   LONDON

We wish to thank Alfred A. Knopf, Inc., for permission to reprint
excerpts from H. D. Aiken, *Reason and Conduct,* copyright
©1962 by Alfred A. Knopf, Inc., and Wallace Stevens, "Sketch of
the Ultimate Politician" in *Collected Poems,* copyright ©1954
by Alfred A. Knopf, Inc., New York.

Library of Congress Cataloging in Publication Data

Frankena, William K
  Perspectives on morality.

  Bibliography: p.
  Includes index.
  1. Ethics — Addresses, essays, lectures. I. Ti-
tle.
BJ1012.F73   170   76-646
ISBN 0-268-01519-8
ISBN 0-268-01520-1 pbk.

Manufactured in the United States of America

Contents

To Harriet and Sadie

Introduction

THE PROJECT OF EDITING AND INTRODUCING A COLLECTION OF ESSAYS by one person, when that person is a) not oneself, and b) very much alive and philosophically active, is a difficult one. The difficulty stems from its being unusual and from certain apprehensions which naturally attend interpreting one's teachers in their presence.

That W. K. Frankena's rather widely scattered published essays should be brought together in a central place (at least a selection of the main ones) has never seemed doubtful to anyone with whom I have spoken — with the predictable exception of Frankena himself. While respecting his judgment on so many topics, I found myself opposed on this one. The compromise was easy, and for students of twentieth century ethics, fortunate.

The essays have been chosen with attention to three different goals:

1) to provide something of a chronological perspective on Frankena's moral philosophical development;
2) to provide a relatively broad sampling of his range of interests; and
3) to make available to a wider audience several papers which have been published in less easily accessible places.

The retrospective remarks in the "Postscript" essay should, in addition, be of great help for understanding Frankena's current views as they relate to his earlier work.

It would be ludicrous, if not impossible, in a short introduction of this sort, to attempt anything like a systematic analysis of Frankena's published work. Besides, such an undertaking would overlook his most recent and ongoing work. Several observations, however, might profitably be made to highlight the originality of his views in the context of the Anglo-American conversation over the past four decades. It is this originality, in my opinion, which has earned him a role of "philosophers' philosopher" — and the highest respect of his colleagues and readers.

II

A great deal of Frankena's most original work falls into two standard categories, and in what follows, I shall attempt briefly to elaborate on his contributions in each. The categories are:

(A) metaethics — analytical criticism of dominant views about the meaning and justification of moral concepts and judgments, together with the development, if necessary, of a viable alternative view, and

(B) normative ethics — criticism of the major normative views, together with the development, if necessary, of a viable alternative view.

Much of Frankena's early published work (pre-WWII) was devoted to the first task under (A) above. His first and widely reprinted article, "The Naturalistic Fallacy," emerges in the wake of Moore's intuitionistic attack on naturalism. And it emerges with a clear and potent lesson: the force of the attack is no greater than the force of its premises. The open-question argument is laid out with precision and shown to depend on intuitionists' antecedent commitments to the indefinability of basic ethical concepts (in Moore's case, 'good'). This theme is orchestrated in several other articles during the forties, and complemented by reflections on the relations between 'good' and 'ought'. Significantly, however, Frankena does not, in these early discussions, offer his analytical criticism as a *defense* for either naturalism or the increasingly popular non-cognitivisms of Ayer and Stevenson. One has the impression that somehow each of the mainline metaethical views is, for Frankena, a kind of window on the nature of moral judgment. Each provides a perspective which has merit, yet each is untenable without modification. The project becomes as simple as it is difficult: how to articulate a clear and consistent account of what C. I. Lewis called "the ground and nature of the right" — one that does justice to the demands of cognitivity and action-guidance, autonomy and self-appraisal.

Some clear hints in the direction of Frankena's more considered thoughts on these matters are at work in "Ethical Naturalism Renovated," a quasi-review article published in 1957. In it, Frankena addresses himself critically (and yet sympathetically) to P. B. Rice's *On The Knowledge of Good and Evil* (1955). The suggestions latent in this critique point toward something like a moral sense theory of basic moral principles, non-cognitivism being combined with a non-relativistic, yet non-inferential, source of justification.[1] This approach is taken up again, and more explicitly, in his potent introductory text, *Ethics* (Prentice-Hall, first edition: 1963), and in "On Saying The Ethical Thing" (1966) and " 'Ought' and 'Is' Once More" (1969). Frankena's own summary in the latter article is clearer than any I might devise:

The similarities and dissimilarities of the three positions I have rejected and the nature of the fourth position which I am proposing may be indicated as follows. Consider four propositions:

(1) Judgments of obligation and value (Oughts) are rationally justifiable, objectively valid, etc.

(2) Judgments of obligation and value (Oughts) cannot be logically inferred from factual ones (Ises).

(3) Judgments of obligation and value (Oughts) cannot be rationally justified, objectively valid, etc., unless they can be logically inferred from factual ones (Ises).

(4) Basic judgments of value and obligation are intuitive, self-evident, self-justifying.

The first position affirms (1) and (3) and denies (2) and (4). The second affirms (1), (2) and (4) and denies (3). The third affirms (2) and (3) and denies (1) and (4). . . . The . . . fourth position toward which I have been working . . . asserts (1) and (2) and denies (3) and (4).

Careful reflection on the sophisticated path along which Frankena is here traveling will make it clear, I think, that for him the ground of moral justification lies in a (shared) department of our conative make-up as human beings, call it "the moral point of view," which provides a non-logical warrant for basic ought-judgments in the presence of rationality and relevant factual knowledge. Small wonder then, that the concept of 'morality' should play such an important role in Frankena's more recent work.[2] Small wonder, too, that controversies over the proper characterization of the moral point of view should make us apprehensive about the reemergence of such familiar issues as indefinability — only now in a new context.

In any case, there can be no doubt that Frankena has managed, in a way that few others can claim to have managed, a metaethical synthesis of significant proportions. The kinds of virtues which, as I see it, underlie such success will be touched on in the third section of this introduction.

With respect to normative ethics, Frankena's contributions have also been both original and salutary. Essentially, his method has been to examine critically the major alternative accounts of obligation and value with an eye toward capturing the merits, while avoiding the pitfalls, of each. The result is what might be called a "controlled pluralism," reminiscent of W. D. Ross,[3] in which a principle of beneficence and a procedural principle of equalitarian justice are juxtaposed as basic *prima facie* moral imperatives. Though this position is laid out most concisely in the second edition of *Ethics* (1973), considerable detail on each of the two principles involved can be gleaned from essays collected here.[4]

The most obvious difficulty attending such a view (a view, incidentally, which walks a thin line between the utilitarianisms of Brandt and Hare and the contractarian views of Rawls) is certainly the problem of conflicting *prima facie* obligations. Frankena is candid about this difficulty (see *Ethics,* second edition, pp. 52-56), but does not take it as lethal. Should cases of conflict arise, a circumstance which one hopes will be rare, appeal must be made to the moral point of view directly (the foundation of the *prima facie* principles in the first place). The verdict of this viewpoint or moral sense, if rational and informed, one implicitly claims will be agreed to by others who invoke it under such circumstances.

Two things keep this approach from slipping into a Rossian intuitionism, and both to its merit, I think. First, Frankena insists that the moral point of view is a conative posture, not a disengaged rational intuition of some sort. It is this feature of his account which locates it generically under the heading "noncognitivism," and which enables Frankena to deal with the emotive or prescriptive dimension of moral discourse. Second, but equally important, is the fact that most intuitionistic accounts, Ross's included, provide nothing in the way of a controlling ethical vision to guide the selection of *prima facie* principles and the resolutions of conflict among them. The point is put by Frankena this way:

> It seems to me that everyone who takes the moral point of view can agree that the ideal state of affairs is one in which everyone has the best life he or she is capable of. Now, in such a state of affairs, it is clear that the concerns of both the principle of justice or equality and the principle of beneficence will be fulfilled. If so, then we can see that the two principles are in some sense ultimately consistent, and this seems to imply that increasing insight may enable us to know more and more how to solve the conflicts that trouble us now when we know so little about realizing the ideal state of affairs in which the principles are at one. Then, while Ross is right in saying that we must finally appeal to "perception," we can at least give an outline of what that perception is supposed to envision.[5]

Actual moral obligation, then, is to be understood in terms of a certain personal and social ideal. At the same time, however, this ideal is not to be construed along the lines of teleological accounts, according to which a given non-moral end warrants whatever means are effective toward its achievement. The ideal functions as exactly what it is, *an ideal* — and one might infer from this that a rational, informed person possessed of it will simply not be prepared on every occasion to move toward it by the shortest apparent path.

III

Frankena's work, epitomized in the articles collected here, exhibits several characteristics which, in closing, it will be useful to isolate for purposes of both deeper understanding and deeper appreciation. In my view, these characteristics account in large measure for Frankena's influence and importance in twentieth-century moral philosophy. And they offer something of a model for philosophical methodology in ethics.

First, *a historical sense*. The careful reader of Frankena's writings becomes aware early on of both his competence in and his respect for the history of ethical thought. This during a period of philosophical reflection which, until recently at least, has been painfully ahistorical. Concerns for temporal perspective and historical precedent, both near-term and long-term, are in evidence in every essay. The net of contemporary ethical categories is, for Frankena, not secure unless it can demonstrate a capacity to interpret the dominant views of the past. And the process of securing that net often yields considerable insight into the issues at hand. Both normative ethical and metaethical tensions take on a different aspect when seen as continuous with themes in Plato, Aristotle, Aquinas, Hutcheson, Butler, Kant, and Sidgwick. Such tensions seem less like impasses and more like dramatic challenges when seen against the backdrop of perennial philosophical inquiry.

Second, *analytical rigor*. From his first published article through to his most recent work, readers have found in Frankena's writing a degree of lucidity and analytical skill second to none. Most moral philosophers and serious students of ethics would require no explanation if told that a given issue needed (or just got) a "Frankena-type" article written about it. For they would appreciate that careful analysis, sharp distinctions, and honest conclusions were the order of the day. It is perhaps for this reason that Frankena's contributions are so often taken as departures for further inquiry, e.g., into the relative merits of various metaethical views, into the concept of morality, and into questions relating moral obligation to motivation, religion, virtue, and education.

It should be noted, however, that the analytical skill so evident in Frankena's work is not, for him, an end in itself. Analysis is a means, not an end: a means to a deeper understanding of the philosophical issues to which it is applied. Frankena's patient and exhaustive examinations of alternative positions, alternative interpretations of a line of argument, putative necessary connections between concepts, etc., are all aimed at exhibiting a problem clearly in all its difficulty, when they are not aimed at solving it.

Third, *normative thrust*. The influences of G. E. Moore and the writings of Ayer and Stevenson had the effect, intentional or not, of muting the traditional normative concerns of ethical theorists. Frankena's work, especially during the fifties and sixties, stands out rather dramatically as a call for normative relevance in metaethical reflection. Indeed, his otherwise sympathetic treatment of the general drift of non-cognitivism seems to stop short at just those points where the emotive character of moral claims begins to be treated as undermining the rationality of normative ethical inquiry. And his discussions, both in articles and in his most widely read book, of egoism, utilitarianism, and social justice make it clear that for him, normative questions are finally the central questions of ethics — and are not to be suspended indefinitely in favor of logical and epistemological investigations.

Fourth, and finally, *philosophical restraint*. It is difficult to define this charactertistic, except to say that it is born of scrupulous fairness and candor about the limitations of "proof." Not that Frankena's views on the issues he addressed are timorous. The point is simply that they are thoroughly considered and often complex, resisting glamour in favor of balance. For Frankena, an opinion which can stand up to contrary argument is worth holding for exactly what it is. Reason asks no more of us — and no less. This virtue becomes a powerful tool in his discussions, since few philosophers have been able to take on the broad conflicting currents of contemporary ethics with such disciplined sympathy.

It is with considerable satisfaction that the essays which follow are presented to the community of scholars, philosophers and non-philosophers alike. It is this editor's hope that they will serve both as a model and as a stimulus for students of contemporary philosophical ethics, as well as those concerned with moral education and theological ethics. The postscript essay, which Professor Frankena was kind enough to write especially for this volume, and the complete bibliography at the end should facilitate interpretation and further study.

K. E. Goodpaster

1: The Naturalistic Fallacy

THE FUTURE HISTORIAN OF "THOUGHT AND EXPRESSION" IN THE TWEN-
tieth century will no doubt record with some amusement the ingenious trick,
which some of the philosophical controversialists of the first quarter of our
century had, of labeling their opponents' views "fallacies." He may even list
some of these alleged fallacies for a certain sonority which their inventors
embodied in their titles: the fallacy of initial predication, the fallacy of simple
location, the fallacy of misplaced concreteness, the naturalistic fallacy.

Of these fallacies, real or supposed, perhaps the most famous is the naturalistic fallacy. For the practitioners of a certain kind of ethical theory, which is
dominant in England and capably represented in America, and which is variously called objectivism, non-naturalism, or intuitionism, have frequently
charged their opponents with committing the naturalistic fallacy. Some of these
opponents have strongly repudiated the charge of fallacy, others have at least
commented on it in passing, and altogether the notion of a naturalistic fallacy
has had a considerable currency in ethical literature. Yet, in spite of its repute,
the naturalistic fallacy has never been discussed at any length, and, for this
reason, I have elected to make a study of it in this paper. I hope incidentally to
clarify certain confusions which have been made in connection with the
naturalistic fallacy, but my main interest is to free the controversy between the
intuitionists and their opponents of the notion of a logical or quasi-logical
fallacy, and to indicate where the issue really lies.

The prominence of the concept of a naturalistic fallacy in recent moral
philosophy is another testimony to the great influence of the Cambridge
philosopher, Mr. G. E. Moore, and his book, *Principia Ethica*. Thus Mr.
Taylor speaks of the "vulgar mistake" which Mr. Moore has taught us to call
"the naturalistic fallacy,"[1] and Mr. G. S. Jury, as if to illustrate how well we
have learned this lesson, says, with reference to naturalistic definitions of
value, "All such definitions stand charged with Dr. Moore's 'naturalistic
fallacy'."[2] Now, Mr. Moore coined the notion of the naturalistic fallacy in his

Reprinted from *Mind*, Vol. 48 (1939), pp. 464-77, by permission of *Mind*.

polemic against naturalistic and metaphysical systems of ethics. "The naturalistic fallacy is a fallacy," he writes, and it "must not be committed." All naturalistic and metaphysical theories of ethics, however, "are *based* on the naturalistic fallacy, in the sense that the commission of this fallacy has been the main cause of their wide acceptance."[3] The best way to dispose of them, then, is to expose this fallacy. Yet it is not entirely clear just what is the status of the naturalistic fallacy in the polemics of the intuitionists against other theories. Sometimes it is used as a weapon, as when Miss Clarke says that if we call a thing good simply because it is liked we are guilty of the naturalistic fallacy.[4] Indeed, it presents this aspect to the reader in many parts of *Principia Ethica* itself. Now, in taking it as a weapon, the intuitionists use the naturalistic fallacy as if it were a logical fallacy on all fours with the fallacy of composition, the revelation of which disposes of naturalistic and metaphysical ethics and leaves intuitionism standing triumphant. That is, it is taken as a fallacy in advance, for use in controversy. But there are signs in *Principia Ethica* which indicate that the naturalistic fallacy has a rather different place in the intuitionist scheme, and should not be used as a weapon at all. In this aspect, the naturalistic fallacy must be proved to be a fallacy. It cannot be used to settle the controversy, but can only be asserted to be a fallacy when the smoke of battle has cleared. Consider the following passages: (*a*) "the naturalistic fallacy consists in the contention that good *means* nothing but some simple or complex notion, that can be defined in terms of natural qualities"; (*b*) "the point that good is indefinable and that to deny this involves a fallacy, is a point capable of strict proof."[5] These passages seem to imply that the fallaciousness of the naturalistic fallacy is just what is at issue in the controversy between the intuitionists and their opponents and cannot be wielded as a weapon in that controversy. One of the points I wish to make in this paper is that the charge of committing the naturalistic fallacy can be made, if at all, only as a conclusion from the discussion and not as an instrument of deciding it.

The notion of a naturalistic fallacy has been connected with the notion of a bifurcation between the 'ought' and the 'is', between value and fact, between the normative and the descriptive. Thus Mr. D. C. Williams says that some moralists have thought it appropriate to chastise as the naturalistic fallacy the attempt to derive the Ought from the Is.[6] We may begin, then, by considering this bifurcation, emphasis on which, by Sidgwick, Sorley, and others, came largely as a reaction to the procedures of Mill and Spencer. Hume affirms the bifurcation in his *Treatise*: "I cannot forbear adding to these reasonings an observation, which may, perhaps, be found of some importance. In every system of morality which I have hitherto met with, I have always remarked, that the author proceeds for some time in the ordinary way of reasoning, and establishes the being of a God, or makes observations concerning human affairs; when of a sudden I am surprised to find, that instead of the usual copulations of propositions, *is*, and *is not*, I meet with no proposition that is not connected with an *ought*, or an *ought not*. This change is imperceptible; but is, however, of the last consequence. For as this *ought*, or *ought not*, expresses some new relation or affirmation, it is necessary that it should be observed and explained; and at the same time that a reason should be given, for what seems altogether inconceivable, how this new relation can be a deduction from others, which are entirely different from it. But as authors do not commonly use this precaution, I shall presume to recommend it to the readers; and am persuaded, that this small attention would subvert all the vulgar systems of morality, and let us see that the distinction of vice and virtue is not founded merely on the relations of objects, nor is perceived by reason.''[7]

Needless to say, the intuitionists *have* found this observation of some importance.[8] They agree with Hume that it subverts all the vulgar systems of morality, though, of course, they deny that it lets us see that the distinction of virtue and vice is not founded on the relations of objects, nor is perceived by reason. In fact, they hold that a small attention to it subverts Hume's own system also, since this gives naturalistic definitions of virtue and vice and of good and evil.[9]

Hume's point is that ethical conclusions cannot be drawn validly from premises which are non-ethical. But when the intuitionists affirm the bifurcation of the 'ought' and the 'is', they mean more than that ethical propositions cannot be deduced from non-ethical ones. For this difficulty in the vulgar systems of morality could be remedied, as we shall see, by the introduction of definitions of ethical notions in non-ethical terms. They mean, further, that such definitions of ethical notions in non-ethical terms are impossible. ''The essential point,'' says Mr. Laird, ''is the irreducibility of values to non-values.''[10] But they mean still more. Yellow and pleasantness are, according to Mr. Moore, indefinable in non-ethical terms, but they are natural qualities and belong on the 'is' side of the fence. Ethical properties, however, are not, for him, mere indefinable natural qualities, descriptive or expository. They are properties of a different *kind* — non-descriptive or non-natural.[11] The intuitionist bifurcation consists of three statements:

(1) Ethical propositions are not deducible from non-ethical ones.[12]
(2) Ethical characteristics are not definable in terms of non-ethical ones.
(3) Ethical characteristics are different in kind from non-ethical ones.

Really it consists of but one statement, namely, (3), since (3) entails (2) and (2) entails (1). It does not involve saying that any ethical characteristics are absolutely indefinable. That is another question, although this is not always noticed.

What, now, has the naturalistic fallacy to do with the bifurcation of the 'ought' and the 'is'? To begin with, the connection is this: many naturalistic and metaphysical moralists proceed as if ethical conclusions can be deduced from premises all of which are non-ethical, the classical examples being Mill and

Spencer. That is, they violate (1). This procedure has lately been referred to as the "factualist fallacy" by Mr. Wheelwright and as the "valuational fallacy" by Mr. Wood.[13] Mr. Moore sometimes seems to identify it with the naturalistic fallacy, but in the main he holds only that it involves, implies, or rests upon this fallacy.[14] We may now consider the charge that the procedure in question is or involves a fallacy.

It may be noted at once that, even if the deduction of ethical conclusions from non-ethical premises is in no way a fallacy, Mill certainly did commit a fallacy in drawing an analogy between visibility and desirability in his argument for hedonism; and perhaps his committing *this* fallacy, which, as Mr. Broad has said, we all learn about at our mothers' knees, is chiefly responsible for the notion of a naturalistic *fallacy*. But is it a fallacy to deduce ethical conclusions from non-ethical premises? Consider the Epicurean argument for hedonism which Mill so unwisely sought to embellish: pleasure is good, since it is sought by all men. Here an ethical conclusion is being derived from a non-ethical premise. And, indeed, the argument, taken strictly as it stands, *is* fallacious. But it is not fallacious because an *ethical* term occurs in the conclusion which does not occur in the premise. It is fallacious because any argument of the form "A is B, therefore A is C" is invalid, if taken strictly as it stands. For example, it is invalid to argue that Croesus is rich because he is wealthy. Such arguments are, however, not intended to be taken strictly as they stand. They are enthymemes and contain a suppressed premise. And, when this suppressed premise is made explicit, they are valid and involve no logical fallacy.[15] Thus the Epicurean inference from psychological to ethical hedonism is valid when the suppressed premise is added to the effect that what is sought by all men is good. Then the only question left is whether the premises are true.

It is clear, then, that the naturalistic fallacy is not a logical fallacy, since it may be involved even when the argument is valid. How does the naturalistic fallacy enter such "mixed ethical arguments"[16] as that of the Epicureans? Whether it does or not depends on the nature of the suppressed premise. This may be either an induction, an intuition, a deduction from a "pure ethical argument," a definition, or a proposition which is true by definition. If it is one of the first three, then the naturalistic fallacy does not enter at all. In fact, the argument does not then involve violating (1), since one of its premises will be ethical. But if the premise to be supplied is a definition or a proposition which is true by definition, as it probably was for the Epicureans, then the argument, while still valid, involves the naturalistic fallacy, and will run as follows:

(a) Pleasure is sought by all men.
(b) What is sought by all men is good (by definition).
(c) Therefore, pleasure is good.

Now I am not greatly interested in deciding whether the argument as here set up violates (1). If it does not, then no 'mixed ethical argument' actually commits any factualist or valuational fallacy, except when it is unfairly taken as complete in its enthymematic form. If it does, then a valid argument may involve the deduction of an ethical conclusion from non-ethical premises and the factualist or valuational fallacy is not really a fallacy. The question depends on whether or not (*b*) and (*c*) are to be regarded as ethical propositions. Mr. Moore refuses so to regard them, contending that, by hypothesis, (*b*) is analytic or tautologous, and that (*c*) is psychological, since it really says only that pleasure is sought by all men.[17] But to say that (*b*) is analytic and not ethical and that (*c*) is not ethical but psychological is to prejudge the question whether 'good' can be defined; for the Epicureans would contend precisely that if their definition is correct then (*b*) is ethical but analytic and (*c*) ethical though psychological. Thus, unless the question of the definability of goodness is to be begged, (*b*) and (*c*) must be regarded as ethical, in which case our argument does not violate (1). However, suppose, if it be not nonsense, that (*b*) is non-ethical and (*c*) ethical, then the argument will violate (1), but it will still obey all of the canons of logic, and it is only confusing to talk of a 'valuational logic' whose basic rule is that an evaluative conclusion cannot be deduced from non-evaluative premises.[18]

For the only way in which either the intuitionists or postulationists like Mr. Wood can cast doubt upon the conclusion of the argument of the Epicureans (or upon the conclusion of any parallel argument) is to attack the premises, in particular (*b*). Now, according to Mr. Moore, it is due to the presence of (*b*) that the argument involves the naturalistic fallacy. (*b*) involves the identification of goodness with 'being sought by all men', and to make this or any other such identification is to commit the naturalistic fallacy. The naturalistic fallacy is not the procedure of violating (1). It is the procedure, implied in many mixed ethical arguments and explicitly carried out apart from such arguments by many moralists, of defining such characteristics as goodness or of substituting some other characteristic for them. To quote some passages from *Principia Ethica:* –

(*a*) "... far too many philosophers have thought that when they named those other properties [belonging to all things which are good] they were actually defining good; that these properties, in fact, were simply not 'other', but absolutely and entirely the same with goodness. This view I propose to call the 'naturalistic fallacy' . . . ."[19]

(*b*) "I have thus appropriated the name Naturalism to a particular method of approaching Ethics . . . . This method consists in substituting for 'good' some one property of a natural object or of a collection of natural objects. . . ."[20]

(*c*) "... the naturalistic fallacy [is] the fallacy which consists in identifying the simple notion which we mean by 'good' with some other notion."[21]

Thus, to identify 'better' and 'more evolved', 'good' and 'desired', etc., is to commit the naturalistic fallacy.[22] But just why is such a procedure fallacious or erroneous? And is it a fallacy only when applied to good? We must now study

Section 12 of *Principia Ethica*. Here Mr. Moore makes some interesting statements:

". . . if anybody tried to define pleasure for us as being any other natural object; if anybody were to say, for instance, that pleasure *means* the sensation of red. . . Well, that would be the same fallacy which I have called the naturalistic fallacy. . . . I should not indeed call that a naturalistic fallacy, although it is the same fallacy as I have called naturalistic with reference to Ethics. . . . When a man confuses two natural objects with one another, defining the one by the other . . . then there is no reason to call the fallacy naturalistic. But if he confuses 'good', which is not . . . a natural object, with any natural object whatever, then there is a reason for calling that a naturalistic fallacy. . . ."[23]

Here Mr. Moore should have added that, when one confuses 'good', which is not a metaphysical object or quality, with any metaphysical object or quality, as metaphysical moralists do, according to him, then the fallacy should be called the metaphysical fallacy. Instead he calls it a naturalistic fallacy in this case too, though he recognizes that the case is different since metaphysical properties are non-natural[24] — a procedure which has misled many readers of *Principia Ethica*. For example, it has led Mr. Broad to speak of "theological naturalism."[25]

To resume: "Even if [goodness] were a natural object, that would not alter the nature of the fallacy nor diminish its importance one whit."[26] From these passages it is clear that the fallaciousness of the procedure which Mr. Moore calls the naturalistic fallacy is not due to the fact that it is applied to good or to an ethical or non-natural characteristic. When Mr. R. B. Perry defines 'good' as 'being an object of interest' the trouble is not merely that he is defining *good*. Nor is the trouble that he is defining an *ethical* characteristic in terms of *non-ethical* ones. Nor is the trouble that he is regarding a *non-natural* characteristic as a *natural* one. The trouble is more generic than that. For clarity's sake I shall speak of the definist fallacy as the generic fallacy which underlies the naturalistic fallacy. The naturalistic fallacy will then, by the above passages, be a species or form of the definist fallacy, as would the metaphysical fallacy if Mr. Moore had given that a separate name.[27] That is, the naturalistic fallacy, as illustrated by Mr. Perry's procedure, is a fallacy, not because it is naturalistic or confuses a non-natural quality with a natural one, but solely because it involves the definist fallacy. We may, then, confine our attention entirely to an understanding and evaluation of the definist fallacy.

To judge by the passages I have just quoted, the definist fallacy is the process of confusing or identifying two properties, of defining one property by another, or of substituting one property for another. Furthermore, the fallacy is always simply that two properties are being treated as one, and it is irrelevant, if it be the case, that one of them is natural or non-ethical and the other non-natural or ethical. One may commit the definist fallacy without infringing on the bifurcation of the ethical and the non-ethical, as when one identifies pleasantness and redness or rightness and goodness. But even when one infringes on that bifurcation in committing the definist fallacy, as when one identifies goodness and pleasantness or goodness and satisfaction, then the *mistake* is still not that the bifurcation is being infringed on, but only that two properties are being treated as one. Hence, on the present interpretation, the definist *fallacy* does not, in any of its forms, consist in violating (3), and has no essential connexion with the bifurcation of the 'ought' and the 'is'.

This formulation of the definist fallacy explains or reflects the motto of *Principia Ethica,* borrowed from Bishop Butler: "Everything is what it is, and not another thing." It follows from this motto that goodness is what it is and not another thing. It follows that views which try to identify it with something else are making a mistake of an elementary sort. For it *is* a mistake to confuse or identify two properties. If the properties really are two, then they simply are not identical. But do those who define ethical notions in non-ethical terms make this mistake? They will reply to Mr. Moore that they are not identifying two properties; what they are saying is that two words or sets of words stand for or mean one and the same property. Mr. Moore was being, in part, misled by the material mode of speech, as Mr. Carnap calls it, in such sentences as "Goodness is pleasantness," "Knowledge is true belief," etc. When one says instead, "The word 'good' and the word 'pleasant' mean the same thing," etc., it is clear that one is not identifying two things. But Mr. Moore kept himself from seeing this by his disclaimer that he was interested in any statement about the use of words.[28]

The definist fallacy, then, as we have stated it, does not rule out any naturalistic or metaphysical definitions of ethical terms. Goodness is not identifiable with any 'other' characteristic (if it is a characteristic at all). But the question is: *which* characteristics are other than goodness, which names stand for characteristics other than goodness? And it is begging the question of the definability of goodness to say out of hand that Mr. Perry, for instance, is identifying goodness with something else. The point is that goodness is what it is, even if it is definable. That is why Mr. Perry can take as the motto of his naturalistic *Moral Economy* another sentence from Bishop Butler: "Things and actions are what they are, and the consequences of them will be what they will be; why then should we desire to be deceived?" The motto of *Principia Ethica* is a tautology, and should be expanded as follows: Everything is what it is, and not another thing, unless it is another thing, and even then it is what it is.

On the other hand, if Mr. Moore's motto (or the definist fallacy) rules out any definitions, for example of 'good', then it rules out all definitions of any term whatever. To be effective at all, it must be understood to mean, "Every term means what it means, and not what is meant by any other term." Mr. Moore seems implicitly to understand his motto in this way in Section 13, for he proceeds as if 'good' has no meaning, if it has no unique meaning. If the motto be taken in this way, it will follow that 'good' is an indefinable term, since no synonyms can be found. But it will also follow that no term is definable. And then the method of analysis is as useless as an English butcher in a world without sheep.

Perhaps we have misinterpreted the definist fallacy. And, indeed, some of the passages which I quoted earlier in this paper seem to imply that the definist fallacy is just the error of defining an indefinable characteristic. On this interpretation, again, the definist fallacy has, in all of its forms, no essential connection with the bifurcation of the ethical and the non-ethical. Again, one may commit the definist fallacy without violating that bifurcation, as when one defines pleasantness in terms of redness or goodness in terms of rightness (granted Mr. Moore's belief that pleasantness and goodness are indefinable). But even when one infringes on that bifurcation and defines goodness in terms of desire, the *mistake* is not that one is infringing on the bifurcation by violating (3), but only that one is defining an indefinable characteristic. This is possible because the proposition that goodness is indefinable is logically independent of the proposition that goodness is non-natural: as is shown by the fact that a characteristic may be indefinable and yet natural, as yellowness is; or non-natural and yet definable, as rightness is (granted Mr. Moore's views about yellowness and rightness).

Consider the definist fallacy as we have just stated it. It is, of course, an error to define an indefinable quality. But the question, again, is: which qualities are indefinable? It is begging the question in favor of intuitionism to say in advance that the quality goodness is indefinable and that, therefore, all naturalists commit the definist fallacy. One must know that goodness is indefinable before one can argue that the definist fallacy *is* a fallacy. Then, however, the definist fallacy can enter only at the end of the controversy between intuitionism and definism, and cannot be used as a weapon in the controversy.

The definist fallacy may be stated in such a way as to involve the bifurcation between the 'ought' and the 'is'.[29] It would then be committed by anyone who offered a definition of any ethical characteristic in terms of non-ethical ones. The trouble with such a definition, on this interpretation, would be that an *ethical* characteristic is being reduced to a *non-ethical* one, a *non-natural* one to a *natural* one. That is, the definition would be ruled out by the fact that the characteristic being defined is ethical or non-natural and therefore cannot be defined in non-ethical or natural terms. But on this interpretation, too, there is danger of a *petitio* in the intuitionist argumentation. To assume that the ethical characteristic is exclusively ethical is to beg precisely the question which is at issue when the definition is offered. Thus, again, one must know that the characteristic is non-natural and indefinable in natural terms before one can say that the definists are making a mistake.

Mr. Moore, McTaggart, and others formulate the naturalistic fallacy some-times in a way somewhat different from any of those yet discussed. They say that the definists are confusing a universal synthetic proposition about *the good* with a definition of *goodness*.[30] Mr. Abraham calls this the "fallacy of misconstrued proposition."[31] Here again the difficulty is that, while it is true that it is an error to construe a universal synthetic proposition as a definition, it is a *petitio* for the intuitionists to say that what the definist is taking for a definition is really a universal synthetic proposition.[32]

At last, however, the issue between the intuitionists and the definists (naturalistic or metaphysical) is becoming clearer. The definists are all holding that certain propositions involving ethical terms are analytic, tautologous, or true by definition, e.g., Mr. Perry so regards the statement, "All objects of desire are good." The intuitionists hold that such statements are synthetic. What underlies this difference of opinion is that the intuitionists claim to have at least a dim awareness of a simple unique quality or relation of goodness or rightness which appears in the region which our ethical terms roughly indicate, whereas the definists claim to have no awareness of any such quality or relation in that region, which is different from all other qualities and relations which belong to the same context but are designated by words other than 'good' and 'right' and their obvious synonyms.[33] The definists are in all honesty claiming to find but one characteristic where the intuitionists claim to find two, as Mr. Perry claims to find only the property of being desired where Mr. Moore claims to find both it and the property of being good. The issue, then, is one of inspection or intuition, and concerns the awareness or discernment of qualities and relations.[34] That is why it cannot be decided by the use of the notion of a fallacy.

If the definists may be taken at their word, then they are not actually confusing two characteristics with each other, nor defining an indefinable characteristic, nor confusing definitions and universal synthetic propositions — in short they are not committing the naturalistic or definist fallacy in any of the interpretations given above. Then the only fallacy which they commit — the real naturalistic or definist fallacy — is the failure to descry the qualities and relations which are central to morality. But this is neither a logical fallacy nor a logical confusion. It is not even, properly speaking, an error. It is rather a kind of blindness, analogous to color-blindness. Even this moral blindness can be ascribed to the definists only if they are correct in their claim to have no awareness of any unique ethical characteristics and if the intuitionists are correct in affirming the existence of such characteristics, but certainly to call it a 'fallacy', even in a loose sense, is both unamiable and profitless.

On the other hand, of course, if there are no such characteristics in the objects to which we attach ethical predicates, then the intuitionists, if we may take them at their word, are suffering from a corresponding moral hallucination. Definists might then call this the intuitionistic or moralistic fallacy, except that it is no more a 'fallacy' than is the blindness just described. Anyway, they do not believe the claim of the intuitionists to be aware of unique ethical characteristics, and consequently do not attribute to them this hallucination. Instead, they simply deny that the intuitionists really do find such unique qualities or relations, and then they try to find some plausible way of accounting for the fact that very respectable and trustworthy people think they find them.[35] Thus they charge the intuitionists with verbalism, hypostatisation, and the like. But this half of the story does not concern us now.

What concerns us more is the fact that the intuitionists do not credit the claim of the definists either. They would be much disturbed, if they really thought that their opponents were morally blind, for they do not hold that we must be regenerated by grace before we can have moral insight, and they share the common feeling that morality is something democratic even though not all men are good. Thus they hold that "we are all aware" of certain unique characteristics when we use the terms 'good', 'right', etc., only due to a lack of analytic clearness of mind, abetted perhaps by a philosophical prejudice, we may not be aware at all that they are different from other characteristics of which we are also aware.[36] Now, I have been arguing that the intuitionists cannot charge the definists with committing any fallacy unless and until they have shown that we are all, the definists included, aware of the disputed unique characteristics. If, however, they were to show this, then, at least at the end of the controversy, they could accuse the definists of the error of confusing two characteristics, or of the error of defining an indefinable one, and these errors might, since the term is somewhat loose in its habits, be called 'fallacies', though they are not logical fallacies in the sense in which an invalid argument is. The fallacy of misconstrued proposition depends on the error of confusing two characteristics, and hence could also on our present supposition, be ascribed to the definists, but it is not really a *logical* confusion,[37] since it does not actually involve being confused about the difference between a proposition and a definition.

Only it is difficult to see how the intuitionists can prove that the definists are at least vaguely aware of the requisite unique characteristics.[38] The question must surely be left to the inspection or intuition of the definists themselves, aided by whatever suggestions the intuitionists may have to make. If so, we must credit the verdict of their inspection, especially of those among them who have read the writings of the intuitionists reflectively, and, then, as we have seen, the most they can be charged with is moral blindness.

Besides trying to discover just what is meant by the naturalistic fallacy, I have tried to show that the notion that a logical or quasi-logical fallacy is committed by the definists only confuses the issue between the intuitionists and the definists (and the issue between the latter and the emotivists or postulationists), and misrepresents the way in which the issue is to be settled. No logical fallacy need appear anywhere in the procedure of the definists. Even fallacies in any less accurate sense cannot be implemented to decide the case against the definists; at best they can be ascribed to the definists only after the issue has been decided against them on independent grounds. But the only defect which can be attributed to the definists, *if* the intuitionists are right in affirming the existence of unique indefinable ethical characteristics, is a peculiar moral blindness, which is not a fallacy even in the looser sense. The issue in question must be decided by whatever method we may find satisfactory for determining whether or not a word stands for a characteristic at all, and, if it does, whether or not it stands for a unique characteristic. What method is to be employed is, perhaps, in one form or another, the basic problem of contemporary philosophy, but no generally satisfactory solution of the problem has yet been reached. I shall venture to say only this: it does seem to me that the issue is not to be decided against the intuitionists by the application *ab extra* to ethical judgments of any empirical or ontological meaning dictum.[39]

2: Obligation and Value in the Ethics of G. E. Moore

G. E. MOORE IN 1903 THOUGHT OF HIMSELF AS ENUNCIATING CERTAIN "principles of ethical reasoning" which had been neglected by most previous moralists and which should serve as "prolegomena to any future ethics that can possibly pretend to be scientific."[1] These principles are the following:

1. Moralists must distinguish three questions: (a) What is meant by 'good'? (b) What things are good in themselves? or, What things ought to exist for their own sakes? and (c) What actions ought to be done?[2]

2. They must also distinguish between means and ends, or between what is good as a means and what is good as an end; and between the relation of means to end and the relation of part to whole.[3]

3. Intrinsic goodness is a simple, indefinable, non-natural intrinsic quality.[4]

4. Judgments of the form "X is intrinsically good" are synthetic, intuitive, incapable of proof or disproof, logically independent of all judgments of existence (natural or metaphysical) and of all judgments about the relations of X to any minds there may be.[5]

5. 'Intrinsic goodness' is the central or basic notion of ethics.[6]

6. The right act or the act which we ought to do is always and necessarily the act which promotes as much intrinsic good in the universe as a whole as possible. It follows that judgments of the form "X is right" are not intuitive but can be proved by inference from premises of which some are judgments of intrinsic value and the rest judgments about causal connections.[7]

7. In answering the question what things are good in themselves two principles must be observed: (a) ". . . it is necessary to consider what things are such that, if they existed by themselves, in absolute isolation, we should yet judge their existence to be good," (b) ". . . the intrinsic value of a whole is neither identical with nor proportional to the sum of the values of its parts."[8]

8. ". . . very many different things are good and evil in themselves, and . . .

Reprinted from The Philosophy of G. E. Moore, The Library of Living Philosophers, Vol. IV, P. A. Schilpp, ed., pp. 91-110, by permission of P. A. Schilpp.

neither class of things possesses any other property which is both common to all its members and peculiar to them."[9]

In these principles Moore is formulating a non-hedonistic utilitarian or teleological ethics of an intuitionistic or non-naturalistic sort. Its core, as a system of ethics, is a certain view of the connection between intrinsic value and obligation, which is expressed especially in principle (6). It is this view which I wish to discuss. It has, however, two parts. The first part is the doctrine that the intrinsically good ought to be promoted, or that a thing's having intrinsic value so far makes it a duty to produce it if possible. This doctrine is an essential part of any utilitarian or teleological ethics, but it may also be accepted by an 'intuitionist' or deontologist like W. D. Ross. The second part is the doctrine that the right or obligatory act is always and necessarily the act which is most conducive to intrinsic good, or that our only ultimate duty is to do what will produce the greatest possible balance of intrinsic value. This is the characteristic doctrine of a utilitarian or teleological ethics, as distinguished from such an ethics as that of Ross. Now my purpose is to discuss the first of these two parts of Moore's view of the relation of obligation and value, in the light of other things which he has said, and in the hope that he may be moved to modify his view at some points and to clarify it at others.

A complete discussion of Moore's views concerning the relation of obligation and value should, of course, include a discussion of the second part of principle (6), that is, of the doctrine that the right act is always and necessarily the act which is most conducive to intrinsic good. This is the doctrine which Moore expresses in the *Ethics* by saying that "the question whether an action is right or wrong *always* depends on its *actual* consequences."[10] It has several noteworthy features. (a) It refers only to *voluntary* actions, and says nothing about the question whether or not any non-voluntary actions (among which Moore groups feelings) are right in any sense.[11] (b) It implies that the rightness and wrongness of actions do not depend in any way on any value which the actions themselves may have, but only on that of their effects.[12] (c) It denies that the rightness and wrongness of actions depend on their intrinsic characters in any sense, for example, on their being cases of promise-keeping or not. (d) It holds that the rightness and wrongness of actions do not depend at all on the motives or intentions with which they are done. (e) It insists that the rightness and wrongness of actions depend entirely on the character of their *actual* effects, and not at all on that of their probable effects or of those which the agent had reason to expect.[13] And, finally, (f) it makes the rightness and wrongness of actions depend entirely on their promotion of *intrinsic* value.[14] Regarding these features of Moore's view many questions might be asked to which the student of his ethics would like to have answers. I have, however, elected not to raise them here. It seems to me that of the two parts of principle (6) the first is the more fundamental, and hence I have limited my paper to its discussion.

My paper, then, will be devoted to a discussion of Moore's view that the good ought to be promoted by us, or that we have, in Ross's terms, a *prima facie* duty to promote what is intrinsically good.[15] Does it follow from the very nature of intrinsic goodness that it ought to be promoted? Or is the connection between intrinsic value and obligation only a synthetic, even if necessary, one?

We may begin by considering the views which Moore expresses in *Principia Ethica*. Here he opens by carefully distinguishing between the notion of intrinsic value and the notion of duty or of what we ought to do (principle 1). So far it seems as if he means to separate obligation and value. Yet I cannot help feeling, as I read on, that Moore really attaches a connotation of obligatoriness to the notion of intrinsic goodness, and regards the good as somehow having a normative significance as such. This is indicated, I should say, by the fact that he regards "intrinsically good" as synonymous with "ought to exist for its own sake."[16] It is also indicated in his discussion of Mill and Spencer by his tendency to take "good as end" or "intrinsically good" as equivalent to "desirable," "ought to be desired," "ought to be aimed at," etc.[17] It is indicated finally by the fact that he goes on to define 'right' as meaning "productive of what is good in itself." For on this definition the obligatoriness of the right must be derived wholly from an assumed obligatoriness of the good.

It appears, therefore, that in *Principia* Moore is maintaining the first of the two alternatives mentioned above, at least implicitly. Here my troubles begin. For if Moore's explicit conception of intrinsic value is correct, then this alternative must be false. This conception of intrinsic value is familiar; it is, indeed, the central point for which Moore has stood in recent moral philosophy. It runs as follows.[18] According to Moore, 'good' is an ambiguous term.[19] Sometimes it means "good as a means," sometimes it means "good as contributing to a whole which is intrinsically good," sometimes it means "morally good" or "morally praiseworthy," and sometimes, "in a very important sense," it means "being the object of a certain feeling on the part of some mind or minds."[20] But in its primary sense, so far at least as ethics is concerned, it means "good in itself," "good as end," or "intrinsically good."[21] We must, therefore, carefully distinguish what is good in the sense of "intrinsically good" from what is good in the other senses.[22] In all of the other senses of 'good', Moore holds, a thing's goodness depends at least in part on its relations to something else. A thing's intrinsic goodness, however, does not depend in any way on its relations to anything else. Intrinsic goodness is a quality and not a relational property,[23] and it is a quality whose presence in a thing is due entirely to that thing's own character.[24] "X is intrinsically good" means "It would be a good thing that X should exist, even if X existed quite alone, without any further accompaniments or effects whatever," or "X is good in a sense such that the question whether X is good in that sense, and in what degree it is so, depends solely on the intrinsic nature of X," or again "X is worth having for its own sake."[25] Moore believes that there are things which are good in the sense indicated by these expressions — good, that is, in the sense of having a goodness which is intrinsic, objective, and absolute.[26] He also believes, of course, that this intrinsic goodness is indefinable and non-natural (principle 3). By saying that it is indefinable he means to say primarily that it is simple or unanalyzable.[27] By saying that it is non-natural he means to say partly that it is not an object of perception, partly that it is not a psychological idea, partly that it depends on a thing's nature in a certain peculiar way, and partly that it is somehow non-existential or non-descriptive.[28]

In short, Moore regards intrinsic value as a quality which is really intrinsic,[29] and which is also simple and non-natural. Now my contention is that if this conception of its nature is correct, then intrinsic value cannot be possessed of any essential normativeness or obligatoriness. It cannot be part of its very meaning that it enjoins us or any other agents to take up a certain attitude toward it. I should even say that if this conception of intrinsic value is correct, then Moore is wrong in saying that ''A is intrinsically good'' is synonymous with ''A ought to exist for its own sake,'' since the notion of what ought to exist for its own sake has a complexity which the notion of intrinsic value is not supposed to have. It involves the notions of obligation and of existence and of a kind of relation of the things in question to existence, and can hardly represent a simple quality. In fact, to say that A ought to exist would seem to mean that someone has a duty to bring A into existence.[30] Then certainly ''intrinsically good'' cannot stand for a simple quality and yet be synonymous with ''ought to exist for its own sake.'' But, however this may be, if intrinsic value is either simple or non-relational, then it cannot contain any obligation in its very nature. For to say that it does is to say that the fact that A is intrinsically good includes or is identical with the fact that certain agents, actual or possible, should do something about A or take a certain attitude toward it. But to say this is to say that intrinsic value may be partially or wholly defined in terms of the notion that certain agents have a duty to do a certain thing — in other words, that it is complex and relational, not simple or qualitative. Intrinsic goodness can have a normative character as such only if it essentially or analytically involves a reference to an agent on whom something is actually or hypothetically enjoined, that is, only if it is not a simple intrinsic quality. If goodness is either simple or a quality, it can be connected with obligation only synthetically. The most that can then be said of it is that it is a characteristic whose presence *makes* things such that they ought to be brought into existence — as pleasantness is sometimes said to be.

What I am saying can also be expressed as follows. Suppose someone asks ''Why should (ought) I bring the good into existence?'' Then, if goodness is a simple intrinsic quality, he cannot be answered by saying, ''Because it is of the nature of the good that it should be brought into existence.'' For, if goodness is a simple intrinsic quality, then it cannot be of the nature of the good that it should be brought into existence.

This point that intrinsic value cannot as such be possessed of any normative character or obligatoriness, if it is a simple intrinsic quality, is worthy of notice even if Moore did not mean to be holding in *Principia Ethica* that it has such a character. I am not interested merely in pointing out what looks like an inconsistency in Moore. If my point is well-taken, then anyone who regards the good as normative, or who holds it to be part of the meaning of the good that it enjoins us to take a certain attitude toward it, must reject the view that goodness is a simple intrinsic quality. Again, if it is well-taken, it will follow, if intrinsic value is a simple quality, that duty cannot be defined in terms of intrinsic value, as Moore in *Principia* holds that it can. It will follow also that there is no place for obligation in the ethics of *Principia*. For if there is no obligatoriness or normative character in the *Principia* notion of intrinsic value, and we have seen that there is none, then there can also be no obligatoriness or normative character in the *Principia* notion of right or duty, since this is defined in terms of the notion of intrinsic value. By regarding goodness as a simple intrinsic quality and defining 'right' as meaning ''conducive to as much good as possible,'' *Principia* transforms statements of the form ''We ought to do X'' into mere statements of fact. For, if goodness is a simple intrinsic quality, as it teaches, then to say that A is conducive to the greatest possible amount of good is not to say that we ought to do A; it is a simple report or prediction of actual occurrence. Thus there is no obligatoriness or normative character in either its notion of intrinsic value or its notion of right or duty, and hence the ethics of *Principia Ethica,* like any naturalistic or metaphysical ethics, is an ethics *sans obligation,* if not *sans sanction.*

This result leads directly to the next main point which I wish to make, namely, that, if intrinsic goodness is not as such possessed of any normative character or obligatoriness, then there is no reason for regarding it as either indefinable or non-natural. Certainly it need not be indefinable or non-natural in order to be a characteristic whose presence makes things such that they ought to be brought into existence. Thus pleasantness is sometimes said to be such a characteristic, for example by Sidgwick, and there is nothing which makes this view impossible in principle. In fact, natural and definable characteristics are generally regarded by Cambridge and Oxford philosophers as being, some of them, good-making or right-making. But if Sidgwick's view is a possible one, then goodness might be identical with pleasantness and yet be a characteristic in virtue of which things which have it ought to be produced. Again, goodness need not be indefinable or non-natural in order to be intrinsic in Moore's sense, granting this to be the case. Pleasantness is an intrinsic quality of certain experiences on Moore's own view, and, if this is so, then goodness might be defined as pleasantness and yet be intrinsic.[31] Moore has, of course, given various arguments to show that intrinsic goodness is indefinable, or at least that it is indefinable in psychological terms. But he has himself admitted the arguments of *Principia* to be inconclusive and fallacious,[32] and those given in his other works can be shown to be no better.[33] Moore has also charged all definist theories of value with committing a fallacy, namely ''the naturalistic fallacy,'' but the procedure which he has in mind is not really a fallacy at all, and it cannot even be called a mistake until after it is known that value cannot be defined.[34]

Thus one can appeal only to inspection or intuition to settle the matter, and I must say that I can discern in the things which I judge to be good in themselves no intrinsic quality of goodness which is unique or non-natural. I do not deny that there is something distinctive or unique about experiences which I judge to be intrinsically good as I am having them, or about experiences in which I judge something else to be intrinsically good. But this something different may be due entirely to the presence in these experiences of a value-judgment, with all of its psychological and emotive associations. It does not follow that there is a unique quality of value, nor that the making of a value-judgment involves an awareness of such a quality. As for experiences which I am not having, but which I judge to be intrinsically good, in them I can descry no character of uniqueness other than that which belongs to every experience or every sort of experience.

So far in dealing with my second contention I have been occupied with disposing of the reasons which Moore has given or might give for his view that intrinsic value is indefinable and non-natural. Now I wish to press my contention more directly. The main point which is involved in the view that intrinsic value is indefinable and non-natural, apart from the doctrine that it cannot be defined in terms of rightness or duty, is the doctrine that it is irreducible to natural or to metaphysical terms. Now, to my mind, what makes ethical judgments seem irreducible to natural or to metaphysical judgments is their apparently normative character, that is, the fact that they seem to be saying of some agent that he ought to do something. This fact, so far as I can see, is the only ground on which ethical judgments can be regarded as essentially different from the factual or existential judgments of science or of metaphysics. If this is true, then the apparently normative character of ethical judgments is the basic fact in the intuitionist or non-naturalist assertion of the indefinability and non-naturalness of ethical notions or characteristics. Hence, if intrinsic value is to be indefinable and non-natural, if judgments of intrinsic value are to be different in kind from non-ethical judgments, then intrinsic value must in itself possess a normative character or obligatoriness. If it does not, then it cannot be regarded as essentially irreducible to natural or to metaphysical terms.

Moore's most recent discussion of the unique nature of intrinsic value is instructive in this connection.[35] There he is discussing the difference between intrinsic goodness and the property of containing a balance of pleasure. Both of these properties, he says, are intrinsic in the sense of ''depending *solely* on the intrinsic nature of what possesses them.'' But he feels that there is some great difference in kind between them. This difference he expresses by saying that the latter seems to *describe* the nature of what possesses it in a way in which the former does not. That is, he regards intrinsic value as somehow non-descriptive. More he confesses himself unable to say. I suggest that this is because an intrinsic quality cannot really be non-descriptive, all intrinsic qualities being essentially descriptive. To be non-descriptive a characteristic must be normative; it must involve a reference to an obligation on the part of some agent. But then it cannot be an intrinsic quality. As long, therefore, as he regards value as an intrinsic quality, Moore must fail to make out convincingly that there is an important difference in kind between it and other intrinsic qualities, or that judgments of intrinsic value are unique in the sense of being somehow non-descriptive or non-existential.

The situation, then, seems to me to be this. If saying that intrinsic value is non-natural is to distinguish judgments of intrinsic value from natural and metaphysical judgments, then the notion of obligatoriness must be part of the notion of non-naturalness. And then intrinsic value cannot be non-natural if it is either simple or an intrinsic quality, or if for any other reason it is capable of having only a synthetic connection with obligation. Again, the real reason for thinking that any ethical notion is essentially indefinable in non-ethical terms is its apparently normative character, and, therefore, if intrinsic value is an intrinsic quality, or if its connection with obligation is only synthetic, then there is no reason for regarding it as essentially irreducible to non-ethical terms. Hence Moore's position that intrinsic value is an indefinable, non-natural, intrinsic quality is an indefensible one. Anyone who holds that intrinsic value is a simple intrinsic quality must also take the second of the alternatives pointed out at the beginning, namely, that intrinsic value can have only a synthetic connection with obligation, and if he accepts this alternative he has no grounds for holding that intrinsic value is indefinable or non-natural. If intrinsic value is indefinable, or if it is an intrinsic quality, then it cannot have any normative character, and cannot, in any distinctive sense, be non-natural. And if it is normative and non-natural, then it is definable in terms of 'ought', and is neither simple nor an intrinsic quality. Finally, if it is an intrinsic quality, or if for any other reason it is not normative, then it is probably not even indefinable in non-ethical terms.

In view of what I have been saying Moore might contend that the notion of intrinsic goodness does have its normative associations, and therefore cannot be defined in non-ethical terms. The premise of this argument may be granted, but its conclusion does not follow. For the normative associations of the term 'good' may be purely emotive, or, if goodness has a synthetic connection with rightness, they may be entirely due to this connection. In fact, Moore must himself explain them in either of these two ways if he continues to regard goodness as a simple intrinsic quality.

All that has been said thus far is about the views which Moore has expressed in *Principia Ethica*, so far as these bear on the topic of this paper. About Moore's later views on such matters as are relevant here it is difficult to speak with certainty. It does seem that in *Ethics* and in *Philosophical Studies* he is no longer regarding rightness and duty as definable in terms of conduciveness to what is intrinsically good. It is quite clear that he still regards intrinsic value as an intrinsic quality.[36] But it is not certain that he holds it to be indefinable.[37] On the whole, however, the view which he seems to favor is the following: (a) intrinsic value is an indefinable non-natural intrinsic quality, (b) obligation is also indefinable and non-natural, and (c) intrinsic value and obligation are related by a synthetic necessary connection. Of this view it does not hold that the ethics based on it must be an ethics without any obligation, for obligation is taken as an ultimate notion. But all the rest of what I have been saying does hold of this view, since it involves the doctrine that intrinsic value is a simple intrinsic non-natural quality which is only synthetically connected with obligation.

My main contentions regarding Moore's position, it will be noticed, are hypothetical in character. Nevertheless, as I have indicated, they lead to the conclusion that his position is indefensible, both in its earlier and in its later forms. In particular, I now wish to point out that they lead to the conclusion that there is no reason for regarding intrinsic value as indefinable, as Moore does. If it has in itself a normative character, then it is definable in terms of 'ought'. If it has not, then it cannot be in principle indefinable in non-ethical terms. There may then still be a practical difficulty in finding a satisfactory definition of the word 'good' in the sort of usage in which it is equivalent to "intrinsically good." But this difficulty by itself hardly warrants the conclusion that 'good' is indefinable in that usage. It may only be that the term 'good' in that usage is ambiguous, or that it is vague, or that its emotive meaning is somewhat peculiar.

I do not claim, of course, to have proved conclusively that intrinsic goodness is definable. This is, perhaps, impossible. At any rate, it could be done, if at all, only by the actual production of a satisfactory definition, and I am not prepared to give such a definition here. What I do claim is that there is no basis for the view that intrinsic value is indefinable, and that everything points in the direction of its definability. If this claim is correct, then there would seem to be two positions open to Moore, if he wishes still to be a non-naturalist or intuitionist in ethics. The first alternative is to hold that 'ought' represents an indefinable and non-natural relation, and that intrinsic value is definable in terms of 'ought'. The other alternative is to hold that 'ought' represents an indefinable non-natural relation, that intrinsic value is definable in non-ethical terms (e.g., in terms of satisfaction), and that intrinsic value, as defined, makes things such that they ought to be promoted. Both of these positions avoid the difficulties which I have found in the view which Moore has been holding. For, on the first of them, intrinsic value is normative and non-natural, but it is not an intrinsic quality; and, on the second, it is or may be intrinsic, but it is not normative or non-natural. On both views intrinsic value is definable. Moreover, either of these views is *prima facie* more plausible than Moore's view. They are more plausible than his earlier view because they take as ultimate the ethical notion which is most likely to be indefinable, but which it regards as definable, namely the notion of obligation. They are more plausible than his later view because they are simpler, since they involve only one ultimate notion, while it involves two. On both of them the non-ethical properties of a thing or experience directly determine whether or not it ought to be brought into existence. But on Moore's later view the non-ethical properties of a thing or experience directly determine only its intrinsic value, and its intrinsic value determines whether or not it ought to be produced or achieved. This is harder to believe. For it is just as likely that the non-ethical properties of a thing should make it such that it ought to be produced as it is that they should make it intrinsically good. And it is just as likely that a thing's non-ethical properties should make it such that it ought to be brought into existence as it is that an ethical quality of goodness should do so, if this is simple and intrinsic.[38]

Now, I have argued that, if value is an intrinsic quality, there is no reason for believing it to be indefinable in non-ethical terms. Hence, if Moore wishes to maintain with any plausibility that value is indefinable in non-ethical terms, he must adopt the view that it is definable in terms of 'ought' or 'right'.[39] And, indeed, I cannot see that he has any good reasons for not adopting this view. Suppose we say that "X is intrinsically good" means "X ought to be brought into existence by us." To this Moore would object that the first expression may be true where the latter is not, since the latter implies that we can produce X while the former does not.[40] What we ought to bring into existence depends on our knowledge, powers, and opportunities, whereas the good does not.[41] This objection may, however, be met by saying that "X is intrinsically good" means "If we are capable of producing X then we have a duty to do so," a form of definition which is not always unacceptable to Moore.[42] Another possible objection is that even if X is intrinsically good and we are capable of bringing it into existence it still may not be our duty to produce it, since we may be able to produce something better.[43] But this can again be met by saying that "X is intrinsically good" means "If we are capable of producing X, then we have a *prima facie* duty to do so," in Ross's sense of "*prima facie* duty."

This brings us to a consideration of an equivalence asserted by Moore in his *Ethics*:

> To say of anything, A, that it is "intrinsically good," is equivalent to saying that, if we had to choose between an action of which A would be the sole or total effect, and an action, which would have absolutely no effects at all, it would always be our duty to choose the former, and wrong to choose the latter.[44]

Why is this statement not a definition? Moore is not certain that it is not,[45] and he must, therefore, be thinking that it may be a definition of "intrinsically good" in terms of 'duty', for the first part of the asserted equivalence can hardly be taken as an analysis of the second part. His only argument for not regarding it as a definition is that it is not a tautology to say that it is always our duty to do what will have the best consequences.[46] But this argument is not conclusive. The fact that a statement seems to be significant does not prove that it is not analytic. Its apparent significance may be due to confusion. Our minds and our usages are not such that we can always recognize an analytic statement as analytic when it is presented to us. In particular, a statement may seem significant to us simply because of the differing connotative meanings of its terms. Now 'duty' and 'good' are precisely terms whose meanings are not at all clear, as is made manifest by the variety of opinion that exists as to their meaning, and they are moreover terms which have emotive meanings which differ in important respects.[47] Hence the seeming significance of the statement in question cannot be taken to show that the second part of the above equivalence is not a correct analysis of the first part. But then Moore seems to have no ground for not accepting this statement as a definition of "intrinsically good."

Moore might argue that it is quite clear that intrinsic value is dependent only on the intrinsic nature of a thing, and that therefore it cannot consist in any normative relation to anything else. Yet, even if we say that "X is intrinsically good" means "Any agent capable of producing X has a *prima facie* duty to do so," there is an important sense in which the intrinsic value of X may depend wholly on its intrinsic nature. For it may be because of its intrinsic nature alone that the agents in question have a *prima facie* duty to produce it.[48]

There remains the possibility of appealing to inspection to show that intrinsic value is a distinct property from that of being right for a competent agent to produce, somewhat as we appeal to inspection to show that the color red is distinct from the color blue or from the shape round or from the relation between. As I indicated earlier, however, the verdict of inspection in my case, as in that of so many others, is negative. I cannot discover in the things which may be considered to be good in themselves any simple intrinsic quality of goodness in addition to their non-ethical qualities and the property of being right for an appropriate agent to pursue or to produce.

My last main contention, then, is that the objections which Moore has given or may give to the view that value is definable in terms of obligation are not conclusive, and can be answered. Moore might reply that the question whether or not value is definable in terms of obligation is not an important one, the important question being whether or not it is definable in non-ethical terms.[49] This may be the import of his statement to the Aristotelian Society that the question whether intrinsic goodness is definable or not is a "comparatively unimportant" one.[50] At any rate, I should say in return that if it is important to hold that value is indefinable in non-ethical terms,[51] then it is also important to hold that it *is* definable in terms of obligation, since it cannot otherwise have any normative character.

Thus we may say the following of the two views between which, as it seems to me, Moore must choose. He can give no convincing grounds for not accepting the first of them, and he must accept it if he wishes to avoid the other. On the other hand, as we saw earlier, he cannot make a very plausible case against this view either, so long as he regards intrinsic value as an intrinsic quality. Neither view, therefore, is refuted by anything which he has to say in favor of his own intermediate view, nor, so far as I can see, by anything which he might say in its favor.

It is not a part of my present purpose to try to determine which of the two views in question is the correct one. To try to decide which of these views is true presupposes a decision on the antecedent question whether or not any non-naturalistic view is true, and this question I am now leaving to one side. My purpose is only to show that Moore's view is unacceptable in either its earlier or its later form. I am inclined to think, however, that there is some truth in each of the alternative views which I have described, in the sense of being inclined to think that the term 'good', in one usage in which Moore is interested, is ambiguous in such a way that it is definable sometimes in terms of 'ought' and sometimes in non-ethical terms, for example, in terms of desire or satisfaction. Some such ambiguity as this has been recognized in one way or another by E. F. Carritt, J. Laird, W. D. Ross, C. A. Campbell, S. C. Pepper, and others, although none of these writers interpret or implement it in the manner in which I am tempted to.

The points which I have tried to make in this paper concerning Moore's view of the relation of obligation and value may be summarized as follows. (1) Obligation cannot be defined in terms of value, as it is in *Principia Ethica,* if value is either simple or intrinsic in Moore's sense. (2) If value is either simple or intrinsic, as Moore holds, then it cannot be normative, non-natural, or definable in terms of obligation, and then there is no reason to regard it as indefinable in non-ethical terms, as Moore does. On the other hand, (3) if value is normative or non-natural or indefinable in non-ethical terms, as Moore believes, then it is definable in terms of obligation; it cannot have only a synthetic connection with obligation, and it cannot be either a simple or an intrinsic quality.[52] Moreover, (4) Moore does not seem to have any adequate grounds for rejecting the view that intrinsic value is definable in terms of obligation. Thus (5) it appears that Moore's view that intrinsic value is an indefinable, non-natural, intrinsic quality (principle 3) is an untenable one, that, in particular, his view that intrinsic value is indefinable is very probably false, and that, if he wishes to be non-naturalist in ethics, he must choose between two other views, against neither of which he has any good arguments, namely, (a) the view that intrinsic value is definable in non-ethical terms, even though it is what makes a thing such that it ought to be pursued or brought into being by a competent agent, and (b) the view that intrinsic value is definable in terms of obligation.

The impact of Moore's thought on twentieth-century moral philosophy has been a powerful one. . . . Possibly no other living moralist has had so great an influence. Certainly, at any rate, no single book of this century has had an effect in ethics or value-theory comparable with that of *Principia Ethica*. Now I am not one of those who hold that this influence which Moore has had has been wholly unsalutary. I am even somewhat inclined to feel that no recent philosopher has had a more salutary effect on ethical thinking, all things considered. I have, moreover, a certain sympathy or predilection for the sort of position in ethics for which he has stood. Nevertheless, I venture to think that the form into which he has put this sort of position, both in *Principia Ethica* and in his later works, is a mistaken one, and must be given up. This is the opinion which I have sought to communicate.

3: Ewing's Case against Naturalistic Theories of Value

IN HIS RECENT BOOK, *THE DEFINITION OF GOOD,* A. C. EWING PRESENTS, among other things, a case against naturalism in ethics. It is my purpose to describe and assess this case, but only insofar as it applies to naturalistic theories of intrinsic value, i.e., to theories which hold that "good," in the usage in which it is short for "intrinsically good," stands for a property and is wholly definable in terms of the concepts of some natural or empirical science, e.g., psychology. Ewing uses the same case against naturalistic theories about "ought" and against theories which define ethical concepts in terms of the concepts of logic, theology, or metaphysics. But with these uses of it I shall not be concerned, though much of what I say will, of course, be applicable to them also.

Ewing's case against naturalistic theories of "good" falls into two parts, not neatly distinguished: (1) his attempt to take the ground from under them, (2) his attempt to show they are false. We may consider (1) briefly first. In this regard, Ewing does rather better than other nonnaturalists in recognizing and counter-ing the considerations which have led people to be naturalists about "good."[1] For example, he argues very neatly against the belief that if one accepts a nonnaturalistic view, one cannot avoid skepticism in ethics.[2]

Still, even he minimizes unduly some of these considerations. For instance, he deals rather too briefly with G. C. Field's claim that goodness must be definable in terms of desire, else it is only a lucky accident if it happens to move us, whereas this should be of its essence. What he says is to the point, but, in view of the number of thinkers who agree with Field, somewhat too cavalier. Again, he is not satisfying in dealing with the empiricism in theory of knowl-edge which causes so many philosophers to reject nonnaturalism.[3] He rightly points out that we must not assume naturalism to be true in ethics because of a theory of knowledge arrived at without any regard for ethics.[4] But he does not

Reprinted from *Philosophical Review,* Vol. 57 (1948), pp. 481-92, by permission of *Philosophical Review.*

do much to answer the various difficulties involved in the doctrine of nonempirical concepts and synthetic a priori truths — difficulties which must at least be mitigated if naturalism is to be left without a leg to stand on or even a hand to hang from.

Hence it must be said that Ewing does not entirely dispose of the grounds for naturalism in value theory, though it may perhaps be granted that he shows the arguments for such a naturalism not to be conclusive. In any case, however, he cannot be content with doing either of these things; he must also try to show that naturalistic theories of "good" are false, and he must make this out the more forcibly just in proportion as he fails to meet the difficulties referred to a moment ago. This brings us to part (2) of his polemic.

Here Ewing's case consists partly of certain "fundamental objections which hold against any naturalist view of good," and partly of more specific objections to various particular naturalistic definitions. I shall deal only with the former. In the past such general objections to naturalistic definitions of "good" have been of three sorts: (a) charges that they involve the commission of certain fallacies, (b) arguments calculated to prove that they are mistaken, and (c) direct appeals to an inspection of what we mean. Now Ewing does not actually accuse naturalistic theories of value of committing any fallacy, naturalistic or otherwise, as many writers still do, following Moore who has himself given up this accusation. But he does not explicitly renounce the use of this charge, and in one place he accuses naturalism (and other attempts to define "good" in nonethical terms) of an "error" which is identical with one of the several procedures which Moore used to call the naturalistic fallacy. He says of H. J. Paton's coherence theory, "if it is intended to give a definition of 'good' . . . in Moore's sense, [it] can . . . fairly be accused of committing the same sort of error as naturalism; that is, of trying to reduce ethics without residuum to the non-ethical. For it is as impossible to get ethical content out of the merely logical as out of the merely psychological . . . ."[5]

This criticism of naturalism can have but little weight. For the reduction of ethical concepts to nonethical ones cannot simply be asserted to be an error; it must, if the question is not begged, be proved to be one. There is no more reason for claiming in advance that the ethical cannot be reduced to or derived from the nonethical than there is for saying in advance that the mathematical cannot be reduced to or derived from the logical, or that matter cannot be reduced to or derived from sense-data. To make such a claim is to say that a certain expression, such as "good" or "number," cannot mean the same as some other expression, such as "being aimed at by all men" or "being the class of all classes similar to a given class." But this one can assert only if one already knows that the two expressions differ in meaning. Until one knows this it is quite possible that "good" and "being aimed at by all men" stand for the same property, as Aristotle held.

Perhaps, however, when Ewing says in Chapter III that naturalism "commits" an "error," he is really thinking that he has already proved in Chapter II that the reduction of ethics to the nonethical is in fact an error. There he lists six general objections to naturalism. These sometimes have the aspect of arguments to prove such naturalism false (b), and sometimes that of an appeal to inspection of what we mean (c). We may consider them in the order in which they are summarized on pages 74-75, though we must make use of other passages in interpreting and discussing them (I shall consider them, of course, only as they apply to "intrinsically good").

The first of these objections, which is borrowed from Broad, may be stated as follows: (1) On a naturalistic theory of value the judgment "A is intrinsically good" is just a vague proposition about statistics, say, about how people feel, or at least it can be established or refuted merely by giving such statistics. But (2) it is clear that "A is intrinsically good" is not a statistical observation and that it cannot be established or refuted merely by collecting statistics. Now, omitting the fact that the first premise applies only to certain forms of naturalism about "good," this argument seems to be singularly dogmatic. Ewing asserts the second premise without taking any value judgments and showing us that they are not statistical observations under the skin, and without taking any disputes about values and showing us that they are not settled by citing statistics. He simply makes an easy appeal to inspection, assuming apparently that if value judgments are statistical this fact will not be disguised but will be written on their sleeves for any runner, no matter how quick, to read. But it seems to me a plain fact that if the character of judgments of value were thus carried on their sleeves, we should not have the controversies we have on this subject. The fact that we find it so difficult to determine their nature means that inspection cannot be so facilely appealed to as it is by Ewing in asserting his second premise.

As a matter of fact, I am not sure that the verdict of inspection, performed a bit more carefully, is on Ewing's side. Take "Knowledge is intrinsically good." It seems fairly plausible to hold that this statement is ambiguous and means now one, now another, of the following: "I enjoy knowledge," "People generally enjoy knowledge," "All men enjoy knowledge," "Everyone would enjoy knowledge if. . .," "If you run upon a piece of knowledge, you will enjoy it." If these assertions are statistical, and Ewing no doubt would say they were, then it is quite possible, so far as I can see, that "Knowledge is intrinsically good" is a vague proposition about statistics. At least this is plausible enough to throw doubt on Ewing's ready assurance.

In any event, I find it hard to see how we can be "clear" that "Knowledge is intrinsically good" is not a disguised assertion about people's likes and satisfactions, and thus "about statistics," if we are not clear first about the meaning of "good," as by hypothesis we are not. Certainly the very people who find a naturalistic theory of the meaning of "good" plausible would find Ewing's second premise doubtful. And so this argument seems to be of little value.

Ewing's next objection, also described as "fatal . . . to any naturalist analysis" is really a restatement of Moore's well-known open-question argument.[6] This argument, he says, must be used with care, apparently because he sees that it can be answered by pointing out that said question is bound to *seem* open just as long and insofar as the suggested definition is not accepted without reservation, which is probably seldom the case even among naturalists and is by hypothesis not the case among the intuitionists who use the argument. I should add, that having said this, Ewing later uses the argument without care at least five times, e.g., when he writes, " 'Good' cannot be defined as harmony. . .for there is no *verbal* contradiction in saying even that war is intrinsically better, though less harmonious, than peace."[7] Here, however, he goes on to state the "valid objection" he believes to be contained in Moore's argument. He says:

> . . . the trouble with the naturalist definitions is that, when we consider them and ask if what has the defining property is always good, we are clearly conscious that we are asking, not a question about what a term means, but the question whether everything which has the defining property has also a different property, signified by "good." It is not merely that it is an undecided question of definition, but that it is not a question of definition at all. The naturalist says that "good" means "desired" or "such that men feel approval" or "such as ultimately to satisfy men"; but it presents itself to us as, at least partly, a contingent question of empirical fact whether what is approved or desired or will ultimately satisfy us is also good.[8]

The answer to this, it seems to me, is still the one just indicated, though it may be supplemented by various other considerations. This is virtually admitted on the next page by Ewing when he confesses, "It is true that an analysis may sometimes express what I mean when I think it does not. . . ." If this is so, the question whether or not what is satisfying is good may present itself as a contingent one even if "good" means "satisfying." Ewing must, therefore, go on to argue (1) that one is not justified in accepting an analysis as expressing his meaning until he reaches the stage at which he can say, "Well, this is what I meant all along, although I did not put it so clearly," and (2) that "we never, with any of the definitions which have been proposed, reach the stage at which it seems at all plausible" to say this. This he does, though somewhat confusingly.[9] (1) must certainly be admitted, and will be dwelt on later. But (2) is questionable. If "we" means the intuitionists alone, it is, of course, true, that's why they are intuitionists. But if "we" means nonintuitionists also, as it should, it is false, for there are naturalists who have reached the stage in question, that's why they are naturalists (Ewing suggests they are naturalists for "extraneous and, I think, wrong reasons," but this is in part precisely the question at issue).

Thus this objection also turns out not to be "fatal" to naturalistic theories of value; in fact, Ewing himself, seemingly in order to clinch it, shifts to another objection[10] which we shall take up last since it is last on his summary list.[11] The next objection to naturalism on his list is stated as follows, supposing x to be something good:

(a) If x has the factual properties it has, it must have the value it has (by a noncausal necessity).

(b) But even if x has the other factual properties it has, it need not be desired, etc. (except in a causal sense of necessity).

(c) Therefore x's being good is not identical with its being desired, etc.

This argument seems to be applied by Ewing only to relational definitions. But it is hardly effective, as stated, even against these, for its premises may be true even if being good *is* identical with being desired. Suppose this to be the case. Then in assuming x to be good we are assuming it to be desired. And then, since being desired is a factual property, x's having the factual properties it has entails (noncausally) that it is good, and the first premise is true. But the second premise, that even if x has the *other* factual properties it has it need not (except causally) be desired, is also true. Hence Ewing's conclusion does not follow.

But the essence of his argument is that goodness is entailed (noncausally) by certain properties which do not entail (except causally) being desired, enjoyed, etc. Thus we may restate it so:

(a) "x is an experience of knowledge" entails "x is good" (noncausally).

(b) "x is an experience of knowledge" does not entail "x is enjoyed" (except causally).

(c) Therefore "x is good" is not identical with "x is enjoyed."

Now it is not subject to the above criticism. But now I am doubtful that the premises are both true if "being an experience of knowledge" is taken in the same sense in both cases, as it must if the argument is to be valid. For that x's being an experience of knowledge (noncausally) entails x's being good seems to me to be true only if by an experience of knowledge is meant a full-orbed experience consisting of a cognition plus the enjoyment which characteristically (I shall not say always) accompanies it. On the other hand, that x's being an experience of knowledge does not entail (except causally) x's being enjoyed can only be true if by an experience of knowledge is meant a mere cognition without the enjoyment that goes with it.

Thus we come to Ewing's fourth listed objection. He says, "The naturalist definitions leave out the essential nature of obligation."[12] This objection arouses a responsive echo in my soul, yet I cannot be sure that it adds up to anything when subjected to analysis, at least as applied to "good." What Ewing sometimes appears to have in mind may be expressed in this way:

(a) "x is good" entails "We have an obligation with respect to x."

(b) But "x is desired" does not entail "We have an obligation involving x."

(c) Therefore "x is good" is not identical with "x is desired."

Similarly for any suggested naturalistic *definiens*. Now, strictly, Ewing does not believe that if *x* is good, we have an *obligation* involving *x*, but only that if *x* is good, it is *fitting* for us to take some pro-attitude toward *x* (and it may be fitting for us to do so where it is not obligatory). But then we must read (b) to say that *x*'s being desired does not entail its being fitting for us to take any pro-attitude toward *x*. Read thus, (b) does not seem to be obviously true. At least there is some plausibility in James's view that any demand ought, for its own sole sake, to be satisfied, if not, prove why not. Ewing's contrary arguments[13] do not seem to be insuperable. In fact, he himself appears essentially to agree with James when he says later, ". . . if I regard something as capable of satisfying desire, I *ipso facto* regard it as in so far and subject to certain assumptions a fitting object of pursuit."[14]

It should also be noticed that this argument is not cogent in the case of any natural property whose presence in *x* makes it fitting for us to take some pro-attitude toward *x*. But there are such natural properties, according to Ewing, even if being desired is not one of them, and so if a naturalist were to propose one or more of these as definitions of good he could not be refuted in this way. Ewing might reply that there is nothing common and peculiar to these right-making properties, but he does not show this, and anyway he himself holds "intrinsically good" to be ambiguous, in which case there need be nothing common and peculiar to them.

Sometimes, however, what Ewing has in mind by his fourth objection is formulated in a different way. He writes, "The naturalist view . . . takes all the point away from morality."[15] This particular formulation is misleading, because it suggests that a naturalistic theory of value cannot show any *motivation* for pursuing the good, which is not necessarily true, and, anyway it is at least as hard for an intuitionist to provide motivation as it is for a naturalist, as has often been pointed out, e.g., by G. C. Field in the discussion referred to above. A better statement is this: ". . . if 'good' were defined naturalistically, it would be no more rational, right, fitting to pursue the good than the bad and . . . good would carry with it no moral obligation to pursue the good."[16] This passage may be interpreted as a version of the argument discussed a moment ago. But it also suggests another line of thought, viz.:

(a) If "good" means "desired" (or any other natural property), then "being the fitting object to a pro-attitude" is no part of the very meaning of "good."

(b) But "being the fitting object of a pro-attitude" is part of the very meaning of "good."[17]

(c) Therefore "good" cannot mean "desired" (or any other natural property).

This reasoning is very persuasive. Yet neither of its premises is unquestionable. The second premise, for instance, asserts that statements of the form "x is intrinsically good" either include or are identical with certain statements about obligation. But this would be denied by Moore and Ross on one side and by most naturalists on the other, and cannot be simply asserted, as it is by Ewing in Chapter II. To argue that "x is morally good" includes "a reference to the non-naturalist ought"[18] is hardly to the point, for Ewing himself distinguishes between "morally good" and "intrinsically good,"[19] and hence it might be that intrinsic goodness can be naturalistically defined while moral goodness cannot. In fact, that is roughly what I should hold. It is true that Ewing later spends much of Chapter V trying to make out that statements of the form "x is intrinsically good" are identical with statements about obligation or, rather, fittingness, but that chapter seems to presuppose Chapter II, and hence it would appear to be something of a circle for him to appeal to it to support this argument. Anyway, ingenious as it is, Chapter V is not entirely convincing in its attempt to show that "x is good" entails "x is a fitting object of a pro-attitude" analytically, and not only in some synthetic sense.

The other premise [that, if "good" means "desired" (etc.), then "fittingness" is not part of the meaning of "good"], I am disposed to accept, but it should at least be pointed out that it assumes, first, that "fittingness" is not part of the definition of "desired," and, second, that "being a fitting object of a pro-attitude" cannot be defined in terms of desire (etc.). For, if either of these assumptions is false, "fittingness" would be part of the meaning of "good" even if "good" means "desired" (etc.). Now the first of them is no doubt true, unless the definition of desire includes a reference to a value or ethical judgment, as is, indeed, sometimes suggested. But the second would simply be denied by many naturalists, e.g., R. B. Perry. Ewing sees this[20] and tries to show that "ought," etc., cannot be defined in terms of "desire," etc., but, of course, his attempt to show this makes use of the same sorts of objection that we are examining, simply applying them to definitions of "ought" rather than of "good." In particular, he uses his sixth objection[21] to which we now turn (I am omitting the fifth as being of little concern).

This objection does not involve any argument or attempted proof that naturalistic definitions are mistaken as most of the others do. It is a direct appeal to inspection, not merely to establish one of the premises of an argument calculated to prove that intrinsic goodness is distinct from all natural properties, but to establish this conclusion itself. Such an appeal to inspection is often made by intuitionists, but Ewing makes it more self-consciously and more boldly than any of his predecessors. He claims to be able to see that intrinsic goodness is a property which is both numerically distinct and different in kind from any natural properties. He writes, "I see that 'good' [etc.] . . . are just not the sort of concepts which can ever be analysed completely in terms of psychology, as I can see that sights cannot be analysed in terms of sound. . . . This awareness is immediate. . . ."[22] He then argues that it is very unlikely that he is peculiar in this respect,[23] shifts from "I" to "we" and from "immediately" to "after careful reflection," and says that "We can, after careful reflection, see that ethical concepts are generically different from, and therefore incapable of reduction to the concepts of psychology or any other empirical science."[24]

Now we come to the crux of the matter. If I am right in contending, as I have been doing, that naturalistic theories of value do not as such commit any "fallacy," and that the various arguments given by Ewing (and others) to prove that such theories are mistaken do not really come off, then inspection is not only the final but actually the sole court of appeal on the issue in hand. Ewing is quite right in appealing to it directly in the end; my point, in a way, has been that he should have been doing so systematically all along, instead of hinting at the "error" committed by naturalism and repeating or devising arguments to disprove it. The question is whether or not "intrinsically good," as we use it, means or says the same (at least as far as nonemotive significance goes) as, or stands for the same property as, "desired," "satisfying," etc., etc. And it can be decided only by an inspective study of meanings and properties. This may be *guided* by such "objections" as those discussed, but it cannot be compelled by them. If we can clearly see that "good" stands for a property different from being desired (or any other natural property), the issue will be decided in favor of the nonnaturalists, but it will be decided by inspective discernment and not by said objections; in fact, these objections become superfluous when this stage is reached. Until this stage is reached, however, they remain indecisive or even question-begging. And if this stage is never reached, if we do not come to see that "good" does not mean "desired," etc., as is the case with naturalists, we must regard the issue as decided against the nonnaturalists. Their arguments are not so impeccable as to be compelling even if inspection does not support their conclusion; and, if they were, they would be merely dialectical.

What of Ewing's appeal to inspection? About "ought" I am still inclined to agree with him, though I am much less confident than he that I actually discern a unique relational property in connection with this term. But in the case of "good" in the sense in which it is short for "intrinsically good" ("good" in the sense of "morally good" is another matter, as indicated earlier) inspection seems to me to point to a naturalistic definition in terms of something like enjoyment or satisfaction. But this is a long story which cannot be entered upon here. Just now, assuming, if I may, that I am not peculiar, I must try to explain what seems to me wrong with Ewing's appeal to inspection. Of course, one might say simply that Ewing is peculiar and really does see that intrinsic goodness is a unique property, but to say this raises many difficulties which it is better to avoid. One can only wager that Ewing does not really see a property of goodness which is distinct from all natural properties, even though he thinks so. And the fact is that when Ewing claims to see this he gives indications of basing his claim on a very questionable theory of meaning and its inspection. He says, " 'What I mean' is . . . 'what I intend to assert,' and I surely can sometimes be immediately aware of my own intentions,"[25] and he appears to imply that

questions of meaning can be settled by simple introspection.[26] "What arguments," he asks, "could be brought to show me that I do not mean what I think I
mean?"[27]

If this theory of meaning were correct, Meno would be quite right in
answering Socrates' question, "What is virtue?" by saying, "Why, there is no
difficulty, Socrates, in telling,"[28] and Socrates' work would be supererogatory
or even deluded. Indeed, the question of the meaning of "good" could not then
be so much a matter of controversy as in fact it is. It may be that what I mean is
what I intend to assert, though this could be disputed, but then what is it I intend
to assert? Is it what I consciously have before my mind at the time, no more and
no less? Even Ewing does not really think so. He admits that "an analysis may
sometimes express what I mean when I think it does not."[29] Is it what comes to
mind when someone asks me what I mean? Then Meno's first answer to
Socrates was the correct one, but he himself admitted after discussion that it was
not. Is it what I will accept as my meaning "after careful reflection," as when I
finally say, "This is what I meant all along, although I did not put it so
clearly"? It would seem so, and Ewing himself sometimes implies as much.
But then although it remains true that "in dealing with attempts at analysis we
are in the last resort forced to fall back on our consciousness that a proposed
analysis does or does not express what we mean,"[30] it is false that any simple
sort of introspection will suffice.

And so we have concluded our review of Ewing's case against naturalistic
theories about "good." In its course we have found, (1) that he does not
entirely dispose of the considerations which lead to such theories, (2) that his
claim that such theories commit the error of reducing the ethical to the nonethical presupposes that his other objections have shown this to be an error, (3) that
his first four objections do not prove it to be an error, each of them involving
steps or premises which may plausibly be questioned, (4) that therefore the
issue lies in an appeal to inspection, and (5) that Ewing's appeal to inspection in
his sixth "objection" is too facile to be satisfactory. Whatever may be true
about "ought," then, his case against naturalism about "good" (in the sense of
"intrinsically good") must be judged to be inconclusive. The matter still rests
in the court of inspection. Ewing's book may well be used as a help in this
inspective investigation, provided that we take his objections only as warning
blinkers and not as eternal stoplights.

4: Arguments for Non-Naturalism about Intrinsic Value

ETHICAL INTUITIONISTS MAY BE DESCRIBED AS HOLDING THAT CERTAIN ethical terms stand for characteristics which are indefinable and non-natural. In twentieth-century literature this claim has been made primarily for the term "good" in the usage in which it is short for "intrinsically good," whereas it had previously been made mainly for such words as "right," "ought," and "fitting." Now, the arguments to prove that "good" (in the sense of "intrinsically good") stands for an indefinable characteristic have been frequently, if not definitively, discussed; but those to show that it stands for a non-natural characteristic, so far as they are distinct from the former, have not, to my knowledge, been dealt with at all. It is, therefore, my purpose to take up these latter arguments here and to show that they quite fail to prove their point.

When they say that goodness[1] is a non-natural characteristic, the intuitionists mean to say one or more of three things: (a) it is nonempirical, (b) it is in a certain sense consequential or resultant, (c) it is in some way nondescriptive.[2] Thus it is one or more of these statements that they are trying to establish when they contend that goodness is non-natural. C. D. Broad, for instance, describes a non-natural property as one the concept of which is nonempirical, and argues as follows to show that goodness is non-natural in this sense, if it is a property at all.[3] (1) It seems evident that goodness is not a characteristic of which we become aware by inspecting our sense-data. (2) It seems equally clear that goodness cannot be identified with any simple psychological characteristic such as we could discover by introspecting our experiences; no one who is tempted to identify it with one of these psychological characteristics will do so if he recognizes the distinction between goodness itself and a good-making characteristic. (3) Therefore, if goodness is a *simple* quality, then it is "almost certainly" non-natural. (4) But no proposed definition of goodness in purely natural terms is in the least plausible. (5) Therefore, if goodness is a *complex*

Reprinted from *Philosophical Studies*, Vol. 1 (1950), pp. 56-60, by permission of D. Reidel Publishing Company.

characteristic, then again it is almost certainly non-natural. (6) Hence, finally, *if* there is such a characteristic as goodness at all, then, "according to our criterion," it will almost certainly be non-natural.

Probably no one except an extreme behaviorist will question step (1). But very many writers would object to step (4), and, in view of the number of able men among them, it seems hardly reasonable to assert that no proposed naturalistic analysis of goodness is in the least plausible. It would be reasonable to say that no such analysis of goodness is correct, but this Broad does not show. In step (2) Broad is similarly dogmatic. If enjoyableness is a simple psychological characteristic, it is not obvious to me, at any rate, that (intrinsic) goodness cannot be identified with any such characteristic; one could, at any rate, identify goodness with enjoyableness and still admit the distinction between goodness and good-making characteristics, just as Broad himself admits the distinction between pleasantness and pleasant-making characteristics. But even if it is true that goodness is not identical with any "other" simple psychological characteristic like enjoyableness, it is by no means clear that it is not an indefinable (simple *and* unique) natural characteristic of an introspectable sort. Merely to affirm that it is not such a characteristic is to beg the question. On the other hand, to assert that inspection reveals goodness not to be on the list of introspectable characteristics may be correct, but it involves admitting that the issue is to be settled by inspection and not by argument, and that what purported to be an argument consisting of six steps was really only an appeal to inspection — which I believe to be the case.

I confess that upon inspection I do not find any indefinable natural property for which the term "good" might be taken to stand when it is used in the sense in which Moore and Broad are interested. Hence I share Broad's opinion to the extent of agreeing that, *if* goodness is a property which is indefinable in natural terms, *then* it is almost certainly non-natural (in his sense, at least). [4] But I must insist that the antecedent of this hypothetical proposition has not been sufficiently well established (certainly not by Broad in the discussion here in question) for anyone to proceed to the assertion of its consequent.

Miss Clarke suggests an argument to show that goodness is non-natural in Broad's sense when she contends that, if goodness is a resultant property, then it would seem that it must be nonempirical. [5] This contention is somewhat cryptic and hypothetical. Suppose we agree that goodness is a resultant property. In which sense? In the Moore-Ross sense? [6] Even in that sense, "P is resultant" does not *logically* entail "P is nonempirical." To get this conclusion we must add the premise, "No empirical property is resultant (in the sense in question)." This premise, however, cannot be asserted until it is known that goodness is *not* an empirical property. It may be true that, if P is resultant in the Moore-Ross sense, then it is not identical with any of the "other" properties which we call empirical (and this only follows if none of these properties is resultant in that sense); this would mean that P is not definable in empirical terms, but it does not follow that P is nonempirical.[7]

Perhaps Miss Clarke means that there is no natural resultant property for which "good" can plausibly be said to stand, so that, if it stands for a resultant property, it must stand for one which is non-natural. Then I can only say that it is not clear, and she does not show, that there is no natural resultant property (definable *or* indefinable) which "good" may be said to denote, or that "good" does denote a property which is resultant (in the Moore-Ross sense, at least).

In his recent reply to his critics, G. E. Moore seems to take a non-natural property to be one which is nondescriptive (in a sense not further specified), and he offers what he calls a "good" argument to show that goodness is non-natural in this sense.[8] The argument, he says, contains two premises; actually, as I understand it, it contains several more, and runs as follows. (1) There are many different natural intrinsic properties which are ought-implying.[9] (2) No natural intrinsic property (except possibly a disjunction of them all) is both entailed by all of these properties and ought-implying. (3) Goodness is not identical with each of these different natural intrinsic properties. (4) It is entailed by each of them. (5) It is not identical with a disjunction of them all. (6) It is ought-implying. (7) Therefore, goodness is not identical with *any* natural intrinsic property.

Moore says that this argument is perfectly conclusive if (1) and (2) are true. This is obviously a slip on his part. It is conclusive only if premises (3) to (6) are also true. But of these premises only (3) is unquestionable. Premise (4) would be denied by those who regard goodness as not being intrinsic in Moore's sense, (5) involves the assumption that "good" in the sense of "intrinsically good" is not an ambiguous term, and (6) was once denied by Prichard and Carritt. However, there may still be good reasons for supposing these additional premises to be true, and I do not wish to question them. Nor am I concerned here to deny (1). What I wish to contend is that in asserting (2) Moore is so far from giving us a "good" argument as to be begging the question. To assert (2) one must know that goodness is not a natural intrinsic property which is both ought-implying and entailed by all the natural properties referred to in (1).

To know this one must know: (a) that goodness is neither a natural property nor a disjunction of natural properties, (b) that it is not entailed by all the natural properties referred to in (1), or (c) that it is not ought-implying.

Now (b) and (c) are ruled out by (4) and (6) respectively. Therefore, if one asserts (4) and (6), then before he can assert (2) he must know (a). Now (a) does not follow from (4) and (6) taken separately or together, for, as Moore admits, a natural intrinsic property may be resultant and ought-implying. Therefore, to know (a) one must know independently that goodness is not a natural intrinsic property. Hence, to assert (2) in conjunction with (4) and (6) is to assume that goodness is not a natural intrinsic property, and so to beg the question.

A.C. Ewing has also contended that goodness is non-natural (in Broad's sense apparently),[10] but I have dealt with his arguments elsewhere.[11] His main point is that the notion of goodness involves that of obligation and is therefore generically different from all natural notions. This, however, assumes that "good" is definable in terms of "ought" and that "ought" stands for a non-natural characteristic; his other arguments do not establish either of these assumptions, any more than they prove directly that goodness is non-natural. In fact, in order to make his point, Ewing appeals, not to any argument, but to inspection. "I see," he says, "that propositions about what is good in some senses of 'good' are propositions which cannot be analysed adequately in psychological terms."[12] This is as it should be, for inspection, if I am right in my estimate of his and other intuitionists' arguments, must in some sense be the ultimate court of appeal in this matter. Even so, his appeal to this tribunal is rather too facile, and others may well, on consulting it, receive a negative verdict, as I do (except in the case of moral value).

However my concern here is with the *arguments* which are alleged to prove that goodness (intrinsic) is non-natural, and I believe I have shown them to be quite inconclusive or even question-begging. Hence, if careful inspection bears us out, we may still be naturalists about intrinsic value.[13] Of course, these arguments cannot serve to establish the non-naturalness of moral value, rightness, or obligatoriness either, if I am right. This result is not entirely to my liking, as I am still inclined to be a non-naturalist about these. But, if one is to be a naturalist about intrinsic value, as I find myself being, one must answer said arguments, and, anyway, if they are in fact inconclusive or question-begging, nothing is to be gained by hiding this. As A. N. Prior has recently said, it is only confusing the issue for non-naturalists to go on misconceiving the grounds of their position.[14]

5: Ethical Naturalism Renovated

NATURALISM HAS HAD TWO MEANINGS IN TWENTIETH-CENTURY DISCUSSIONS relating to ethics. In a wider sense "naturalism" has stood for a general philosophical point of view the essence of which is a denial of supernaturalism, including most forms of idealism. "The ethics of naturalism" in this sense is any ethics forming part of a philosophy which rejects all supernaturalistic conceptions of the world. But since the publication of G. E. Moore's *Principia Ethica* in 1903, and especially in the writings of his intuitionist and non-cognitivist successors, "naturalism" has had also a more special meaning when used in ethics; it has meant any ethical theory which holds that an ethical judgment is simply a true or false ascription of a definable and natural (or empirical) property to an action, object, or person. Opposed to ethical naturalism in this usage is not supernaturalism but a pair of positions: (a) intuitionism, also called "non-naturalism," which holds that an ethical judgment is a true or false ascription to something of an indefinable and non-natural (or non-empirical) property, and (b) non-cognitivism, which in its extreme forms claims that an ethical judgment is not a true or false ascription of any property to anything, but something very different, like an interjection, a command, a wish, a resolution, or a prescription.

Thus ethical theory has been involved in a double controversy, the general controversy between naturalism and supernaturalism, and a more special one between naturalism, intuitionism, and non-cognitivism. These two debates have been variously mingled. Naturalists in the one sense have not always been naturalists in the other. Some naturalists in the broad sense have also been naturalists in the narrower (John Dewey, R. B. Perry), but some of them have been intuitionists (G.E. Moore, B. Russell before 1912), and many of them, especially recently, have been non-cognitivists (A. J. Ayer, C. L. Stevenson). Again, supernaturalists have sometimes been intuitionists (H. Rashdall), sometimes non-cognitivists (some religious existentialists and neo-orthodox theologians), and sometimes naturalists (J. B. Pratt, Thomists).

Reprinted from *The Review of Metaphysics*, Vol. 10 (1957), pp. 457-73, by permission of *The Review of Metaphysics*.

Now Rice is a naturalist in his general philosophical position, but he does not argue for this naturalism in the present book.[1] It is assumed and is present as a background all the time. Thus there is a Garden of Eden motif, as the title indicates, but without any Christian theology, though not without natural piety. No doubt Rice thinks of himself as reasserting naturalism in this wider sense also, in the face of the resurgent Catholic and Protestant moral philosophies of Berdyaev, Brunner, Maritain, Niebuhr, Tillich, and others. Still, it is the more special controversy which is in the center of his stage here, and it is naturalism in the narrower sense which he is particularly concerned to reaffirm, though, in so doing, he gives it a "radical restatement."

It is worth noticing that in refurbishing ethical naturalism Rice is not alone. We are today, in fact, having a kind of revival of such a naturalism, which has not had it as easy in this century as one might expect. First there was a period during which many books and articles reviewed critically metaphysical ethics and naturalism, and came out with intuitionism, as Sidgwick and Moore had. Next came a period when philosophers took a critical look at naturalism and intuitionism, and emerged with an emotive theory, as Ayer and Stevenson did. Then for a time it was the fashion, set by S. E. Toulmin, to take up naturalism, intuitionism, and emotivism in turn, and to decide for a sophisticated form of non-cognitivism which Rice calls "informalism." In all of these discussions naturalism was under attack, but now things are different. We have, for the first time, a number of books in which philosophers review naturalism, intuitionism, emotivism, and informalism; and whatever this may portend, they all end by reasserting naturalism![2]

Of these works Rice's is surely one of the most important, and I shall concern myself with it. It is a book by a philosophical statesman; the author takes part seriously in ethical controversy, but reflectively and with a large vision which embraces opposing views and keeps the larger setting of moral judgments constantly in mind. It is also the work of a man of letters, and is written with more literary taste and general sensitivity than are most recent books in ethics. Both of these virtues are manifested in the existence here of many passages in which wise substantive insights and valuable reflections on method and perspective are expressed in such a way as to make the book worthwhile for their sake alone.

In dealing with Rice's book, however, I shall not go over the whole question of the tenability of ethical naturalism as restated by him. I shall only concern myself with some points in his restatement of it which will be involved in any estimate of its tenability. And I shall consider only what he says about judgments of moral obligation, leaving to one side his views about judgments of value. A short summary of his position is required before we can proceed.

The first question for the ethical naturalist is this: is an ethical judgment simply a true or false ascription of a naturalistically analyzable property to some object? The intuitionist and non-cognitivist both argue (the naturalistic fallacy, the open question, etc.) that it is not, and Rice finds their arguments convincing. Simple naturalism must be given up. But intuitionism, with its essential dogmatism and its non-empirical epistemology, cannot be accepted. The mistake of the simple naturalist is only in thinking that an ethical judgment is *merely* a statement to the effect that a certain object has a certain natural property — if anyone ever thought this. (In a plausible chapter Rice argues that so-called naturalists like Mill, Santayana, Perry, and Dewey did not in fact think this.) The nature of the revision needed is made clear by the non-cognitivist; naturalism must explicitly recognize that there is an important non-cognitive element in an ethical judgment, though it may and should retain its claim that there is also a cognitive one (as a constituent of the judgment, and not merely as a reason for it). Non-cognitivism, in inferring that an ethical judgment contains in itself no true or false assertion, is going farther than the argument requires, and throws into jeopardy the whole structure of reasoning in ethics (for if it were true, there would be nothing in an ethical judgment which could be supported logically by inductive or deductive methods, and the suggestion of a third logic is "crypto-intuitionist" and "unintelligible").

In saying that an ethical judgment has both a cognitive and a non-cognitive constituent, Rice has not yet distinguished himself from Stevenson, who is willing to grant, though he does not *insist,* that an ethical utterance has a cognitive *constituent,* as well as being supportable by factual *reasons.* He does this mainly by arguing for a kind of monism. Where Stevenson holds that the properties which are asserted in a moral judgment are many and variable, and can be fixed only by "persuasive definition," Rice plugs for the view that there is basically a single property which is asserted of actions by all judgments of moral obligation, and that the identification of this property is not merely a process of "persuasion."[3]

Thus, while Rice borrows something from each of the houses he visits — simple naturalism, intuitionism, and non-cognitivism in its various forms — he ends by declaring a plague on them all. But it is only a very light plague which he declares on naturalism, for he proceeds to build right next door. He does this, he says, not only for the reasons indicated above, but because he believes "that the intuitionists and non-cognitivists, for all their contributions, have reached the limits of advance by the methods they have used hitherto, and that solution of the riddles in which ethical theory is bogged . . . can be made only by renewed attention to the larger natural and social context of valuations, emphasized by naturalism and largely neglected by recent schools of analysis for more restricted questions of logic and meaning" (p. 100).

Briefly, then, Rice's view is this (see pp. 13, 120 f., 271 f., 281): a moral judgment like "A is right or obligatory," so far as its "primary" meaning goes, consists of two parts: an assertion that A has a certain natural or empirical IP or Identifying Property, and a non-cognitive Matrix Meaning or MM!. That is,

A is right = A has IP; MM!

Here a particular moral judgment is being analyzed. The schema for a "maxim" like "We ought to be just" would be:

Every just act (probably) has IP; MM!

As for a basic "principle" like "We ought to promote the greatest general good," Rice seems to think that it will have the same schema:

Whatever promotes the greatest general good has IP; MM!

But this cannot be, for on his view the IP in question just is the property of promoting the greatest general good, and the principle would, on such a reading, say:

Whatever promotes the greatest general good promotes the greatest general good; MM!

No, for Rice this principle (and he does not believe any others are ultimately valid) must be represented as follows:

Whatever promotes the greatest general good; MM!

or perhaps

(x), if x promotes the greatest general good, then MM!

A number of questions arise. (1) What is the nature of the MM!, the non-cognitive aspect of a judgment of obligation? Rice speaks of it both as a "force" and as a "job" or "function" of the judgment, and he carefully recognizes that "ought" sentences may have a variety of forces or functions, cognitive or non-cognitive. But he believes that there is one job or force which is "primary," namely, a non-cognitive one which he calls the "trigger function." "The 'ought' or the 'right' . . . *expresses the fact that a choice has been made, and serves as a signal to release the action"* (109). "The 'ought' signifies that the alternatives have been explored as thoroughly as feasible, and expresses a decision. The decision then, assuming that the relevant conditions have been fulfilled, releases or triggers the act" (232). Saying that the "ought" is prescriptive or imperative serves approximately, but only approximately, to identify this "central force," which is "to set in motion an act after a process of deliberation" (112).

One could ask about the mechanics involved here. Presumably it is my *utterance,* "I ought to do A," which has this force. But how does it express a decision or release an action? Through some "emotive meaning" which it has or through some information which it conveys? Can it both "express" and "release"? Is it the utterance or the decision expressed which releases the action? Are "prescribing" and "triggering" as similar as Rice seems to think? But the real question is whether this kind of account of the central function of "I ought," which is similar to that of Nowell-Smith, can be correct or not, however the details are worked out. I do not believe that it can. When one is faced with a decision and asks, in a non-moral sense, "What should I do?" this may be equivalent to asking, "What shall I do?" and the answer, "I should do A" equivalent to "I shall do A," as Rice implies. But it is "What morally ought I to do?" and "I morally ought to do A" that we are concerned with, and I cannot see that they are equivalent in force to "What shall I do?" and "I shall do A." Their force is more like that of "What am I justified in doing (or unjustified in omitting)?" and "I am justified in doing (or unjustified in omitting) A."

If "I morally ought to do A" expresses a decision, it is not, so far as I can see, a decision to do A but a decision about what should be done — a decision made, as it were, by a part of me and not by my whole will — so that I may conclude that I morally ought to do A and yet not do or even try to do A. Rice admits that "I ought" may fail to release action because of weakness of the flesh. In this case it does not have all the force one would like to see it have, but it remains a full-fledged *moral* "I ought" nevertheless. If so, "I morally ought" is not primarily a trigger. It is true, as Rice points out, that even "I morally ought" normally appears in a context of decision, and that asking "What morally ought I to do?" and answering "I ought to do A" are *in a sense* "useless unless they eventuate in the firing itself." The normal point of moral deliberation and judgment is the effective direction of action. But that "I morally ought" is essentially triggering does not follow, even *if* it is so normally. It may still be appropriate and useful to say "I morally ought to do A," before one decides to do it, to express the fact that one thinks he is justified in doing (or unjustified in not doing) A. Here "I morally ought" appears not as an expression of decision, nor as a trigger of action, but as a *guide* to decision and action, perhaps even as *one* determinant of the outcome. If one's flesh is not too weak, etc., it may serve to release action, but this is not of its essence. Rice himself claims that "I morally ought" not only triggers action but does so with the implication that the action is justified by appropriate considerations; it seems to me that its moral force lies in this implication, not in the triggering. A moral judgment seeks to guide and even to trigger conduct, but it may fail. Then it may not have the desired *force,* but its moral *meaning* is complete, as a guidepost has its uses and meanings even if it is not always followed. A moral judgment is not as such a movement of the entire will, though it hopes to be, just as "There is a car coming" is not as such a warning, though it may have this purpose.

In what Rice says about justification there are, as we shall see later, the makings of a rather different (and in my opinion more tenable) view of this matter.

(2) As has been indicated, Rice holds that there is a single IP for all judgments of moral obligation, that this IP is not merely a reason for such judgments but a constituent in their primary meaning, and that it is the property of promoting the

greatest general good. Thus he offers us a kind of utilitarian "definition" of "morally ought":

I morally ought to do A = A promotes the greatest general good; MM!

This definition he does not regard as merely "persuasive." He does not lay it down in advance, and he does not answer the question, "Why ought we to promote the general welfare?" by saying that this is the very meaning of the term, as Moore thinks naturalists must. Neither does he advance conduciveness to the general good as what we explicitly have in mind when we use "ought" in a moral sense; Moore's arguments, he thinks, show that this is not the case. He offers his definition as the very tentative conclusion of a reflective inquiry into our moral judgments. What kind of an inquiry? As I understand it, an inquiry into the reasons which may be advanced in order to justify judgments of moral obligation. It is generally agreed that to justify morally such a judgment as "I ought to do B," we show that B is just, keeps a promise, prevents harm, etc. (in short, that B has some Conferring Property or other). But we may ask for a justification, Rice thinks, of the "maxims" requiring us to be just, keep our promises, etc., and he argues that such a justification can only lie in the claim that justice, etc., promote the greatest general good. Here, of course he must answer the arguments of the deontologists, and, indeed, a discussion of them forms a large part of his defense of his "definition." I cannot say that I am convinced by this defense of utilitarianism, but his discussion is a good one as far as it goes.

I can raise only a few questions about this. Is such an inquiry a normative one, that is, is Rice contending that our only duty ultimately is to promote the greatest general good; or is he arguing that the promotion of the greatest general good is ultimately the only reason which we in fact give in justification of our moral judgments? But suppose that we agree that *the* justifying reason in morality is conduciveness to the greatest general good. Why should we go on, as Rice does, and say that an assertion of such utility is a constituent of, and not merely a reason for, the judgment "A is morally right." This does not follow; Hutcheson accepts Rice's findings that the justifying reason for a moral judgment is utility, but holds that a moral judgment is simply an expression of a peculiar sentiment. That "I ought to do A" is justified by showing A to be optimific does not entail that it asserts A to be optimific — at least if we do not assume that "justified" has a logical force here, which would be begging the question. Rice may reply, "Yes, but, since moral judgments are justified by an appeal to utility and only by such an appeal, let us say that they assert utility of their subjects." But would we gain anything by doing this? If "p asserts that A is optimific" only means that p is justified by showing that A is optimific, we make no advance. Then "being a constituent of" is the same as "being a reason for."

Perhaps the proposal is that we should henceforth mean to assert that A is optimific when we say it is right. I am not sure that Rice's naturalism does not come to this. To say that it does would, of course, not be to condemn it. But why should we adopt this proposal? Why not remain non-cognitivists with a "monistic" conception of ethical reasoning, as Hutcheson did? Rice's reply would be that, on a non-cognitivist view, there is only a psychological connection between an ethical judgment and the reasons for it, not a logical one; or, in other words, that moral conclusions can be logically supported by inductive or deductive reasoning only if they include an assertion of some sort. Let us assume that, other things being equal, it is desirable that judgments should have logical connections with the reasons given for them, and that no third "logic" is available. Still, on Rice's view, it will be only the cognitive component of an ethical conclusion which will follow logically from the reasons offered; the rest of it follows, if at all, only psychologically, and the rest is essential to its being an *ethical* conclusion. The MM! in the conclusion will follow only if there is an MM! in the premises, and even then it will not follow logically. Simply to show that A is for the general good will not logically entail any sort of triggering; in fact, it may not even suffice causally to release action, in which case other "persuasive" considerations will be required.

Rice argues in support of his naturalistic proposal that it keeps us closer to "the larger natural and social context of valuations." Historically this may be true, since so many of the non-cognitivists have limited themselves to analysis. But this relative neglect of the larger context of moral judgments is due to the view that moral philosophers should stick to analysis; it is not necessarily implied by non-cognitivism, as Stevenson has shown.[4] In fact, S. E. Toulmin has a good deal to say about this larger context.[5] In saying this he may be breaking through the boundaries of analysis, but he is not doing anything inconsistent with his non-cognitivism.

(3) Rice's radically restated naturalism appears then to have no essential advantages over a monistic non-cognitivism. It is even tempting to ask if there is any real difference between these two positions, when both of them include a utilitarian theory of justification (i.e., of what Rice calls "validation") and a triggering conception of the primary job to be done by a moral judgment, so that they differ only on the question whether utility is asserted or merely presupposed in such a judgment.

Let us suppose, however, that these two positions are really different. Is there any reason for regarding Rice's as a form of naturalism rather than as a form of non-cognitivism? True Rice's position is monistic, and non-cognitivism has usually been pluralistic. But the latter may be monistic and even utilitarian, as the examples of Hutcheson and Hume show.[6] More to the point is the fact that on Rice's view "I ought to do A" has a constituent which is true or false, and follows logically (by induction or deduction) from empirical premises. We have seen, however, that this does not imply that the methodology of justifying A is any more logical than it is for Stevenson, especially if justifying A involves bringing me to the point of deciding to do A (as it does on Rice's stated view of the force of "I ought," though not on the view implied in his account of justification). Saying that "I ought" has a cognitive constituent is not enough to make one a naturalist in any important sense, even if one is a monist where Stevenson is a pluralist. Whether one who concedes that moral judgments have an important non-cognitive meaning is a naturalist or not must depend on his conception of the relation between the cognitive and the non-cognitive elements in such judgments. If one regards the non-cognitive aspect as primary, one can hardly be called a naturalist, except in the broader sense of being opposed to supernaturalism (if one is); but if one conceives of the cognitive aspect as primary, it would still seem appropriate to call him a naturalist even in a narrower sense. Unfortunately Rice's account is not very clear. Sometimes he speaks of the cognitive and non-cognitive elements as both belonging to the primary meaning of "I ought"; sometimes he says that the primary or central job of such expressions is to trigger action. On the former view, we shall need to know more about how the two are related before we can answer our question; on the latter, we seem to be forced to regard Rice as a non-cognitivist. But Rice also speaks of the considerations asserted by an ethical judgment as justifying the releasing of the action, which is the non-cognitive function of the judgment, and this seems to give the cognitive element at least a moral primacy. In one place he even passes the whole problem off as unimportant ["All that matters is to include both elements" (271 f.)], and perhaps it is, but not if one wishes to be a naturalist rather than a non-cognitivist.

Rice must mean to hold that a sentence like "I ought to A," in its primary use, (1) asserts that A has a certain property, and (2) releases A into the world. If he does not hold that it does (1), he cannot be regarded as a naturalist. But his holding that it does (1) is not enough to make him one; we must still know how its doing (1) is related to its doing (2). It will not suffice to say that its doing (1) justifies its doing (2), for this a non-cognitivist may allow. Perhaps Rice is thinking that "I ought to do A" accomplishes (2) by way of doing (1); or more accurately that my belief that A has the property in question (utility) causes A to be released (notice, this is to say that it is not the whole utterance with its non-cognitive aspect that triggers the action, but only the cognitive part of it). He might then maintain either that this belief by itself produces A, or that it does so by enlisting some desire of mine. But then the case of "I ought to do A" seems to be very like that of "There is a car coming" said to another as one is crossing a street. In the latter case, too, one can speak of a cognitive job of asserting and conveying information, and a non-cognitive one of releasing (or inhibiting) action. The non-cognitive job is (or at least may be, if the sentence is spoken in a somewhat matter-of-fact way) accomplished simply by way of doing the cognitive job, if this enlists a desire to live on unhurt, as presumably it will.

Now, if "I ought to do A" is like "There is a car coming" for Rice, then he can regard himself as a naturalist, for this is what naturalists have been concerned to maintain. However, he must then give us his insistence that a certain kind of non-cognitive force is an essential part of the primary meaning of "I ought to do A." For one would not claim and could not plausibly argue that any particular kind of non-cognitive force was an essential part of the meaning of "There is a car coming" (other than that of releasing belief), even though one might contend that "There is a car coming" is always used for some non-cognitive purpose or other (other than that of expressing or arousing belief).

If "I ought to do A" does not achieve its end simply by virtue of asserting what it asserts (and enlisting whatever desires this information enlists), but also by virtue of some other potency it owns (e.g., "emotive meaning"), what is this potency and how does it operate? Is it the presence of this factor which determines the methodology of ethical reasoning, as Stevenson maintains, or is it the presence of the cognitive factor, as a naturalist must insist?

I have no quarrel with Rice's interesting discussion of the logic of justification in ethics. (His view is that a particular judgment like "I ought to do A" is morally justified by appeal to a maxim like "We ought to keep our promises," which is justified by appeal to a principle, viz., the principle "We ought to promote the greatest general good.") I fully sympathize with his insistence on appealing to principles, and on looking for a single principle, though, as I said, I stop short of following him to his utilitarian conclusion (which he himself holds only tentatively). Of more importance for us here, and really very stimulating, is what Rice says about the justification of principles. He maintains that a principle cannot be justified in the sense of being demonstrated or "validated," just because it is the ultimate premise of moral reasoning. Nor can it be self-evident or self-justifying. Yet it stands in need of some sort of justification, for one may ask with respect to what it enjoins, "Why should I?" Rice's suggestion is that it can be "vindicated," and what he says here is a valuable contribution to contemporary discussion, even if it is not entirely clear or conclusive. He goes beyond what recent non-cognitivists have done; in fact, this seems to be one reason why he regards himself as a naturalist, since the non-cognitivists have generally stopped short of a quest for vindication and have sometimes abjured it. I share Rice's sense of the legitimacy of such a quest, but actually nothing that he does in pursuit of it is inconsistent with non-cognitivism. A non-cognitivist may not only join in this quest; he may even make "the appeal to human nature" which Rice does, as will become clear later.

The problem is to justify the principle, "We ought to promote the greatest general good." Now this principle, as I indicated earlier, does not include a factual assertion, as lesser judgments of obligation do, though Rice sometimes suggests that it does. Its schema is:

Whatever promotes the greatest general good; MM!

It signifies "a linkage of the factual or descriptive and the normative or prescriptive elements" (278), but it does not assert such a linkage, else it would be capable of empirical validation; and neither of its parts is an assertion. Rice seems to take it as equivalent to the "definition" or "definitory principle":

X is morally obligatory = A promotes the greatest general good; MM!

But this is not an assertion of purported fact, and contains no such assertion. In any case, though one may accept this definition if he regards the utilitarian principle as vindicated, he need not do so, for he may prefer to consider an assertion of utility merely as a reason for a moral judgment and not as a constituent of it. The prior question is about its vindication as the basic principle of moral validation.[7] We have already described Rice's case to show that it is the basic premise of such validation; now the question is about its own status, and my point is that, since on Rice's view the principle is not an assertion, vindicating it is not showing that it is true. It is more like persuading us to accept it, that is, to commit ourselves to the promotion of the good.

Rice explores the notions of vindication (a) by an appeal to "the congenital a priori" (i.e., to a commitment which is a necessary ingredient in human nature), and (b) by an appeal to acquired life-involvements or "second nature" (he seems to equate this with "pragmatic justification," but I do not find the use of this phrase very clear here). There is a third possibility, which Rice touches on but does not distinguish from the other two, viz., (c) an appeal to a drive which is innate in human nature but not necessary in the way in which the congenitally a priori is, e.g., altruism (cf. 177). The principle "Seek ends," he argues, is congenitally a priori and thus vindicable, but it and other such congenitally a priori principles do not suffice for ethics; no ethical first principle can be wholly justified in this way. "Vindication may appeal to the human make-up, but it must finally be the human make-up as shaped by a social situation" (190), i.e., "second nature." "[The] linkage [between MM! and the general good] is made neither by empirical verification nor by sheer stipulation, but partly by our congenital structure and partly by our life-involvements, or rather by the two in interaction" (278).

But what form is vindication to take then? It might consist in showing that we already are in fact committed by our nature (first or second) to the principle in question. Some of what Rice does runs along this line, e.g., his contention that the principle of utility is the "structural presupposition" of our pre-discursive and lower-level moral judgments. But Rice does not think that such a demonstration can constitute vindication, though it may contribute to it. "We cannot deduce or induce principles from our best verified theories as to what human nature is, though these exercise restraint upon us and offer guidance" (192). A principle cannot be fully justified in our sight by a line of argument which a spectator standing outside the normative process and seeking to understand it might use. They must be espoused by us as participants; they must pass the scrutiny of our "moral consciousness" or "global sense of directedness," and this may on occasion "reject or modify the presuppositions that have guided us hitherto" (190-194).

For Rice, then, the "vindication" of the principle of utility must consist in moving us to commit or recommit ourselves to it. Nothing is involved that a non-cognitivist cannot allow. Now, we may ask if it makes any difference what means are used to lead us to wed or re-wed this principle. For Rice, once the principle is admitted, only appeals to it are good or relevant reasons for other moral judgments, but what about it? Does anything go here, so long as it is effective? Rice need not take this view, and I do not believe that he does, though his identification of the non-cognitive aspect of moral judgments with trigger-ing seems to imply it. Rather, he appears in this part of his discussion to think of vindication in the following way. There is in us something often referred to as "conscience" or "moral consciousness," which he prefers to call our "global sense" of moral adequacy. This he thinks of as part of our "second nature," as a "compounding of active forces" which is "shaped by long buffeting from the world," or "pounded into us by social compulsions, but is also critical of them" (cf. 186, 190 f., 194 f.). A principle is "vindicated," once this question has been raised, if and only if this element in our nature reaffirms it after having been presented with whatever considerations may be deemed relevant, among them, perhaps, facts about human nature and implicit previous commitments. This global sense may "err" but only it can judge its own aberrations (195).

Here there is an "appeal to human nature," but the vindication does not proceed so much by establishing facts about human nature (first or second), as by appealing to something in human nature (mainly "second") as a kind of judge or tribunal. And only a part or aspect of human nature is so appealed to. Hence only considerations which will move *it* to espouse or re-espouse the promotion of the general good are relevant in the process of vindication. It is not required that we be persuaded to commit ourselves to it with our whole souls; and *additional* considerations or methods which are calculated to do this are strictly irrelevant. Espousing a moral principle does not entail acting upon it.

The problem of passing from factual reasons to an ethical conclusion has been much discussed, and some have introduced the notion of a "third logic," peculiar to moral reasoning, to deal with it. But such a view as Rice's (if the above is Rice's view, as I think) has an answer to it. No *inference* from factual premises to ethical conclusions, in any logical sense, is involved in ethical reasoning. What happens in the case of a principle is that our moral sense is *moved* to a favorable or unfavorable response, which it expresses by saying "We ought" or "We ought not." And once a principle has been accepted (consciously or unconsciously) it serves as an ethical premise for the derivation of lower order judgments with the help of factual considerations.

But if this is Rice's view, then, in the analysis of judgments of moral obligation, he should not have identified the element signified by "MM!" with the capacity to release action (which involves a decision of the whole will) but with the taking of a favorable (or unfavorable) stand by the moral sense or whatever it is in us that is committed to the promotion of the general good (which is not the entire self).

Of course, there is much that could be said or asked concerning such views about the vindication of ethical principles. It would be interesting to compare Rice's appeal to human nature with that of Lewis.[8] And one might ask about the "global [moral] sense." How can it be a product of social life and yet be capable of criticizing social rules and institutions? How is it related to our commitment to rationality? Can it be identified with the sentiment of sympathy? Whence comes its authority, especially its authority over other elements in our nature? I do not mean to imply, however, that Rice would have any difficulty with such questions; it is just that I wish he had gone on to consider them more explicitly. He does give us a chapter on "the moral authority" which is well worth reading on this difficult subject, but it is not so clear as one would like, and does not really raise the question just indicated.

This, then, is Rice's naturalism restated. Whether it is tenable or not in general I have not considered, except for trying to show that there is no reason for preferring it to a monistic form of non-cognitivism, if, indeed, it can be distinguished in any important way from such a position — and I am not at all sure that this would have disturbed Rice very much. My main criticism has been directed at his view that the primary force of "I morally ought" is to express decision and trigger action, and I have found support for my criticism in what Rice himself goes on to say about justification. Apart from this I find many points which are unclearly treated, and many inquiries which are not pushed quite far enough to be convincing. But Rice offered his book as "simply an effort to propose a general scheme which may help to get ethical theorizing started again from the stalemate in which it has been bogged" (270), and I do think that he has put moral philosophy farther on its way by the lines of thought which he has thrown out and helpfully explored. All the topics taken up are suggestively dealt with, and every direction taken needed taking. Someone had to do just what Rice tried to do, and while one wishes that he could have given us a more finished work, we may all be glad that he put his studies in book form when he did, for they are the fruits of rich reflection and full of insights and inquiries which must be taken seriously.

6: Obligation and Motivation
in Recent Moral Philosophy

This paper will be concerned with a problem about the analysis of judgments of moral obligation, that is, of judgments in which an agent is said, by himself or others, to have a certain moral duty or obligation in a certain situation or kind of situation. It will not offer an analysis of such judgments, but will occupy itself with a study of a particular opposition between two points of view as to their analysis. The character of this opposition may be indicated as follows. Many moral philosophers have said or implied that it is in some sense logically possible for an agent to have or see that he has an obligation even if he has no motivation, actual or dispositional, for doing the action in question; many others have said or implied that this is paradoxical and not logically possible. The former are convinced that no reference to the existence of motives in the agent involved need be made in the analysis of a moral judgment; the latter are equally convinced that such a reference is necessary there.

Roughly, the opposition in question is between those who regard motivation as external and those who regard it as internal to obligation. We may, therefore, borrow W. D. Falk's labels and call the two points of view externalism and internalism, respectively.[1] It should be noted, then, that the question is not whether or not moral philosophers may or must introduce the topic of motivation. Externalists have generally been concerned about motivation as well as about obligation; they differ from their opponents only about the reason for this concern. Internalists hold that motivation must be provided for because it is involved in the analysis of moral judgments and so is essential for an action's being or being shown to be obligatory. Externalists insist that motivation is not part of the analysis of moral judgments or of the justification of moral claims;

Reprinted from *Essays in Moral Philosophy*, A. I. Melden, ed. (1958), pp. 40-81, by permission of the University of Washington Press, Seattle.

for them motivation is an important problem, but only because it is necessary to persuade people to act in accordance with their obligations.

Again, the issue is not whether morality is to be practical. Both parties agree that it is to be practical in the sense of governing and guiding human behavior. That is, it should supply the rules of human practice, and it should not do this out of idle curiosity, but with a real concern for their being followed. But the one party insists that judgments of obligation must be practical in the further sense that their being efficacious in influencing behavior is somehow logically internal to them, and the other denies this. The question is whether motivation is somehow to be "built into" judgments of moral obligation, not whether it is to be taken care of in some way or other.[2]

Here is an old and basic issue. It may be regarded as involved in Aristotle's critique of Plato's Idea of the Good, and is certainly present in Hume's polemic against cognitivists and rationalists in ethics. It is different from, and to a considerable extent cuts across, the issues which have been discussed so much recently (intuitionism versus naturalism, cognitivism versus noncognitivism, humanism versus supernaturalism, relativism versus absolutism, deontologism versus teleologism), for proponents of almost every one of these embattled points of view can be found on either side in this controversy. Indeed, I am disposed to think that it is more basic than most of these other issues, since answers to it are often taken as premises for settling them, for example they are frequently taken by naturalists and noncognitivists as premises for refuting intuitionism.

Yet, ancient and fundamental as it may be, this opposition has seldom been made explicit or studied in its own right, even in recent times when so many of the other oppositions which were latent in earlier moral philosophy have been underlined and debated. Its ghost was raised and given something like form by H. A. Prichard, but only, as he vainly hoped, to be laid forever.[3] R. M. Blake and Falk are perhaps the only others to make a separate study of it.[4] For the rest, however, the opposing positions involved have simply been assumed, it seems to me, without adequate analysis or defense. Hence it is my purpose here to call attention once more to this issue, to consider its present status, and to do something to clarify it and the methods by which it is to be settled.

My sympathies have always been with the first of the two positions described. It has not seemed to me inconceivable that one should have an obligation and recognize that one has it and yet have no motivation to perform the required act. But I am less sure of this than I used to be, and shall therefore explore the problem now with the goal, not of arriving at any final conclusions, but of taking some steps in that direction. I shall not proceed, however, by making an independent study of the matter, but by reviewing analytically and critically a number of passages and discussions in the literature of the last two or three decades.

I

Externalism may take various forms, as has been indicated. Intuitionism, holding that obligation is indefinable and nonnatural, is the most striking example of it, and internalism has cropped out most frequently in refutations of intuitionism. But many other views have held that moral judgments can be analyzed without any reference to the conations of the agent involved,[5] for instance, any form of naturalism which regards "I ought to do B" as equivalent to "B is approved by most people" or "B is conducive to the greatest general happiness," and any form of noncognitivism which identifies moral require-ments with social or divine imperatives.[6] For all such theories, obligation represents a fact or requirement which is external to the agent in the sense of being independent of his desires or needs.

Against them, internalists have a number of arguments which are more or less related and which they usually attribute to Hume, sometimes correctly. It is to a study of these arguments that the first main part of this paper will be devoted. In all of them the theme is that externalism has a problem about motivation, and is therefore false. The first to be considered is an argument by G. C. Field to the effect that, if an obligation represents an external fact about an agent in the sense explained above, then its presence entails no "reason for action."[7] But it is "one of the most deeply recognized characteristics of the moral fact" that it is in itself and necessarily "a reason for acting." Therefore the views of Kant, Moore, and other externalists are false.

We need not question Field's claim (1) that, if an action is obligatory, this is a reason for doing it, since an externalist can accept it. But Field assumes in his discussion (2) that a reason for action is a motive, and this may well be doubted. It seems to me, at any rate, that we must distinguish two kinds of reasons for action, "exciting reasons" and "justifying reasons," to use Hutcheson's terms.[8] When A asks, "Why should I give Smith a ride?" B may give answers of two different kinds. He may say, "Because you promised to," or he may say, "Because, if you do, he will remember you in his will." In the first case he offers a justification of the action, in the second a motive for doing it. In other words, A's "Why should I . . . ?" and "Why ought I . . . ?" are ambiguous questions. They may be asking for an ethical justification of the action pro-posed, or they may be asking what motives there are for his doing it. "Should" and "ought" likewise have two meanings (at least) which are prima facie distinct: a moral one and a motivational one.

Thus a motive is one kind of reason for action, but not all reasons for action are motives. Perhaps we should distinguish between reasons for acting and reasons for regarding an action as right or justified. It is plausible to identify reasons for acting with motives, i.e., with considerations which will or may move one to action, and perhaps this is why Field assumes that all reasons are motives, but it is not plausible to identify motives with reasons for regarding an action as morally right or obligatory. At any rate there is a prima facie distinction to be made between two senses of "ought" and two kinds of reasons, and, if this distinction is valid, then Field's case as he states it collapses. For then an externalist can reply that (1) is obviously true only if "reason" means "justifying reason" and not "motivating reason," and that (2) is true only if "reason" means "motivating reason"; and he may go on to claim that "obligation" is ambiguous, being indeed susceptible of an internalist analysis in its motivational sense, but not in its moral sense. He may even contend that the plausibility of internalism rests on a failure to make this distinction.

The internalist, then, must either show that the above distinction is invalid, which Field does not do, shift to a different argument, or move the entire discussion to another level.

II

W. T. Stace and others use a similar argument against intuitionism and Platonism, contending boldly that, on any such analysis of "A ought to do B," A can admit that he ought to do B without its following that he has an *obligation* to *do* B. Stace's version of this contention may be paraphrased as follows.[9] On an externalist analysis of judgments of obligation, such a judgment merely asserts a kind of fact, simple or complex, natural or nonnatural. Then, even if the judgment "A ought to do B" is true, it does not follow that A has any obligation to *act,* any *practical* obligation, but only an obligation to *believe.* Why should he do anything about B? An obligation to act follows only if A desires to do something about it, and then it follows from this desire alone. Moreover, he may not desire to do anything about it, and then he has no obligation of any sort to act. But a moral judgment necessarily entails an obligation to act; therefore externalist theories are false.

This argument, which seems so plausible to Stace, has always been puzzling to me. Let us begin, as he does, by supposing that a moral judgment *is* just a statement of some kind of "external" fact. Then one cannot admit such a fact about oneself, and still ask sensibly if one has a moral obligation to act. For to admit the fact is then to admit the obligation. One cannot in that case ask, "Why morally ought I do the act in question?" except to gain an insight into the *grounds* of the admitted obligation. One can still ask, "Why should I do the act?" but only if one is using "should" in the sense in which one is asking for motivation, or in some third sense. No doubt, as Stace says, one *will* do it only if he desires to do what has the given kind of "external" characteristic. Then one's desire obliges him in the sense of moving him. But the admitted moral judgment asserts a *moral* obligation nonetheless, and whether one will in fact perform the act in question or not does not bear on his having this obligation.

Even if one may not desire to do what is right (i.e., what has the characteristic referred to by "right" on our hypothesis),[10] this does not change the fact that one has a moral obligation; it means only that one has no motivation, at least occurrently. That one has no moral obligation does not follow unless having an obligation entails having a motive. But this Stace does not show, and it is obviously true only in one sense of "obligation."

In fact, it is clear that Stace is assuming that to have an obligation is to have a motive, just as Field did, and his argument is essentially the same, though verbally different. And again the answer is that, until the contrary is shown, one must distinguish between two senses of "should" or "ought." For, if this distinction is valid, it can be claimed that Stace's argument reduces to this: even if I ought in one sense, it does not follow that I ought in the other sense, which is true but refutes no one. Stace, like Field, has failed to observe or consider the possible ambiguity of "should."

What he has noticed is that one apparently can ask, "Why should I do what I morally ought to do (if this represents some fact independent of my interests)?" But one can ask this sensibly only if "should" and "morally ought" are used in different senses. One cannot ask, "Why morally ought I to do what I morally ought to do?" even if "morally ought" does stand for an objective property. But neither can one ask, "Why should I do what I morally ought to do?" if "I should" and "I morally ought" *both* mean "I have a motive" or "It is necessary for my happiness," as they do on Stace's own view. For the question to be sensible, "I should" and "I morally ought" must have distinct meanings, whatever these are; and, while one may entail motivation, the other need not.

III

The fullest and most recent version of this argument is to be found in P. H. Nowell-Smith's book.[11] He remarks with interest that the intuitionists "have but repeated Hume's argument" about the gap between the *is* and the *ought* in refuting naturalistic theories.[12] Then he goes on to contend that intuitionism itself may be disposed of by essentially the same argument, namely, that it likewise fails to bridge the gap; and in making this striking contention good he elaborates the argument that, no matter what "fact," natural, metaphysical, or nonnatural, one may establish about an action, it will still not follow that one ought to do the action.

The intuitionist's answer to the question "Why should I be moral?" — unless, like Prichard, he rejects it as a senseless question — is that, if you reflect carefully, you will notice that a certain act has two characteristics, (a) that of being obligatory and (b) that of producing a maximum of good or of being a fulfilment of a promise . . . etc. . . . But suppose all this has taken place. . . . Does it follow that I ought to do the action . . . ? . . . a world of non-natural characteristics is revealed to us by a . . . faculty called *"intuition."* . . . And from statements to the effect that these exist no conclusions follow about what I *ought to do*. A new world is revealed for our inspection . . . it is mapped and described in elaborate detail. No doubt it is all very interesting. If I happen to have a thirst for knowledge, I shall read on. . . . But what if I am not interested? Why should I do anything about these newly-revealed objects? Some things, I have now learnt, are right and others wrong; but why should I do what is right and eschew what is wrong? . . . Of course the question "Why should I do what I see to be right?" is . . . an absurd one. . . . But . . . [this question], which [is] absurd when words are used in the ordinary way, would not be absurd if moral words were used in the way that intuitionists suppose . . . if "X is right" and "X is obligatory" are construed as statements to the effect that X has the non-natural characteristic of rightness or obligatoriness, which we just "see" to be present, it would seem that we can no more deduce "I ought to do X" from these premises than we could deduce it from "X is pleasant" or "X is in accordance with God's will."

This passage needs discussion here, even at the risk of some repetition. To begin with, it seems to me that Nowell-Smith is confusing two arguments, both suggested by Hume.[13] One says that conclusions involving "ought" cannot be derived from premises involving only "is" and not "ought." The other says something like this: conclusions involving "ought" cannot be derived from premises stating only *truths*, natural or nonnatural, even if one of these truths is what is meant by an ought-statement. Now it is the first of these which is used by the intuitionists against their opponents, and *it* cannot be turned against them. For its point is valid even if ought-statements assert truths as the intuitionists claim, provided only that the truths they assert are different from those asserted by any is-statements. Insofar, then, as Nowell-Smith is trading on whatever validity this argument possesses, his case against intuitionism breaks down. It is the other argument on which he must rely.

This one is harder to deal with. We must first eliminate another point on which Nowell-Smith seems to trade. He supposes that "X is obligatory" stands for a nonnatural property and then argues that it does not follow that I ought to do X. Of course, it does not follow that *I* ought to do X, since it was not specified for whom X is obligatory. Let us take "I have an obligation to do X" instead, and let us suppose that it asserts a fact about me and X, natural or nonnatural. Then the argument is that, even if it is true, it does not follow that I have an obligation to do X. Whether this is correct or not, however, depends on the meaning of "I have an obligation to do X" when it appears after the words "it does not follow."[14] If it here also stands for the fact in question, as cognitivists hold and as we are for the moment supposing, then it does follow that I have an obligation to do X, for the "conclusion" simply repeats the "premise."

Nowell-Smith may, of course, reply that no truth, natural or nonnatural, can entail an *obligation.* My point has been that it can *if* an obligation is a certain fact, as cognitivists claim. Nowell-Smith may go on to contend that an obligation is not identical with *any* such fact, but then he must show this independently, and cannot do so by the present argument. His contention may seem plausible when it is applied to naturalistic theories, as intuitionists have always thought. But it is not obviously true, if one does not identify obligation and motivation, that an obligation cannot be identical with any peculiar kind of "fact" such as the intuitionist believes in, for he claims that it is such a peculiar "fact" precisely to account for its obligatoriness. He has, as it were, built obligatoriness into his "fact." Possibly this cannot be done or is too pat a solution, as Nowell-Smith suggests. But this must be shown independently; Nowell-Smith must argue directly that such a fact is inconceivable or is not what is meant by "obligation," remembering as he does so the prima facie distinction introduced above. For if it is conceivable and is what is meant by "obligation," his present argument is not cogent.

The real reason why Nowell-Smith thinks that no set of truths or facts entails my having an obligation to act is, of course, the fact that he implicitly assumes that my having an obligation implies my having a motive. This comes out when he says about the intuitionist's brave nonnatural world, "But what if I am not interested?" And again the answer is that, while there is a sense in which having an obligation equals having an interest, there is prima facie another sense in which it may stand for a truth of another kind, natural or not. It is true that motivation will not follow logically from this truth (though it may follow causally from a recognition of it);[15] it will not follow any more than "Y is a fellow traveler" follows from "Y is tickled pink." In this sense Nowell-Smith's point is correct. I can contemplate all the facts pointed out by the intuitionists and externalists and still ask sensibly, "Ought I?" if I am asking about motivation. But it may still be nonsense to ask, "Ought I?" in the moral sense, as the cognitivist would claim.

Here Nowell-Smith insists that, when words are used in the ordinary way, it is absurd to ask of an act which it is admittedly right for me to do, "Why should I do it?" And of course it is, if "should" is used in its moral sense. But in this sense, the intuitionist may contend, his usage involves no gap either, as we have been seeing. It is only if "should" is used in its motivation-seeking sense that he must allow that there is a gap, and in this sense, he may claim, there really is a gap, which is not noticed because of an ambiguity in the word "should" as it is ordinarily used.

Again, then, it becomes apparent that the internalist must either challenge this distinction between two uses of "should," or show independently that "should" implies motivation even in its moral use.

IV

The internalist arguments discussed above depend on the claim that obligation and its recognition entail the existence of motivation, but they depend on it indirectly, through an identification of a reason for acting, or of an obligation to act, with a motive for doing so. Frequently, however, the internalists make this claim in so many words, and conclude directly that externalistic theories are mistaken. Thus Field argues against Moore that "the moral fact" is in itself and necessarily of interest to us when apprehended, but this it cannot be on Moore's view, and therefore Moore's view is false.[16] Likewise for all forms of externalism. Suppose we take Field's first premise in a psychological sense, as asserting (1) that, if one acknowledges an obligation to do something, then it is psychologically impossible for him not to have some tendency to do it, and (2) that his recognizing his obligation by itself produces this tendency. Then it can be denied with some plausibility, for not everyone's moral experience witnesses to the truth of either of these assertions, let alone of both of them. But suppose it is true. Must an externalist give up his position? Only if we can add two further premises: (3) that, no matter what external fact we may become acquainted with, it is always psychologically possible for us to be indifferent to it, and (4) that "the bare knowledge of anything can never move us to action." Now (4) is plausible, as Field shows at some length in attacking "the Kantian fallacy." But most externalists would admit that knowledge can move us to action only by awakening an already existing desire, in this case, perhaps, a desire to do the right.[17] As for (3), it is obviously false, since there are external facts to which, given the conative natures we have, we cannot remain wholly indifferent. And, this being the case, an externalist like Moore might insist that we are so constituted that we cannot be wholly cold in the presence of the particular external fact which he regards as constituting obligation — a claim which Field does nothing to disprove.

However this may be, Field gives us no grounds for accepting his premise that the recognition of an obligation is by itself and necessarily a motive. He seems simply to infer this from the fact that such recognition is by itself necessarily a reason for action. But we have seen that, at least prima facie, "reason" is ambiguous here, and something may be a reason without thereby being a motive. Field must then show that his assertion is true independently of any possible confusion between two senses of "reason," which he does not do. And, if he is not going in for the longer kind of reasoning to be described in our last section, he must show that it is true in a logical sense, as asserting that it is logically impossible to have an obligation to which one is indifferent.

Another use of the argument occurs in C. L. Stevenson's important first article,[18] where he employs it against "any attempt to define ethical terms without reference to the interests of the speaker" — in favor, not of an internalistic cognitive theory, as in Field and Stace, but of an emotive one.

Stevenson contends, among other things, that ethical terms "must have, so to speak, a magnetism," and that any analysis of them must provide for this. By saying they have magnetism he means that "a person who recognizes X to be 'good' [or 'obligatory'] must *ipso facto* acquire a stronger tendency to act in its favor than he otherwise would have had." He then writes:

> This rules out the Humian type of definition. For according to Hume, to recognize that something is "good" is simply to recognize that the majority approve of it. Clearly, a man may see that the majority approve of X without having, himself, a stronger tendency to favour it.

The same reasoning, of course, will rule out intuitionism and other forms of externalism. On all such views, to assent to a moral judgment is to assent to a fact which involves no reference to one's interests; therefore this assent does not *ipso facto* or necessarily lead to a stronger tendency to favor the action in question.

This is essentially Field's argument over again, as Stevenson himself recognizes. The crucial premises are two: (1) that anyone who assents to a moral judgment must *ipso facto* or necessarily acquire a stronger tendency to do the action in question, and (2) that assenting to a fact which involves no reference to one's own interests will in no case *ipso facto* or necessarily produce such a tendency. Now these statements may be understood in a *causal* or psychological sense. But, if so, they should be shown to be true before they are used to rule out entire theories. The first is certainly not obvious in the case of all kinds of ethical judgments; it may be true of value-judgments but is it true of all ought-judgments? That it is seems particularly doubtful if we must distinguish between two kinds of ought-statements, for then one kind might be incitive in tendency and the other not; yet Stevenson takes no account of the possibility of such a distinction. Again, as was just said, it is hard to believe that in the case of every "external fact" about an action it is *psychologically* possible for us to be indifferent to it. If this were so we could have no "primary appetites" in Butler's sense; all of our interests would be washing-women taking in each others' laundry. But, if there are interests whose objects are "external," then Hume can plausibly claim that it is a psychological law of human nature that we invariably feel *some* tendency to do what we believe the majority to approve, or an intuitionist that it is psychologically necessary that we pursue a nonnatural right or good, as Plato thought.

Now Stevenson does nothing to refute such psychological theories. He must, then, be thinking that assenting to a moral judgment in some sense *logically* entails its having a tendency to affect one's action — that an analysis of a person's moral judgment or recognition that something is obligatory must in some way involve a reference to his tendencies to do the action in question. That is, motivation must be "built into" the analysis of ethical utterances. This dictum, however, cannot simply be assumed, if the issue is not to be begged, especially if the distinction referred to earlier holds. Moreover, it is ambiguous. It may mean that a reference to the agent's desires is to be built into the *descriptive* meaning of ethical judgments, or it may mean that part of what is meant by *assenting* to a moral judgment is a disposition to respond accordingly. The first of these alternatives is taken by Field and Falk[19] but rejected by Stevenson. The second, as we shall see in a later section, can be accepted by an externalist.

                                         V

A somewhat novel form of the present argument has been advanced by H. D. Aiken in a well-known article.[20] He maintains (1) that judgments of obligation are normative in the sense that they influence the will and determine conduct, and (2) that "the relation between cognition and motivation, on any theory of motivation whatever, is a causal, not a logical, relation"; and he concludes that all "descriptivist" analyses of judgments of obligation are therefore mistaken, whether naturalistic or nonnaturalistic (including internalistic forms of naturalism such as those of Field and Stace). (2) is an important point and needed to be made, but it may be admitted. (1) is a premise already familiar to us in other forms, but, whereas his predecessors regard it as empirical, Aiken makes it analytic. He defines a judgment of obligation as one which influences conduct "by whatever means." This, however, has a curious effect, namely, that what are usually called ethical judgments may not be judgments of obligation in his sense, since they will be so only if they influence the will. But then, even if his argument shows that his "judgments of obligation" cannot be descriptively analyzed, it proves nothing about the so-called moral judgments with which the rest of us have been concerned.

Aiken is tacitly assuming that judgments of the form "A should . . . ," "B ought . . . ," and so forth, in the uses with which we are concerned, are all causally efficacious, at least normally, and so fall under what he calls "judgments of obligation." This may be doubted, especially if we keep in mind our distinction between two kinds of "should" sentences, but let us accept it for the sake of the argument. Then his conclusion still does not follow. For a judgment that causally affects behavior may be susceptible of a cognitivist analysis, and even of an externalistic one. That is, a statement may be a "judgment of obligation" and yet be descriptive. For its moving power may be due wholly to the information, natural or nonnatural, which it conveys to our desires. If I say to you as we cross the street, "There is a car coming," my statement will influence your actions, and it may do so simply in its informative capacity (given your desire to live). Then it will be a "judgment of obligation" and yet be capable of a descriptivist and externalist analysis.

The matter may be put thus. Consider "I ought to do X" in any safely ethical use. The question is whether or not this is to be given an internalistic analysis. Aiken does give us such an analysis of the meta-sentence, " 'I ought to do X' is normative." But this is not an analysis of the sentence, "I ought to do X," itself, and so all of the standard theories about its analysis remain open. It is, however, this sentence which constitutes our problem; we want to know the function or meaning of "obligatory" as it is used in, "It is obligatory on me to do X," not in, " 'It is obligatory on me to do X' is obligatory." Aiken's attempt to sidestep the dispute about ethical sentences is no doubt a laudable one; the moral of my critique is only that, if one does sidestep it, one must not draw any conclusions about it, as he seems to do.

VI

The above kinds of argument against externalism all depend on the claim that obligation or judgments of obligation somehow entail motivation, perhaps directly, perhaps by identifying motivation and reasons for acting or by identifying motivation and obligation to act. I have tried to dispose of each argument individually, but my main point has been that there is a prima facie distinction to be made between moral or justifying reasons and exciting or motivating ones, or between moral and nonmoral obligation; that this distinction is usually ·neglected by internalists when they use such arguments; and that if this distinction is valid the arguments lose their cogency. For then the externalist can reply that, while there is a motivational sense of "ought" which *is* "internal," there is another sense of "ought" which is moral and which may be "external" for all that has been shown so far.

In making this point I have but echoed an old intuitionist refrain, which to my knowledge was first sung by Samuel Clarke and last by R. M. Blake, but which may also be sung by nonintuitionists. Clarke, observing the rising conflict between internalism and externalism of his day, distinguishes "the truest and formallest obligation," which is moral, from "the Dread of Superior Power and Authority, and the Sanction of Rewards and Punishments . . . which is . . . really in itself only a *secondary* and *additional* Obligation, or *Inforcement* of the first." Then he remarks that a failure to notice this ambiguity of the term "obligation" has blinded some writers to the (externalist) truth that "the original *Obligation* of all . . . is the eternal *Reason* of Things. . . . " He says drily, in parentheses, " . . . the ambiguous use of which word [Obligation], as a *Term of Art,* has caused some Perplexity and Confusion in this Matter" — the perplexity and confusion being, of course, in the minds of the internalists.[21] It seems to me, as it seemed to him and to Blake, that neglect of this ambiguity has been a serious mistake in recent moral philosophy.

Even if the distinction is valid, however, it does not follow that internalism is false, but only that externalism may be true if it cannot be refuted on grounds other than those so far considered. One may admit the distinction and still claim that both kinds of judgment of obligation, the moral as well as the nonmoral, are susceptible of an internalistic analysis. In fact, some recent internalists do distinguish moral from nonmoral obligation in one way or another, though apparently without seeing that the above kind of argument does not establish the internality of the moral ought, when this is distinguished from the nonmoral one. It may then be held that, independently of such a distinction and of the above arguments, it can be shown that moral obligation is internal. We must now in the second main part of this paper take up some considerations that seem calculated to show this.

It will be helpful, first, to sort out a number of propositions that internalists have held or may be holding, particularly since they have rarely been distinguished in the literature. All of the above writers, and many others, are convinced that having or acknowledging an obligation to do something involves having, either occurrently or dispositionally, some motivation for doing it; and they infer that externalism is false. But this proposition can be taken to assert several things, namely: (1) that the state of having an obligation includes or is identical with that of being motivated in a certain way; (2) that the statement, "I have an obligation to do B," means or logically entails the statement, "I have, actually or potentially, some motivation for doing B";[22] (3) that the reasons that justify a judgment of obligation include or are identical with the reasons that prove the existence of motivation to act accordingly; (4) that the reasons that justify a judgment of obligation include or are identical with those that *bring about* the existence of motivation to act accordingly; (5) that, although justifying a moral judgment does not include giving exciting reasons for acting on it, it presupposes the existence, at least potentially, of such excitement; (6) that *saying* or being *said* to have an obligation presupposes one's having motives for doing the action in question; (7) that *assenting* to an obligation entails feeling or having a disposition to feel at least some inclination to act in the way prescribed; or (8) that one can know or "see" or think that one has a certain obligation only when one is in a favorable conative state with respect to performing the act in question.

Even these formulations are not very rigorous, but perhaps they will suffice to make clearer the opposition we are discussing. The externalist is concerned to deny (1) through (4), which the internalist will assert. If they are true, externalism is untenable. However, as far as I can see, the internalists have not shown them to be true to such a degree that they can be safely used as premises for refuting externalism; indeed, they are plausible only when the distinction between two senses of "ought" and "reason" that we have been stressing is not borne in mind.

As for (5) through (8), an externalist may accept them, though they may also be denied with some plausibility (and would be denied by a really "compleat" externalist). It is obvious that he can admit (8), for it makes only a psychological assertion about the conditions of moral insight; in fact, (8) is maintained by such externalists as Scheler and Hartmann.[23] (5), as we shall see, may also be agreed to by an externalist, though only if "presupposes" is understood in some psychological or "contextual" sense, and not in a strictly logical one.

The arguments to be dealt with here generally involve (1), (6), or (7), and we may take first those that use (1) in some form or other. In one of them Falk appeals to the familiar principle that "I morally ought" implies "I can," adding that "I can" implies "I want to (in the sense that I have, at least dispositionally, some motivation for doing)," and then drawing an internalist conclusion.[24] Suppose we admit, though both claims may be disputed, that "I morally ought" in all its sense implies "I can," and that "I can" implies "I want to." Even then this argument will be cogent only if the "implies" involved is a logical one in both cases. But is it in " 'I can' implies 'I want to' "? To say, "I cannot whistle a tune while standing on my head, unless I feel some inclination to do so," is perhaps an odd thing to say about an odd bit of behavior, but it seems at most to state a physical fact, not a logical necessity. One may, of course, so define "I can" as to include "I have some impulse to," but it is not obvious that one should, and it is not clear that "ought" implies "can" as so defined.

But *"ought* implies *can"* need not be construed as asserting a strict logical implication. It may plausibly be understood as saying: (a) moral judgments "presuppose," "contextually imply," or "pragmatically imply" that the agent is able to act as proposed or is believed to be, but do not assert or state that he is; or (b) the *point of uttering* moral judgments disappears if the agents involved are not able to act as proposed or at least believed to be; or (c) it would be morally wrong to insist that an agent ought to do a certain action, if he is or is thought to be unable to do it. If Kant's dictum is interpreted in one of these ways the externalist need have no fear, for then it will not serve to refute him.

VII

In a somewhat similar argument, Aiken reasons that obligation presupposes responsibility and that this presupposes motivation:

> Hume's argument can be stated in another . . . way. We assume that no person can be held morally responsible for actions which he did not willingly perform. We do not address such judgments as "Killing is wrong" to cyclones. . . . In short, we regard only responsible beings as moral or immoral. But . . . responsibility *presupposes* a motive for or interest in any act for which a person is held "responsible." If this is so, the very notions of "moral" and "immoral" involve a reference to feeling or sentiment; and every moral judgment states or implies such a reference.

Aiken then asserts that this argument "disqualifies all theories whatever which

. . . deny that moral categories are to be construed in terms of human feeling or interest. . . ."[25] In another place he claims that obligation and desire are intimately related, "For . . . it is doubtful whether the term ['ought'] is ever properly applied to anything save motivated activity." Here too he takes this conviction as a criterion to be met "by any adequate analysis of 'ought'."[26]

Now, the argument from obligation to responsibility to motivation is like the argument from obligation to ability to motivation, and the same points hold about it. Instead of repeating, then, let us take up the conviction that moral obligation and judgment presuppose motivation. It does seem correct to say that my having moral duties implies that *others* have desires and feelings, but this externalists need not deny. It is also plausible to hold that my having duties, or being a moral agent whose acts are right or wrong, presupposes *my* having interests and motives. To this extent Aiken is, in my opinion, correct. But an externalist can agree, and still insist that, although one can ascribe obligation only to a motivated being, to ascribe an obligation to such a being is not to talk about his motives but to assert some external fact about him.

More crucial is Aiken's further claim that A's having an obligation to do B presupposes his having not only interests *überhaupt* but, directly or indirectly, an interest in doing B (though not necessarily a predominant one). If this means that A's having a duty to do B logically entails his having an interest in doing B, or that establishing his obligation to do B logically entails showing him that he has such an interest or producing such an interest in him, it may be denied. A man who is seeking to determine if he has a duty to do a certain deed need not look to see if he has any motives for doing it, and he cannot claim that he does not have the duty simply on the ground that he finds no supporting motivation. Aiken may reply that, nevertheless, A's having an obligation to do B in some sense presupposes his having a concern to do B, at least dispositionally, and I am inclined to agree that it does, but only in the sense that *ascribing* this duty to A "contextually" or pragmatically implies that, if A sees he has it, he will have some concern to perform it (6). This, however, does not mean that A's having this concern is a condition of his having a duty to do B, and it can be admitted by an externalist. In *Principia Ethica* Moore says, "If I ask whether an action is *really* my duty or *really* expedient, the predicate of which I question the applicability to the action in question is precisely the same. In both cases I am asking, 'Is this event the best on the whole that I can effect?' " Yet, although "duty" and "expedient" have the same conceptual meaning for Moore, he maintains that there is a difference in their use, "duty" being applied to those useful actions "which it is more useful to praise and to enforce by sanctions, since they are actions which there is a temptation to omit."[27] Then "B is A's duty" *means*, "B is the best thing on the whole that A can do," but it *presupposes* that A is tempted not to do it. Perhaps moral judgments only presuppose motivation in a similar sense.

VIII

Two other considerations seem to have been regarded as showing that having an obligation entails having a corresponding motivation. One is a conviction that a man cannot have an obligation unless he accepts it as such and "beats responsive and not irresponsive to the claim" in what James calls the "everlasting ruby vaults" of his heart.[28] This is expressed in the following quotation from Falk: " . . . Even the commands of God could only constitute moral obligations for somebody who considered it a *law unto himself* to respect what God bids him to do."[29] Now it does seem in some sense correct to say that a man cannot actually have a moral duty if he does not see and accept it. At the same time, this is an odd thing to say unless we are using "duty" in two senses, for we are saying that A has no duty to do B if he does not recognize that he has a duty to do B. The same double usage occurs in the sentence, "You ought to do what you think you ought to do." The matter can be cleared up using the distinction, long accepted by externalists, between what one *subjectively* ought to do and what one *objectively* ought to do. The point, then, is that A subjectively ought to do B only if he accepts this as his obligation. It still may be, however, that B would be objectively right for him to do anyway. In fact, when a man thinks that something is his duty, what he thinks is that it is a duty independently of his thinking so (and independently of his wanting to do it); and when he asks what his duty is, he implies that he has a duty that he does not yet recognize, and what he is seeking to know, as it were, is what it would have been his duty to do even if he had not discovered it. Thus there is a sense in which one has a moral obligation even if one does not recognize it as such.

It has also been insisted by internalists that the moral will is autonomous, and R. M. Blake believed that this doctrine should be repudiated by externalists as incompatible with the existence of any categorical imperative. Nowell-Smith is especially persistent in asserting such autonomy. " . . . The feature which distinguishes moral obligations from all others is that they are self-imposed. . . ." "The questions 'what shall I do?' and 'what moral principles should I adopt?' must be answered by each man for himself; that at least is part of the connotation of the word 'moral'."[30] In spite of what Blake says, it is hard entirely to reject this "moral protestantism," as Margaret Macdonald has called it,[31] common as it is to Kant, existentialism, and Nowell-Smith. But I am not persuaded that a recognition of autonomy necessarily leads to internalism. In areas outside of ethics we also believe in autonomy, e.g., in our scientific beliefs, and, in "religious protestantism," in our theological beliefs. Yet here the "facts" in which we freely believe or disbelieve are "external" ones — facts which are independent of us but about which we are nevertheless left to make up our own minds. It may then be that obligations are external facts of a similar sort. Certainly intuitionists and naturalists can allow us the same kind of autonomy in ethics that we claim in science and religion, without thereby going over to the enemy. They may hold that what we objectively ought to do is self-imposed only in the sense of being self-discovered or self-recognized, as scientific facts are, and that only what we subjectively ought to do is self-imposed in the more radical manner indicated earlier.

IX

However, even if *having* a moral obligation does not always and in every sense depend on the agent's accepting it and feeling motivated to do it, it may nevertheless be maintained that *assenting to* a moral obligation entails a feeling of motivation on his part. This brings us to (7), which is widely insisted on by internalists.[32] It may be put in various ways, but the essential point of it is either (a) that one cannot assent to or be convinced of an obligation of one's own without having some disposition to act accordingly, or (b) that we should regard it as odd or paradoxical if someone were to assent to an obligation without feeling any motivation whatever for fulfilling it. In the first case, there is a direct assertion that a certain sequence of events is not possible; in the second, there is only a claim that we should be puzzled if we observed such a sequence or, rather, do not believe that one can occur.

Now, taken in its first form, (7) does not seem to me to be obviously true. In any case, as we have noticed, it is ambiguous in a way that its proponents do not recognize. Taken as an assertion of a psychological law, it can be admitted by any externalist who does not hold our conative nature to be *totally* depraved.[33] It must then be regarded as asserting a logical truth, if it is to say anything inconsistent with externalism. Here again there are two alternatives. (m) It may be meant that part of what a judgment of obligation *asserts* or *states* is that the agent referred to feels a responsive beat in his heart. Then (7) is identical with (2), and simply to assume it is a *petitio*. (n) The other alternative is that motivation is to be built, not into the content of a moral judgment, but into the process of assenting to it. On this view, it is not "A ought to do B" that logically implies his having some tendency to do B, but "A is convinced that he ought to do B." That is to say, part of what is meant by "assenting to an obligation" is that one feels a responsive stirring.

Most recent internalists, I believe, would prefer this formulation of (7) to that represented by (m). I am not at all sure that (7), so interpreted, is true, but I should like to suggest that an externalist can accept it if it is. An externalist may agree, it seems to me, that we cannot, in the sense in which we use these words in connection with moral judgments, "accept," "recognize," or "be convinced of" an obligation without thereby having at least some motivation to fulfill it. He may hold, for example, that judgments of obligation have a conceptual content of an "external" kind, but add that we do not speak of a man's *assenting* or *sincerely assenting* to them unless he not only apprehends the truth of their conceptual content but is at least to some extent moved to conform to it. He would then admit that it is *logically* possible that one might have a "mere intellectual apprehension," as Field calls it, of their truth, but he would recognize the generally practical function of language (which his opponents have made so much of), especially moral discourse. There is no reason why he cannot change his ways enough to do this; even an intuitionist need not insist that the *actual* use of moral language is merely to report the news of a nonnatural world and is in no way adapted to the interests of the reader. It may be part of the ordinary "grammar" of such words as "assent," when used in connection with ethical judgments, that they are not to be employed except when "mere intellectual apprehension" is accompanied by a responsive beating of the heart. Even in the case of nonethical judgments it has been held that one does not believe unless one is in some sense disposed to act accordingly in appropriate circumstances. But, even if this is not so, it might be argued that because ethical discourse is more particularly concerned to guide human action than is nonethical discourse, such terms as "believe" may be presumed to obey different rules here.

Of course, the internalist may still complain that on his opponent's view it is logically, if not actually, possible to have a "mere intellectual apprehension" of an obligation. But, if the position just described is tenable, then he cannot support his complaint by appealing to the dictum that we cannot really assent to an obligation without having a disposition to respond. And simply to assume that it is not even logically possible to have a "mere intellectual apprehension" of an obligation is a *petitio*.

Consider now (7) in form (b). Here there is an appeal to certain data about our ordinary moral consciousness and its ways of thinking; these data are supposed to show that internalism is true or at least is embedded in moral common sense. Thus Falk has argued that externalism fails to account for such facts as the following:[34] (p) that "we commonly expect that in thinking ourselves obliged we *ipso facto* feel some constraint to do what we think we ought to do"; (q) that, "when we try to convince another that he ought to pay his bills, we expect our argument if accepted to effect some change of heart in him"; (r) that "we should think it odd to receive the answer: 'Yes, I know now *that* and *why* I ought to pay my bills, but I am still without any incentive for doing so.' "

I am not so much concerned to question these facts, though I do not myself find the answer in (r) entirely odd, as to point out that they do not, as stated, prove obligation and motivation to be *logically* connected. If we have the expectations and feelings of oddity described, this may only mean that we commonly believe that all men are *psychologically* so constituted as to be moved by the recognition that something is right. It need not mean that this is *logically* necessary or even that we believe it to be so. And we have already seen that one may hold rightness to be an external characteristic and yet claim that we are so made as necessarily (causal) to take an interest in it.

Falk's facts may also be explained in another way by the externalist. For, until evidence is given to the contrary, the externalist can argue that the common moral consciousness feels the expectations and oddities mentioned only because it does not distinguish at all clearly or consistently in its thinking between two senses in which one may be obliged, so that it links to the one feelings and thoughts appropriate to the other. This seems to me plausible, for we do frequently fail to see any difference between the two kinds of reasons for action, and often shift from one to the other without noticing.

Still a third explanation is possible. As we have indicated before, when one asks what he ought to do, he is not or at least need not be asking what he already accepts as his duty, but what is his duty although it is not yet accepted as such; and he is not or need not be asking what he has or may have a motive for doing, but what he is morally required to do and may not have any motive for doing until after he sees that it is his duty. But, of course, one would not normally ask the question unless one was concerned about the answer and felt some motivation to do his duty, whatever that might turn out to be. And so, when one concludes that such and such is what he ought to do, he can be expected to feel some motivation to do such and such and even to decide to do it. The whole process of moral question and answer normally takes place in this atmosphere of moral concern. This is all that such facts as those mentioned prove, and this much an externalist may and no doubt should admit, though he may add that it is logically possible that the case should be otherwise. Normally, then, when assent occurs in the course of a moral inquiry, it can be expected to involve commitment. But it does not follow that it is a condition of one's having an obligation to do a certain action that he should have a motive for doing it apart from discovering that it is his duty, nor that discovering it to be his duty logically entails his having a motive for doing it.

It has been argued that, if a man says he believes that he has a duty to do a certain action but feels no conation at all in favor of it, then he does not understand the sentence, "I have a duty," or its use.[35] If by this it is meant that he does not understand what an obligation is, then simply to assert this is to beg the question against the externalist. If it is meant that he does not understand what it is to *assent* to an obligation, the externalist can agree and give the explanation indicated above in our discussion of (7). But it may be that what is intended is that he just does not know in what circumstances to *say*, "I ought to do so and so," and this an externalist may also concede.

X

This brings up a number of points made by internalists, not so much about *having* an obligation or *assenting* to one, as about *uttering* sentences to the effect that one has an obligation or that someone else has — in short, (6). For example, it is said (a) that my uttering a sentence beginning with "I ought" always or normally "expresses" a pro-attitude or decision on my part or "contextually implies" one.[36] But this an externalist may grant even if he holds that such a sentence "asserts" an external fact. The sentence, "There are flying saucers," expresses the speaker's belief, but for all that it purports to assert an external fact. Thus, W. D. Ross, who holds that "good" *means* an external characterisitic, is "inclined to think" that we *use* or *apply* the term in such a way "that in each case the *judge* has some feeling of approval or interest towards what he calls good."[37] It is also said (b) that my uttering a sentence starting with "You ought" expresses or contextually implies a pro-attitude on my part toward your doing the act specified, as well as one on yours.[38] But Ross could admit this too. If I say, "There is a tidal wave coming up behind you," I "express" a concern about your welfare and "presuppose" that you also have one, but what I assert is still an external fact or purports to be.

In a similar vein internalists contend (c) that it would be absurd, odd, or "logically odd" to say things like: "You ought to do A, but don't"; "I ought to do A, but shall I?"; "I ought to do A, but I shall not."[39] Now these would, perhaps, be unusual uses of language, but are they logically impossible? "There are flying saucers, but I don't believe it" would be an unusual contribution to any serious and sober conversation, but it is not a logically self-contradictory one, since both parts of what is asserted may be true together; the apparent conflict is not between parts of what is asserted but between part of what is asserted and one of the presuppositions of asserting the rest.

Logically, as far as I can see, "I should" and "I shall" are distinct, and one can admit that he ought and still not resolve to do. One would not then be very likely to *say,* "I ought but I shall not," for one probably would not be that interested in the morality of what one was doing, but logically the situation would be such as to be describable in those terms. No doubt, as Nowell-Smith and P. B. Rice claim, a firsthand "I ought" does normally express commitment or decision on the speaker's part, for one would not normally go through the process of moral deliberation that concludes with "I ought" if he were not sufficiently devoted to the moral enterprise for this conclusion to coincide with his decision. This does not mean, however, that "I ought" logically entails "I shall"; it may only pragmatically presuppose or contextually imply this.

Nowell-Smith's discussion of "I ought" and "I shall" is interesting in this connection.[40] According to him, "I (morally) ought" expresses a decision, just as "I shall" does, although it is a decision based on rules, and therefore "I ought but shall I?" is logically odd unless "shall I?" is used in a predictive sense. Yet he admits that "I ought" is "also used, not to express a decision, but in the course of making up one's mind before a decision has been reached," and it is this use that interests me. It seems to me that in this use one *could* say, "I ought but shall I?" and one might go on thinking he ought and yet decide not to. Nowell-Smith seeks to avoid this conclusion by turning the "I ought" here into the Voice of Conscience or "self-hortatory 'you ought' " — a neat device but question-begging in this context. The main point, however, is that there is an "I ought" which does not express decision. It is true that this "I ought" is normally replaced by "the verdict-giving 'I ought' " *if* desire does not win out over conscience. But desire may win, and then there is a situation which can be described by "I ought, but I shall not," where "shall" is not predictive but decisive, though if one is in this situation one is not likely so to describe it until later, and then in the past tense.

XI

So far our study of the opposition between internalism and externalism in moral philosophy has fallen into two main parts. In the first (sections I through V) we reviewed one family of arguments against externalism and saw that they are not successful, mainly because they can for the most part be answered by distinguishing two senses of "obligation," corresponding to two meanings of, "Why should I?" In the second (sections VI through X) we found that another set of considerations that are relatively independent of this distinction can, insofar as they are valid at all, be met or accepted if certain other distinctions are made — between what we objectively and what we subjectively ought to do; between having an obligation, assenting to an obligation, and saying one has an obligation; between what is stated or logically implied and what is "presupposed" or "implied" in some not strictly logical sense by a moral judgment, and so forth. In short, we have seen that externalism is not refuted by these arguments and considerations and can be maintained if there are not yet other grounds on which it must be given up.

We might now go on to consider corresponding arguments against internalism. It is, however, difficult to find such arguments explicitly set forth in recent literature, and perhaps we may assume that they too would turn out to be inconclusive. The distinction between two senses of "should" and "ought" to which we have appealed, for example, cannot, even if it is valid, be used as an argument to refute internalism, although it disposes of some arguments used in its support.[41] For it is possible to admit this distinction and still maintain a kind of internalism. One might hold, for instance, that moral judgments are expressions of some specifically moral attitude, such as love, sympathy, an internalized sense of social demand, an attitude of impartial spectatorship, and so forth, and regard justifying reasons as reasons calculated to appeal to this attitude, exciting reasons as those that appeal to other attitudes and desires. One would then regard this attitude as conative (unlike Hutcheson's moral sense), and moral judgments as *ipso facto* to some extent motivating. But one would not claim that this attitude is always dominant, and so could admit that I may agree that I ought to do a certain action and yet say, "But I shall not!" In this very important respect one's position, though a form of internalism, would be like externalism.

The main result yielded by our discussion, then, is that the opposition we are studying cannot be resolved, as so many seem to think, by such relatively small-scale logical or semi-logical arguments as we have been dealing with. But we have also achieved some clarity about the exact points at issue. The externalist can admit that there is a nonmoral obligation and even a "subjective" moral obligation that logically entails motivation. He can accept any statement that says that having an obligation, assenting to one, or being said to have one causally or *psychologically* involves the existence of a corresponding motivation. He may also agree that assenting to an obligation *logically* entails the existence of motivation for acting accordingly. He may even allow, and perhaps should, that having or being said to have an obligation presupposes in some not strictly logical sense the existence of such motivation. What he must deny, and the internalist assert, is that having objectively a certain moral obligation logically entails having some motivation for fulfilling it, that justifying a judgment of objective moral obligation logically implies establishing or producing a motivational buttress, and that it is logically impossible that there should be a state of apprehending a moral obligation of one's own which is not accompanied by such a buttress (even if this "mere intellectual apprehension" is never actual and does not amount to what is called "assenting to" or "acknowledging" an obligation).

Now one may, if sufficiently hardy, choose to defend a form of externalism that does not make any of the concessions just indicated, or a form of internalism that does not incorporate the distinction between two senses of "Why should I?" or between exciting and justifying reasons. Personally, it seems to me that the choice must in practice be between an externalism that makes such concessions and an internalism that recognizes such a distinction. But, in any case, how is the issue to be settled? If arguments of the kind we have been reviewing are inadequate, are we then at an impasse here, too, as so many think we are on other questions? This does not follow. It does follow that neither kind of moral philosophy can be decisively refuted by the other, and that we must give up the quest for certainty in the sense of no longer hoping for such refutations. But it does not follow that nothing can be said for one view as against the other. What does follow is that the whole discussion must consciously move to another level.[42]

This does not mean that it must become even more "meta" than it already is. What this shift involves, and that it is necessary, can best be made clear by taking a look at Falk's best-known paper.[43] Here he first seems to argue very much as he does in the earlier articles already dealt with. But soon it becomes apparent that something different is going on. Falk finds in the controversy between Prichard and his opponents and in moral common sense a tension between two positions, namely, "that morality needs some additional psychological sanction'' and ''that what sanction it requires, it necessarily carries with it.'' That is, moral philosophy and ordinary moral thinking have been a confused combination of, or alternation between, externalism and internalism. Falk suggests that this situation ''has its origin in uncertainties and contradictions in the common use of words like 'ought' or 'duty'; in an unnoticed juxtaposition of meanings each of which entails a different relation to motivation.'' It is due to the fact that ''ought'' is used in both an externalist and an internalist sense, which ''remain undifferentiated and are imperceptibly juxtaposed and confused,'' so that ''there may be an unnoticed switch from the one use of 'ought' to the other.'' This is why the questioner's ''Why should I be moral?'' has been so puzzling. In one sense of ''ought'' it is ''legitimate and in need of some factual answer,'' in the other it is absurd; and where the two senses are confused ''no answer can satisfy,'' and the way is open for the skeptic to draw his disturbing conclusion.

In other words, Falk, although he is an internalist, is explicitly recognizing the ambiguity we have made so much of — indeed, he goes further and says that one of the senses involved *is* external, a claim we have not made. He uses this ambiguity to explain the rise of our two points of view and their juxtaposition in moral common sense and philosophy. All this I cannot but approve. I have only wanted to add that it is the internalists rather than the externalists who have failed to notice the ambiguity, and that this failure vitiates much of their argument. Falk does not deny this; he simply does not repeat his earlier arguments for internalism, apparently recognizing their insufficiency. Instead, he proceeds to a new line of attack.

Falk contends that we cannot be satisfied, as an externalist would be, with uncovering the confusion and replacing it with an avowed use of ''ought'' in two senses, one external and one internal, one moral and the other motivational. In fact, he insists that the external use of ''ought'' cannot be accepted by a mature reflective person who is ''aware of a capacity of reasoned choice and intent on using it,'' because such a person cannot ''easily agree to a use of [moral] words for any demand on him that still left him to ask whether he also had a sufficient reason for doing the act.'' He then argues that one internal use of ''ought'' bears ''at least a sufficient resemblance to what ordinary usage expects of a normative term'' for it to qualify as moral.[44] He calls this ''the purely formal motivational 'ought.' '' To say one ought in this sense is to say he has a reason or motive for acting with regard to which no further question can be asked, or which is compelling no matter what considerations reason may advance, and so is ''formally sufficient.'' This ''ought,'' Falk holds, can be identified with the moral ''ought,'' since it is normative in the sense of influencing ''the direction of people's volitional attitudes and actions,'' it is not simply a function of occurrent wants, and it is categorical, not hypothetical. It is, in fact, confused with the external moral ''ought'' in ordinary thinking. It *should* be taken as *the* moral ''ought'' because it must be recognized in any case, and because ''in using moral language we mean to denote something that when known, can conclusively serve to direct what we do, and we cannot obey two masters.''

Now I am not convinced by what Falk says, all too briefly, even here. He says that ''we cannot avowedly use 'moral ought' both for an external and an internal state of affairs, as if a man might have one but not another sort of moral duty in respect of the same act.'' Yet he has not shown that we ever do use the *moral* ''ought'' for an internal state of affairs, but at most that we ought to. Besides, in the distinction between a subjective and an objective ''ought'' it seems to be possible to use even ''morally ought'' in two senses, one more internal and one more external, without thereby having to serve two masters. Moreover, it does not appear that his substitute will do as the moral ''ought.'' As far as I can see, an act may be morally wrong even though I am impelled to do it after full reflection. What one is impelled to do even after reason has done its best is still dependent on the vagaries of one's particular conative disposition, and I see no reason for assuming that it will always coincide with what is in fact right or regarded as right. As for Falk's assertion that ''in using moral language we mean to denote something that when known, can conclusively serve to direct what we do'' — this is ambiguous. It may mean that moral judgments are intended to serve as conclusive *guides* or that they are meant to serve as conclusive *goads*. In the first case Falk is clearly right, but an externalist can agree. In the second he is either forgetting his own admission that there is an external use of ''ought'' in ordinary discourse or begging the question. His further claim that a reflective person cannot accept as a moral duty anything which he does not have a ''formally sufficient'' motive for doing seems to me to beg the question as it stands.

What interests me here about Falk's paper, however, is the fact that he has moved the controversy to another level, a less merely logical and larger scale level. The issue, he says in conclusion, is not settled merely by distinguishing ''between normative facts of different kinds, confusedly referred to by the same name''; ultimately what is necessary is ''clarity and decision about what fact would most nearly correspond to our intentions in the use of moral language and which words like 'ought' and 'duty' should be made to denote.'' This is the problem as it shapes itself at the end of our study. Externalism versus internalism, yes, but on a macroscopic rather than a microscopic plane. These are not small positions that may be decisively established or taken in a brief action recorded in a page or two. They are whole theories of ''our intentions in the use of moral language,'' past, present, and future.

To see this let us glance at the internalist case, as it must be made if the above discussion has been correct. Central in it must be the contention that externalism leaves a gap between perceived obligation and motivation. Now, we have seen that externalism does not *logically* entail the existence of a *psychological* gap here. By itself it entails only that it is logically possible that one should in some sense perceive (though perhaps without giving a full-fledged *assent*) that one has an obligation and yet have no disposition to fulfill it. That is, the argument that externalism logically involves a gap does not come off; externalism implies only that there is a logical gap or that it is logically possible there is a psychological gap, and it is simply begging the question to begin with the opposite premise. But instead of reasoning in this way, as in effect the writers we have dealt with do, the internalist may and should elaborate his case as follows.

1. Externalism does not by itself logically imply that there may (psychologically) be a gap between perceived obligation and motivation, but it implies that such a gap is logically possible. This is true in the qualified sense just indicated.

2. An externalist may claim that there is in fact no gap — that actually there is always some possibly adequate motivation for doing what one perceives to be right — and he may offer various psychological theories in his support. He may hold that a "mere intellectual apprehension" of one's duty is itself moving, that there is in human nature a desire to do what is right, that the sentiment of benevolence is always on hand to support the call of duty, and so forth. But all such theories are false; there is no external fact which the externalist may plausibly identify with obligation which is also such that its apprehension is always, let alone by a psychological necessity, accompanied by a responsive beating of the heart. Therefore, there is in fact a psychological gap between obligation and motivation if any form of externalism is true, in the sense that then one actually might perceive an obligation and have no corresponding motivation.

3. At this point the internalist may argue either that there is in fact no psychological gap, that the existence of such a gap is intolerable from the point of view of morality, or that our moral common sense does not believe there is such a gap, concluding that externalism is false or inconsistent with common sense.

Such a line of reasoning involves first establishing (2), and this requires a full-scale psychological inquiry, which is more than internalists have yet gone in for. Suppose that it is established. All that follows is that, if externalism is true, human beings may sometimes lack all motivation to do what they apprehend as right. One who is willing to admit this need follow the argument no farther. This brings us to (3). To argue here that there is no gap is to make a factual, psychological claim, the establishing of which again calls for an empirical inquiry, one as difficult to handle as the question whether Socrates was correct in believing that we always do what we think is right. It is hard to see how it could be carried out without taking some position with respect to the definition of obligation, assenting, and so forth, and it is just this that constitutes our problem. In any case, the record of human conduct is not such as to make it obvious that human beings always do have some tendency to do what they regard as their duty. The contention that our common moral consciousness supposes that there can be no gap will be met by conflicting evidence, as Falk admits, and, in any event, one may reply that common sense may be mistaken, thus opening the whole question again. If the contention is only that it is a rule of ordinary moral discourse that a person shall not be *said* to have an obligation unless there is or may be presumed to be in him some disposition to respond favorably, then, as we have seen, the externalist may admit it, but he may also contest it or argue for a change in the rules.

It seems to me, therefore, that in the end the internalist must argue, as Falk does, not only that externalism involves a gap between obligation and motivation, but that such a gap cannot be tolerated, given morality's task of guiding human conduct autonomously. Then, however, the externalist will counter by pointing out that internalism also entails a danger to morality. Externalism, he will say, in seeking to keep the obligation to act in certain ways independent of the vagaries of individual motivation, runs the risk that motivation may not always be present, let along adequate, but internalism, in insisting on building in motivation, runs the corresponding risk of having to trim obligation to the size of individual motives.

Here the true character of the opposition appears. Each theory has strengths and weaknesses, and deciding between them involves determining their relative total values as accounts of morality. But such a determination calls for a very broad inquiry. It cannot be based on individual preference. We must achieve "clarity and decision" about the nature and function of morality, of moral discourse, and of moral theory, and this requires not only small-scale analytical inquiries but also studies in the history of ethics and morality, in the relation of morality to society and of society to the individual, as well as in epistemology and in the psychology of human motivation.[45]

The battle, if war there be, cannot be contained; its field is the whole human world, and a grand strategy with a total commitment of forces is demanded of each of its participants. What else could a philosopher expect?

7: Love and Principle in Christian Ethics

I

A PHILOSOPHER READING ABOUT IN THE LITERATURE OF CHRISTIAN ETHICS, especially if he is steeped in that of recent philosophical ethics, is bound to be struck, not only by the topics discussed and the claims made, but by the relative absence of careful definition, clear statement, or cogent and rigorous argument, as these are judged by the standards with which he is familiar in his own field (even if he does not himself always conform to them). It seems all too seldom to occur to its writers that they should seriously try to expound and defend Christian ethics in terms of what Matthew Arnold called culture — "the best which has been thought and said in the world" — and in particular in terms of the best philosophical thinking of the time. As H. D. Lewis has put it,

> Much that is peculiarly instructive has been written about these matters by notable ethical thinkers of the present day, and the progress that has been made recently in ethics is one of the most distinctive and promising features of modern thought. But religious thinkers, in the main, have been curiously indifferent to these important advances in a field closely akin to their own.[1]

Indeed, they have not only been "curiously indifferent" to the work of the philosophers; many of them take the position, at least implicitly, that any recognition of its importance would be dangerous — a sinful concession to the intellectual pride of the natural man or the old Adam. At any rate, they reflect the same attitude and manner of thought and expression that were castigated by ancient Celsus, and by Arnold after him, as "the want of intellectual seriousness of the Christians." The issues they are dealing with are all too rarely clearly formulated or rigorously reasoned about. It may be that the philosopher who criticizes them can also be charged with some kind of want of intellectual

Reprinted from *Faith and Philosophy,* A. Plantinga, ed. (1964), pp. 203-25, by permission of Eerdman's Publishing Company, Grand Rapids, Michigan.

seriousness, or even with spiritual pride, but his criticism may be correct nevertheless.

This essay represents an attempt, by a philosopher who feels that its theological proponents may be selling Christian ethics short by their manner of expounding and defending it, to do something toward remedying the situation. In it I shall make only a beginning, however, hoping that others who can speak with more authority will follow suit. I shall only try to state what seem to me to be some of the main issues and positions in Christian ethical theory, keeping away from practical issues of the sort that theologians have been writing about so much (more, I admit, than philosophers have). And I shall limit myself to issues and positions in Christian normative ethics, leaving for another occasion the problems and points of view of Christian metaethics, if there is such a thing.[2] As for answers — in stating the issues and positions I shall be indicating those that are possible, but I shall not be doing much to settle on any of them. To do so would involve my venturing farther into theology than I can go with anything like the kind of intellectual seriousness which I am advocating. Anyway, one can only try to throw a certain amount of light at any given time.

In doing what I am doing I make an assumption — that the function of reason and philosophy for the Christian is not simply to serve as an instrument for refuting or otherwise disposing of gentiles, pagans, and unbelievers, but also and especially to serve as a colleague in helping him to understand and deepen the faith that is in him. Some may say, on reading what follows, ''Why should we bother to think in such terms as these? What is good but to do justly, and to love mercy, and to walk humbly with thy God? And what is pure religion and undefiled but to visit the fatherless and the widows in their affliction, and to keep oneself unspotted from the world.'' But the writers on Christian ethics that I have in mind can themselves hardly make this reply, for they have already ventured out beyond the fold of such simple faith and duty into the forum of rational formulation and defense. My only complaint is that they have not been as careful as they should be if they are going to venture out in this way. As for those who would decry even such venturing into the forum, I can only remind them that the same Book that says,

''We are fools for Christ's sake. . . .''

also says,

''Buy . . . also wisdom, and instruction, and understanding,''

and

'' . . . whatsoever things are true, whatsoever things are honest, whatsoever things are just, whatsoever things are pure, whatsoever things are lovely, whatsoever things are of good report, . . . think on these things.''

II

Actually, as I have indicated, there has been a good deal of thinking on these things by Christians. But we cannot consider it all here, and, in fact, I shall limit myself to one of its main themes. Much of this thinking has been about the role of moral rules and principles in Christian ethics. The ensuing debate is especially lively in Protestant circles, but Pope Pius XII and Dietrich von Hildebrand found it necessary not long ago to admonish young Catholics to beware of a "new morality" which they call "circumstance ethics" and which seeks to eliminate general principles from Christian morality, declaring "every moral decision to be based on a unique situation and to be the result of a confrontation of the 'I' of the person with the 'I' of God."[3] No doubt the debate is also present in Jewish ethics. At the one extreme are views variously referred to as antinomian, nominalist, existentialist, situationalist, or contextualist, which hold that each moral decision about what to do is to be a direct function of faith, love, or the experience of God together with a knowledge of the facts in the case, with no ethical principles coming into the matter. At the other, apparently, is the Thomist or near-Thomist view that many, if not all, moral decisions should involve, at least in part, an appeal to certain moral principles whose validity does not depend on faith, love, revelation, or the knowledge of God. It is with the topic of this debate that I wish to deal here, first, because it seems to me to be most unclearly dealt with by theologians, and, second, because philosophers have been discussing somewhat similar subjects with a good deal more clarity and in terms which may, it seems to me, be of some use in the debate in question.

Before we begin, however, five preliminary remarks must be made. (1) A distinction is often made by philosophers and theologians alike between moral rules and ethical principles. A rule is relatively concrete and small, like "We ought to tell the truth," a principle relatively abstract and big, like "We ought to promote the general happiness." This distinction is important in certain contexts, but may here be kept in the background. Unless otherwise specified, then, I shall use "rule" and "principle" synonymously, to mean any general judgments about what is *morally* right, wrong, obligatory, or good, whether abstract or concrete, formal or material. (2) One may speak of love or "the law of love" as a rule or principle in the sense just indicated. Indeed, some of the debate has been on precisely the question whether this way of speaking of love is proper or not. But what interests me here is not so much the question whether love or the love-command is itself a rule or principle as the question whether there are *other* rules or principles which do not mention love, what their status is, and how they are related to the ethic of love (whether this is conceived as a principle or not). (3) The term "law" we may take here as meaning a rule or principle or a set of rules or principles, except perhaps when it is used in the phrase "the law of love." (4) I shall disregard the question whether the "law of love'' enjoins or excludes love of self and the question how love of neighbor is related to love of God. It will be convenient to take it simply as enjoining love. We must also leave open the question whether the love enjoined is ''an emotion or affection'' or ''primarily an active determination of the will,''[4] trying so to express what we say that it may be true either way. The main point is that, either way, love is aimed at an object and seeks it or its good. (5) Some may take faith or commitment to God as the basic virtue or posture of Christian ethics, rather than love, but even then most of what I shall say will hold with ''faith'' or commitment to God'' substituted where I say ''love.''

III

Our subject, then, is the theological debate about the relation of love and principles in Christian (and similar religious) ethics. To deal with it we must first look at the parallel debate which I indicated was going on among philosophers. Here the issue is not love versus principle or love versus natural law. Roughly speaking, where theologians talk about love, philosophers talk about beneficence or general utility. At any rate, among the latter, the main debate in normative ethics (as vs. metaethics) has been between the deontologists or formalists on one side, and the teleologists on the other. The latter hold that all rights and duties, particular or general, are to be determined directly or indirectly by looking to see what is conducive to the greatest balance of good over evil, and they are ethical egoists, nationalists, or universalists (utilitarians) depending on whose good they say is to be promoted, that of the agent, that of his nation, or that of the universe as a whole. The deontologists insist that there are rights and duties, general or particular, which hold independently of any conduciveness they may have to promote a balance of good over evil for agent, nation, or universe. Among the deontologists the main issues are whether beneficence or utility is a duty at all or not, whether all moral rules of right and duty fall under justice, and whether the basic judgments of right and duty are formal or material, general or particular. Most teleologists lately have been utilitarians of one sort or another, and here there has been a particularly lively debate between the extreme or act-utilitarians and the restricted or rule-utilitarians (also in another dimension, not directly relevant here, between the hedonistic and the ''ideal'' utilitarians). This needs a brief explanation here.

We may, in fact, distinguish three utilitarian positions for our purposes, according to the view taken about moral rules. (1) Pure act-utilitarianism is the view which has no place whatsoever for such rules, holding that one is to tell what is one's right or duty in a particular situation simply by an appeal to the principle of utility, that is, by looking to see what action will produce or probably produce the greatest general balance of good over evil, counting all of the consequences which it itself causes or will probably cause and no others, and in particular ignoring the consequences which might be brought about if the same thing were done in similar situations (i.e., if it were made a rule to do that act in such situations). (2) Pure rule-utilitarianism holds that one is to tell what is one's right or duty in a particular situation by appeal to some set of rules like "Keep promises," "Tell the truth," etc., and not by appeal to the principle of utility. In this respect it is like extreme deontological theories. But, as against all deontological theories, it holds that we are to determine what rules should govern our lives by an appeal to the principle of utility, i.e., by looking to see what rules are such that always acting on them is for the greatest general good. That is, we are never to ask what act will have the best consequences in a particular situation, but either what the rules call for or what rule it is most useful always to follow in that kind of a situation. And it may be obligatory to follow the rule in a particular situation even if following it is known not to have the best possible consequences in this particular case. (3) Modified act-utilitarianism would allow us to formulate rules and to use them as guides, but they would be rules which say, not that always-acting in such and such a way in such and such a kind of situation is socially more useful than always-acting on any other rule would be, but that it is always or generally for the greatest good to act in a certain way in such situations. Take

"Keeping-promises-always is for the greatest general good"

and

"Keeping promises is always for the greatest general good."

The first is the rule-utilitarian's way of formulating his rules, the second that of the modified act-utilitarian. The main difference is that the latter cannot allow that a rule may ever be followed in a particular situation when following it is known not to have the best possible consequences in this particular case.

Of course, one may combine two of these forms of utilitarianism in one way or another; one might maintain, for instance, that in particular situations we are to appeal to rules justified by their utility in certain kinds of cases and directly to the principle of utility in certain other kinds of cases. I think it will also be clear that ethical egoism may take similar forms: pure act-egoism, modified act-egoism, pure rule-egoism, etc. What concerns me now, however, is to point out that a love-ethic, which I shall call agapism, may take parallel forms. Agapism is the view which assigns to the "law of love" the same position that utilitarianism assigns to the principle of utility; it allows no *basic* ethical principles other than or independent of the "law of love." It can take any of three main forms: pure act-agapism, modified act-agapism, and pure rule-agapism. These will be described more fully in the next section.

One might ask here whether there really is any difference between the ethics of love or agapism and utilitarianism. Theologians generally assume that there is, without discussing the point very carefully. Philosophers, on the other hand, seem to assume that there is no basic difference between them — see, for example, J. S. Mill or A. C. Garnett. This is an important question, and the answer is not very obvious, not at least until one has made some distinctions, and then it seems to me the answer is yes or no depending —.[5] But we must leave it to one side here, and rest with pointing out parallels. Even if the parallels turn out to be identities, however, all that we shall be saying about them will still be true.

But Christian "schemes of morality," as ethical systems were called in the eighteenth century before the word "scheme" came to mean something nefarious, need not be wholly agapistic. Just as a philosopher may hold that some or all rights and duties are independent of utility, so a theologian may hold that some or all rights and duties are independent of the "law of love," or, in other words, that love is not enough to give us all of morality even when taken together with all relevant factual belief or knowledge (empirical or theological).[6] If he does hold this, then his position is like those of the deontologists rather than like those of the utilitarians. In fact, there would be a position for him to take parallel to each of the various deontological positions. And here again we may distinguish three pure positions: pure act-deontologism, modified act-deontologism, and pure rule-deontologism. The first will say that every moral decision is somehow to be a function of a knowledge of the particular situation without any appeal to rules or to utility. The second would allow us to use rules, but would insist that the rules are mere inductions from particular cases and so may never contravene a clear direct verdict in any such case. What Henry Sidgwick called "perceptual intuitionism" might take either of these forms. Pure rule-deontologism would assert that we are always to tell what is right or wrong wholly by appeal to a set of rules or principles, insisting, of course, that these rules and principles are not mere problematic inductions, and that their validity does not depend on their utility. Both what Sidgwick called "dogmatic intuitionism" and what he called "philosophical intuitionism" would be forms of this view, differing only in the number and abstractness of the rules or principles regarded as basic. Again, of course, one might combine two of these forms of deontologism; one might, for example, combine perceptual and dogmatic intuitionism as Sir David Ross does. These are all pure forms of deontologism, and, apart from questions of orthodoxy, positions of all these sorts are open to the theologian who is not being an agapist. If, however, one regards the principle of utility as one of the principles to be used in making moral decisions, though not the only basic one, then one is still a deontologist (not a teleologist) but an impure one. Similarly, if a theologian regards the "law of love" as one of the principles to be used, but not as the only basic one, then he is holding an impure or mixed view, only it will be more convenient in this case to call it an impure form of agapism or mixed agapism.

IV

Now, against this background and using my fragmentary knowledge of the literature of Judeo-Christian ethics, I can try to characterize various possible views about the place of principles and their relation to love — various "schemes" of Christian or religious ethics — and do something to relate them to positions actually taken in the literature. In fact, the following outline of positions will be my main contribution to the discussion I am trying to help along. For my conviction is that theologians would be much clearer and much more cogent if they were to state their issues and positions in such terms as these, and then make evident precisely why we should accept their answers. It may be that the Christian ethical thinker cannot be wholly content with the terms, methods, or conclusions of the mere "moral philosopher," as G. F. Thomas and many others before him have urged; but, even so, one may perhaps insist that his thinking ought at least to meet the standards which such a moral philosopher, at his best, sets himself.

It should be pointed out here that, whichever of the following schemes of morality a Christian thinker adopts (if any), there will be a question about just what he is claiming for it. (1) He might be claiming only that said scheme is *the* proper form for Christian or Judeo-Christian ethics to take, or at at least that it is *a* proper form for it to take. (2) He may also be claiming, as H. Rashdall does in *Conscience and Christ,* that the Christian normative ethics, as he conceives it, is a satisfactory one in the eyes of the most enlightened moral consciousness and so is tenable by modern man. But if he makes only these claims, he may still be allowing that there are other valid schemes of morality (even of Christian morality) or part-schemes of morality, such as St. Paul seems to ascribe to the Gentiles. Hence a Christian may and often seems to make a stronger claim, namely, (3) that the normative ethics he subscribes to, or something very close to it, is the only adequate and tenable scheme of morality there is. This claim would be harder to defend, but theologians have been known to rush in where angels (not to mention philosophers) would be wary of treading. However this may be, let us get on with our outline. I merely wanted to point out that different claims may be made for the scheme adopted — and to add that theologians do not always make clear just what claim they are making or on what grounds they are making it, just as they do not always make clear precisely what the scheme is that they are adopting in the first place.

The first group of positions I shall call *pure agapism.* They all hold that the "law of love" is the sole basis of morality — that on it hang "the whole law and the prophets," i.e., that the rest of the moral law can and must be derived from love together with relevant non-ethical beliefs and knowledge, empirical, metaphysical, or theological. In Bertrand Russell's words, pure agapism holds that "the [morally] good life is a life inspired by love and guided by knowl-edge."[7] Its most extreme form is *pure act-agapism.* This admits no rules or principles other than the ''law of love'' itself, and it also does not allow that there are any ''perceptual intuitions'' about what is right or wrong in particular situations independently of the dictates of love. It insists that one is to discover or decide what one's right or duty in a particular situation is solely by confronting one's loving will with the facts about that situation, whether one is an individual or a group. Facts about other situations and ethical conclusions arrived at in other situations are, for this extreme view, simply irrelevant, if not misleading. It adopts with complete literalness, as the whole story, St. Augustine's dictum, ''Love, and do as you please.'' Here belong at least the more drastic of the views sometimes referred to as antinomian, nominalist, existentialist, situationalist, simplistic, or contextualist. Thomas ascribes such a view to Emil Brunner, if I understand him, though he correctly points out that Brunner sometimes seems to hold one of the views to be described later.[8] Paul Ramsey, like Thomas and von Hildebrand, has been attacking such theories lately, but in *Basic Christian Ethics* he appeared to come very close to agreeing with them.

The other forms of pure agapism all take rules or principles to be necessary or at least helpful in guiding the loving Christian individual (or group) in the determination of his (its) rights and duties in particular cases. But, being forms of pure agapism, they regard all such rules or principles as somehow derivative from love. First of these forms is *modified act-agapism* or ''summary rule'' agapism.[9] This admits rules but regards them as summaries of past experience, useful, perhaps almost indispensable, but only as rules of thumb. It cannot allow that a rule may ever be followed in a situation when it is seen to conflict with what love dictates in that situation. For, if rules are to be followed only in so far as they are helpful as aids to love, they cannot constrain or constrict love in any way. But they may and perhaps should be used. I am not sure I know of any good cases of this modified act-agapism, but perhaps some of the so-called contextualists or ''circumstance'' moralists belong here; some of them at any rate do mention rules or principles on occasion without making clear just how they conceive of them, e.g., J. Sittler in *The Structure of Christian Ethics*.[10]

Pure rule-agapism is analogous to pure rule-utilitarianism; it maintains that we are always to tell what we are to do in particular situations by referring to a set of rules, and that what rules are to prevail and be followed is to be determined by seeing what rules (not what acts) best or most fully embody love. For modified act-agapism the proper way to state a rule is to say, for example,

''Keeping promises is always love-fulfilling.''

For pure rule-agapism one must say, rather,

''Keeping-promises-always is love-fulfilling.''

The difference is that on the latter view we may and sometimes must obey a rule in a particular situation even though the action it calls for is seen not to be what love itself would directly require. For pure rule-agapism, in other words, the rules may in a sense constrict the direct expression of love. For if love is, in fact, constrained to fulfill itself through acting according to rules, as Ramsey puts it in his more recent writings,[11] love must be "in-principled," or, as philosophers would now say, it must be "rule-governed."

If we ask here why love is thus constrained to express itself through rules or principles rather than by doing in each case the act which is most loving in that case,[12] the rule-agapist may answer in three apparently different ways which are usually not distinguished. (1) He may argue that love is constrained to cloak itself in principles, not by anything outside of itself, but by its own nature or "inner dialectic," as some might prefer to say. This is not an easy view to get clear — I am not even sure it can be made out — but it is suggested by 1 John 3:17,

> But whoso hath this world's good, and seeth his brother have need, and shutteth up his bowels of compassion from him, how dwelleth the love of God in him?

This suggests that it follows from the very nature of love that the rich should help the poor, and one might argue that all the rules of Christian morality can be derived from the nature of love in this direct way. Rashdall seems to try to follow this course in deducing the "corollaries and consequences" of the law of love: love to enemies, forgiveness, self-sacrifice, purity, repentance, etc.[13] In a somewhat similar way J. S. Mill reasoned (mistakenly, I think) that justice and equality are entailed by the principle of utility as such; a theologian might claim the same for love, possibly with more justice.[14]

(2) The second possibility is to claim, not that the rules are somehow contained in the very nature of love, but that love must act through rules because the world is so constituted that it can fulfill itself or attain its object more fully if it conforms its actions to rules than if it does not. On this view love is constrained to adopt rules, not by its own nature alone, but by its nature together with the facts about the world in which it is seeking to fulfill itself or reach its object. In a similar way a rule-utilitarian might contend that, although no rules are contained in the principle of utility, rules must be followed if the greatest general good is to be achieved, which rules to follow being determined by a consideration of the relative utility of certain rules as against others.

(3) On the third view, the fact that love must adopt rules is due neither to its own nature nor to the nature of the world, but to the nature of reason or of morality. The argument would be that if love is to be the matrix of the *moral* life, then it must follow maxims which it wills to be universally acted on (i.e., embody itself in a set of "universal laws"), since this is a necessary condition of rationality, or of morality, or of both. The affinities of such a position with Kant's is obvious, for both insist that reason and morality require rules which are willed to be universal laws; the difference is in the method of determining

which rules make up the moral law — for Kant the method is to see what rules we can will to be universal laws independently of whatever motives or ends we may have, but for the present view it is to see what rules we can or must will to be universal laws when our motivation is *love*. That it is to be rule-governed is required if it is to take the form of reason or morality, but what the rules shall be is still for it to say. They will still be determined as in (1) or (2).

Of these three views the third is suggested, to my mind at least, by some passages in Reinhold Niebuhr,[15] but, in general, they have not been distinguished by the more rule-agapistically minded writers. Presumably what Ramsey calls "in-principled love-ethics" falls under one of them, but I have not been able to tell which. I do not have labels for these three forms of rule-agapism. Enough is enough, and I am doing enough labelling here as it is. What matters is that the three views should not be confused by either friend or foe. I should point out, however, that it is only the second that is strictly analogous to what is usually called rule-utilitarianism, though rule-utilitarianism could also take forms analogous to (1) and (3).

The remaining forms of pure agapism are *combinations* of act-agapism and rule-agapism. Here would fall, for instance, the view that, while we may and should appeal to rules when we can in deciding what should be done in a particular case, as the rule-agapist holds, we may and should appeal to the "law of love" directly in cases for which there are no rules or in which the rules conflict, just as the act-agapist does. Such combinations may, in fact, be more plausible than either pure act-agapism or pure rule-agapism by themselves.

V

We may now look at what I shall call *pure non-agapistic theories*. These hold that *all* of the basic judgments of morality proper, whether these are particular or general, are independent of any "law of love" — that any such law of love, if it is valid at all, is neither necessary nor helpful in morality, and, in fact, does not belong to morality at all. These views are analogous to (or identical with) the forms of pure deontologism described in III, which do not recognize any moral obligation to be beneficent or to follow the principle of utility. There will be a purely non-agapist theory corresponding to each of the purely deontological theories mentioned there. Speaking roughly, they all identify morality with justice and regard justice as determinable independently of either the principle of utility or the "law of love." It might seem that no such scheme of morality can be accepted by a Christian, since these schemes all regard the entire substance of morality as coming from some source other than love. But even Christians have "sought out many inventions," and there are at least two types of pure non-agapism which are approximated by what some of them have invented. One is a view which agrees that "love is the fulfillment of the [moral] law,'' but holds that the whole content of the law is discernible independently of love. In effect, it takes acting in accordance with an independently ascertainable moral code as the criterion or perhaps even as the definition of what love is. Thus it is only verbally and not in any substantive way agapistic.[16] It may therefore turn out to be a wolf in sheep's clothing, but at least some intuitionistic moralists of the past, Samuel Clarke, for example, have meant to be Christians while holding a view which can be described in some such terms as these. The other purely non-agapistic conception of morality to be mentioned here has a rather different character. It involves making a distinction between the moral life or ''mere morality'' and the religious way of life, adding that morality is to be conceived in a non-agapistic way, and then proposing that it should be supplanted by the religious way of life, this being conceived as a life of love and as transcending ''mere morality.'' Like Nietzsche it goes ''beyond good and evil'' in the moral sense; unlike him it does so in the interest of religion. Its drift is agapistic, since it advocates a life of love (and its agapism may take any of the forms described in IV), but its conception of morality is not. Something of this sort is suggested in different ways by at least some passages in Kierkegaard and Brunner.[17]

Very similar in substance is the ''two morality'' theory variously intimated or proposed by Henri Bergson, Lord Lindsay, and Eliseo Vivas. According to it there are two independent moralities, one the morality of love, the other that of social pressure, one's station and its duties, claims and counter-claims, or what have you. Each is complete and valid in its fashion, but the first is superior to and should supplant the second. This view thus combines a purely agapistic conception of one morality with a purely non-agapistic conception of the other. And, of course, it may conceive the former in any of the ways described in IV and the latter after the fashion of any of the forms of pure deontologism distinguished in III. Yet it is in a sense still a form of agapism since it proposes to replace the non-agapistic morality, where feasible, with that of love. Its ideal is the ethics of love. The only difference between it and the previous theory is that it speaks of two moralities where that theory speaks of two ways of life but calls one of them morality and the other religion.

VI

There are also, as I indicated earlier, mixed theories which I shall call *impure or mixed agapisms*. They are combinations of agapism and non-agapism but not along the lines of the ''two morality'' theory. For them there is only one morality by which we are to live but it has two parts. One of its parts is the ''law of love,'' the other consists of judgments about right and wrong which are independent of the ''law of love,'' judgments which may be either general (rules) or particular. It should be noted here that saying these judgments are independent of the "law of love" means only that they are not derivative from the "law of love" in any such way as agapists think they are (see IV); it does not mean that they are knowable apart from revelation, grace, or religion. Confusion here is easy and frequent, but the two points are distinct. The "law of love" may or may not be revealed, and the alleged independent ethical insights also may or may not be revealed. Whether they are or not is a question, not of normative ethics, but of metaethics or, if you will, of the epistemology of ethics.

Impure agapism is analogous to Ross's impure deontological theory. Ross holds that the principle of utility (non-hedonistically conceived) is one of the valid principles of ethics, but that there are others also whose validity is independent of the principle of utility. Substitute the law of love for the principle of utility here and you get impure or mixed agapism. But Sir David also holds (1) that the principle of utility and the other principles may conflict on occasion, (2) that in that case the former does not always take precedence over the others, and (3) that, partly for this reason, both are necessary for the guidance of our actions. Similarly, an impure agapist might take the position (1) that the "law of love" and the other principles of ethics may conflict, (2) that in such cases the former does not always take precedence, and (3) that, partly for this reason, both the "law of love" and the independent principles are necessary.[18] But he need not accept such an impure form of impure agapism. He may deny that the other principles can conflict with the law of love; or he may agree that they do conflict with it on occasion but contend that then it always takes precedence over them. In either case he would be maintaining that the other principles, while valid, are not necessary for the guidance of our conduct, though they may be helpful. Or he may argue that they are not even helpful — except to those who do not know the "law of love." If he takes any of these three lines, he remains pretty much an agapist in effect though not in strict theory. But he may — and some theologians do — go even farther. While admitting that there *are* ethical insights which are independent of the law of love, he may contend that, though they leave natural man "without excuse," they are so far from being helpful as to be positively misleading — that they are unclear, inaccurate, incomplete, corrupted, etc., and hence not standards of any "true virtue" at all and so not to be relied on by anyone who knows the law of love. For him then the ethics to work by is even more imperatively that of love, at least for those to whom it is available.

There are other, rather different, possible theories for which it is hard to find a label, but which must be mentioned because theologians do sometimes seem to subscribe to them. In all of the above theories, if the law of love is recognized at all (in a non-verbal way), it is regarded as a *basic* norm. But it is not necessary so to regard it if one recognizes it; one may consider it to be derived from some other more basic principle which is in itself non-agapistic. Some thinkers, among them some theologians, take as the ultimate norm of our conduct the requirement of realizing ourselves, completing our natures, or fulfilling our beings, and then argue that the (or at least *a*) way to do this is through love. A. C. Garnett reasons thus in his little book *Can Ideals and Norms Be Justified?*

> . . . this discussion . . . has shown that utilitarianism (in its non-hedonistic form) [which he identifies with Christian agapism] has correctly pointed to the *end* at which ethically right conduct must aim, while the self-realization theory has correctly stated the *ground* or *reason* why conduct aiming at that end is ethically required.[19]

Similar lines of thought may be found in Tillich and in both Niebuhrs, though less clearly and explicitly expressed.[20] Here the ideal of love is derived in one way or another from what is basically a form of ethical egoism. But the outcome may still be a working agapism, depending on whether or not love is taken to be the only avenue to self-realization or fulfillment of being. If it is, then, of course, the resulting *derived pure agapism* may take any of the forms described in IV. If it is not, the outcome will be some kind of *derived impure agapism*.

There are, however, other schemes of morality in which the "law of love" is derivative and not basic. Suppose we hold, as some religious people do, that we have one and only one basic duty, namely, to obey God's commands. Then we might well go on to argue that God has summed up his will in the command to love, and thus again come out with a working agapism to live by (which again can take any of the forms described in IV). This line of thought appears in Reinhold Niebuhr's characterization of the ethics of Jesus. It is, he says, "oriented by only one vertical religious reference, to the will of God; and the will of God is defined in terms of all-inclusive love."[21] Here, too, agapism is deduced from a principle which in itself is non-agapistic. We might also, however, reason in one of the following ways, both familiar to Christians:

(a) We ought to imitate God ("Be ye perfect as I am perfect").
   God loves us.
   Therefore we ought to love one another.
(b) We ought to be grateful to our benefactors.
   God has sent his Son into the world to save us, etc.
   Therefore we ought to love him.

If I remember correctly, Niebuhr suggests both of these lines of thought too.[22] In all such patterns of reasoning, however, the law of love is derivative from some principle which is independent of and basic to it. Whether the result is a working agapism or not depends again on whether one holds that there are other duties coordinate with or more basic than love (besides the one stated in the first premise). If one does not, one is a derived agapist of one of the kinds described in IV; if one does, one is some kind of a mixed agapist.

VII

Well, there in all its, I fear, boring but, I hope, clarifying detail is my outline of possible schemes of Christian ethics considered as bearing on the debate about love and principle. I am sure, to parody one of my favorite texts again, that some will say at this point, "God made man upright, but Frankena has sought out many inventions." Even so, I have no doubt missed some possibilities. No doubt also, in my quest for philosophical clarity, I have blurred some theological refinements and subtleties. Nevertheless, I do think that it would help greatly if theologians and religious thinkers were to use some such table of views as I have sketched, and some such terms as I have employed, in stating their issues, their positions, and their arguments for their positions — all without trying to preach to us at the same time (though there is a time for that too). Throughout, in the interest of relevance, I have sought to relate the positions described to positions actually taken or suggested in the literature, and now, before going on, I should like to add a little along this line. I have mentioned Ramsey, but am not clear just what his position is. It seems to be a form of pure agapism — or possibly of derived agapism — but it is not clear just what kind of pure agapism it is, and it may even be a kind of impure or mixed agapism. G. F. Thomas's position too is not entirely clear. In arguing against Brunner he is certainly rejecting act-agapism, but whether he is a pure rule-agapist or a mixed agapist of some sort I cannot tell for sure. It depends on what he means when he talks about "principles derived from an analysis of the various kinds of human needs and relationships and the best methods of dealing with them"[23] and whether he takes the principle of love as one of the premises needed in deriving them. The position of St. Thomas, with its emphasis on natural law, is, on the other hand, pretty clearly what I have called a mixed theory, though it may involve a rule-utilitarian conception of "human law." Brunner's position I have referred to in one or two connections. It seems to me quite ambiguous; sometimes it looks like a form of act-agapism, but at others like a form of mixed agapism or even like a species of non-agapism. As for Reinhold Niebuhr, he appears to me to suggest, in one place or another, almost every one of the positions I have described; whether this spells richness or confusion of mind I shall leave for others to judge. As for me and my house, the most plausible position seems to me to be a certain kind of mixed theory — roughly, one which takes as basic in ethics (1) the "law of love" and (2) the "principles of justice" conceived as independently arrived at.

Here I must also notice the position of A. C. Garnett, one of the few philosophers who have taken part in the debate which is our topic. In the last chapter of *Religion and the Moral Life* he contends that Jesus did not conceive the agapistic point of view in ethics as "devoid of principles" for (1) he built "the principles of universality and impartiality" into the injunction to love — the former by interpreting "neighbor" to include enemies, and the latter by specifying that one is to love each neighbor *as oneself*. Garnett also argues (2) that Jesus "implies a place for principles of secondary generality," viz., "the moral laws that 'hang upon' the law of love" or which spell out "the implications of the law of love for certain specific human relations." Now, in our terms, which position is it that Garnett is thus ascribing to Jesus and accepting for himself? So far as (1) is concerned, it looks like a pure rule-agapism of the first sort distinguished in IV, for the two principles involved are represented as being contained in the injunction to love itself. And this does seem to be true for the principle of universality. But what about the principle of impartiality or justice? It is not clear whether it is being thought of as analytically entailed by the bare command to love our neighbors or as being added as a qualification of that command. It seems to me it must be the latter, and, in that case, the injunction to love really is equivalent to "Thou shalt love all men and thou shalt do so justly." And, then, it seems to me, the position is a form of impure or mixed agapism of the sort I myself have just proposed. As for (2) — here, so far as "principles of secondary generality" go, the position seems to be a rule-agapism of the second kind described in IV, though it may still be simply a modified act-agapism. Incidentally, Garnett's proposed view shows, in any case, that one may hold one kind of theory for some ethical principles and another kind of theory for others — a point I did not make clear before.

   I should also like to take this occasion to say a little about two well-known and relevant dicta of Christian and other religious moralists. The first is, "Love is the *fulfillment* of the law." I cannot try here to interpret St. John and St. Paul, both of whom use this formula. I wish, however, to point out that the formula can be interpreted in various ways, and may be accepted by all or almost all of the above views, even by non-agapistic ones. Thus, (1) the dictum may be taken to say that the moral law is simply to love, that the content of the moral law is wholly given by love. Agapists, pure or derived, accept it in this sense. (2) The dictum may also be understood as saying that the moral law is incomplete without the "law of love," that this law is necessary to make the moral standard complete. Impure, pure, and derived agapists may all understand it in this sense, though each will do so in his own way. (3) Again, the dictum may be conceived as meaning that loving is *formally* (in Descartes's sense) equivalent to fulfilling the law, i.e., not that the criterion of fulfilling the moral law is loving (agapism) but that the criterion or definition of loving is fulfilling the law. This view, which was introduced earlier, presupposes that the content of the moral law consists of principles and particular judgments which are arrived at independently of love, though not necessarily independently of Scripture or of special revelation. Only a non-agapist can interpret the formula in this sense. (4) But one may also interpret the formula as meaning that love or loving *eminently* (again in Descartes's sense) fulfills the law — that if one loves one fulfills the law and more, one does not fulfill it literally, one fulfills it or overfulfills it but at a higher level and in a different mode. Here again the content of the law itself is independent of the requirement to love, and a non-agapist therefore can accept the dictum in this sense, while an agapist cannot. But it is also implied that one may live by love alone and need not literally (formally) live by the law. In this sense this interpretation yields a working agapism; in fact, this interpretation yields the view, mentioned before, that there are two ways of life, the moral and the religious, the latter being the better in some way. It adds only that following the latter also "fulfills" the former. (5) Our first dictum may, however, also be construed as saying that love is to the law as Jesus Christ is to John the Baptist, as is suggested by Jesus' words, "I am not come to destroy [the law] but to fulfill [it]." But this is neither clear nor unambiguous. One might say this and hold that love is to *supplant* the law. Or one might say it and hold only that love fulfills the law in the sense of completing it [i.e., in sense (2)], or that it fulfills the law eminently in the sense just explained.

The second dictum I wish to say something about is, "Love is the *spirit* of the law." This is also vague and ambiguous, though in a different way. (1) It may mean that love is the motive with which one should obey the law. This does not make love the source of the content of the moral law, and hence non-agapists and mixed agapists can agree that love is the spirit of the law in this sense. (2) It may mean, however, that the rest of the moral law is or may be derived from the "law of love" and corrected in the light of it. In this sense it will, of course, be accepted by agapists (except perhaps derived agapists). If all that is claimed is only that "the whole law and the prophets" *can* be derived from the "law of love," then even mixed or non-agapists may agree (for them it may still be that some or all of "the law and the prophets" can also be independently derived). (3) Or it may mean that love fulfills the law eminently in the manner explained a moment ago. (4) Finally, it may mean that love is not a principle which can serve as a major premise for deriving the rest of morality, but a spirit of approaching questions about what to do which also somehow helps us to answer them though it cannot be encapsuled in any verbal formula — i.e., it is a conative and directive attitude or disposition. As indicated at the beginning, I have tried to avoid the issue about whether love is a principle or an attitude. I believe that with the proper distinctions, it can be both. All that needs to be said here, however, is that one can agree that love is the spirit of morality in this fourth sense on any of the views described above.

VIII

The end cometh, but it is not even yet. For we must still look, at least briefly, at the question how one is to decide which of the above schemes of Christian morality is the correct or most tenable one. How or by what method is the Christian thinker to tell whether he must admit principles in addition to love, how is he to conceive these principles, and which principles is he to admit, if any? By what means is the debate we have taken as our topic to be settled? This methodological matter the theologians have also been none too clear about, perhaps in part because they have not been very clear about the issues and possible positions involved. We must, therefore, consider it before we can close.

There are at least two questions here: (1) whether or not there are any ethical rules or principles (or any particular ethical judgments, for that matter) which do not merely repeat the "law of love" and which are authoritative, necessary, or helpful, (2) whether these ethical rules or principles (or particular judgments) are ascertainable independently of the "law of love" or not, and, in either case how they may be or are to be ascertained. In dealing with the first question, we must note that it is important to be clear just what one is claiming about the rules or principles (or particular judgments) in question. For they may be helpful without being necessary, and they may be authoritative or valid without being either necessary or helpful. But, whatever is being claimed, one method of settling the question at once suggests itself to the Christian thinker, namely, a direct appeal to Scripture, especially the teachings of Jesus and the Apostles. Thus Lindsay Dewar argues directly from the New Testament that Jesus did in fact "legislate certain rules or principles."[24] This sort of appeal seems to me to show only that there are some rules and principles other than the "law of love" (though perhaps not independent of it) which are authoritative or valid, not that they are necessary or helpful, unless it is assumed that Jesus would not have legislated them if they were not necessary or at least helpful (and the Bible does not tell us *this*). Indeed, it seems to me that such appeals do show, to the extent that they show said principles to be authoritative, that a Christian cannot be satisfied with pure act-agapism as a normative *theory* — in practice, however, unless the principles in question are necessary or at least helpful as well as authoritative, he may still proceed as a pure act-agapist would. But this seems to me the most that an appeal to revelation can show; in principle it can establish anything for a Christian, of course, but in fact it establishes only what is actually revealed, and Scripture does not actually tell us that the disputed rules or principles are necessary or helpful as well as authoritative (and this it tells only to one who accepts it as a divine revelation). To show (or refute) this, therefore, one must resort to "moral philosophy," for example, to a logico-empirical argument calculated to prove (or disprove) that the bare injunction to love, even taken together with relevant factual knowledge about particular situations, is insufficient to give us adequate guidance of a moral kind.

In connection with the second question, we must first observe that whether the alleged ethical rules and judgments are independent of the "law of love" or not, there are various possible alternative theories about how they may or are to be ascertained. If they are not independent of the "law of love," we must still try to decide between modified act-agapism and the various forms of rule-agapism; if they are independent we still have to decide between various possible kinds of mixed agapisms and non-agapisms — and here all sorts of theories are possible: natural law theories, intuitionism, revelationism, social approval theories, etc. In effect, the second question is how to decide between the various normative theories described above. And, again, a Christian theologian may seek to do so by appeal to Scripture; if Scripture were full enough in what it says, this would for him be decisive. But the texts are not full enough in a philosophical sense; some point one way, some another. Perhaps the most crucial is Romans 2:14-15, in which St. Paul says that the Gentiles, who presumably do not have the "law of love," yet have a moral law "written in their hearts." This appears to show that there is moral insight which is independent both of special revelation and the "law of love" — and so to establish the correctness of some kind of mixed or non-agapistic theory. Yet even this passage is hardly explicit and elaborate enough to settle such a theoretical point, and the same is still more true of all the other texts — they are not theoretical enough in their message to help the Christian to decide with any conclusiveness between the rival theories open to him, except perhaps to rule out pure agapism (*if* they can be claimed to do even this). Here again the theologian must resort to "moral philosophy" as well as to revelation, if he means to try to settle such points of theory at all on anything like intellectually sufficient grounds, as he seems to.[25]

If, however, the theologian does resort to moral philosophy, how is he to decide between rival normative schemes? Unfortunately, contemporary moral philosophers are no more in agreement on this point than the theologians are. But I believe that at their best at any rate, they debate about it more clearly and more rigorously than theologians ever do, perhaps in part because they are not tempted to preach or to fall back on any scriptural or ecclesiastical revelation. In any case, the thinking theologian has no alternative but to become more adequately acquainted with "the best that has been thought and said in the world" of moral philosophy and then try to draw his own conclusions. In particular, he must make himself at home in the most rarified reaches of recent metaethical discussion, for his problem is not merely one within normative ethics; it includes the question how one scheme of normative ethics can be justified as against another, or if it can be justified at all. At this level I think theologians and Christian moralists have been much too unclear and much too unrigorous in their thinking. They almost invariably maintain that morality depends on religion or theology but they are rarely, if ever, very careful in their formulation of this claim or in their arguments in support of it. I myself doubt that it can be established, except perhaps in some greatly and carefully qualified sense, and believe that there are at least some "principles of justice" which are logically independent of the "law of love," of revelation, and of religion and theology. But that is another story which cannot be told now.[26]

It may be objected here that Jesus had no metaethics and hence that we need none. And it is, no doubt, true that the ethics of Jesus, and even of the Bible as a whole, is compatible with a variety of metaethical theories; the history of Judeo-Christian thought seems to show this. But, as I said at the outset, I am assuming that the theologians I have had in mind are right in feeling impelled to "think on [all] these things." If this is a mistake — and it too is a point which Christians have debated — then the mistake is as much theirs as mine.

8: Some Beliefs about Justice

"Masters, give unto your servants that which is just and equal."
St. Paul, Colossians 4:1.

THE TOPIC OF THIS LECTURE IS SOCIAL JUSTICE, MORE SPECIFICALLY, DIS-
tributive justice. One of the good things about this topic is that one does not
have to be kind to it; one has only to be just. Having twice in the past sought to
do it justice without success,[1] I now propose to try once more. If I fail to do it
justice this time — and I am sure I shall — at least it will not be for lack of
trying.

Now, as Aristotle points out, one can conceive of justice as covering the
whole area of morality, of moral virtue, or at least of moral rightness; Plato,
Kant, and, more recently, C. I. Lewis come close to conceiving it thus. But this
seems to be distributing justice a little thin. As J. S. Mill says, we must
distinguish between justice and "other obligations of morality" like "charity
or beneficence."[2] Even if, like Lewis, we refuse to regard charity or beneficence as obligations of morality, we still cannot identify distributive justice
with the whole requirement of the moral. For, as Aristotle also says, the justice
we are investigating is only a part of virtue, as is shown by the fact that, if a man
throws down his shield in battle, uses abusive language, refuses to assist a
friend with money, or commits adultery, we accuse him, not of injustice
(certainly not of distributive injustice), but of cowardice, bad temper, mean-
ness, or profligacy.

"Well," it may be said at this point, "this is true of justice as ascribed
to *individuals;* there are other things that morality requires of individuals
besides justice. However, all that can be required of a *society* or *state* is
that it be just — that it distribute justly what it is within its power to
distribute. That is, in the case of society or the state virtue equals justice,
distributive justice." This view has a good deal of plausibility, but it raises the
problems of the relation of justice to welfare and of welfare to the state, and we

Lindley Lecture (1966), reprinted by permission of the Department of Philosophy,
University of Kansas.

cannot discuss these here. Our concern now is with the question when a society or state is distributively just, not with the question whether this is all it should be.

I

There is one principle of distributive justice on which there seems to be general agreement, namely, that like cases or individuals are to be dealt with in the same way or treated alike, or that similar cases are to be treated similarly. Chaim Perelman calls this the *formal* principle of justice.[3] Now, it does seem clear that an act of distributing is at least *prima facie* unjust if it involves treating differently, or discriminating between, individuals whose cases are similar in all important respects. If my case is substantially like yours but it is treated differently, one of us has grounds for crying that injustice has been done, as any child seems to see instinctively. In this sense, the formal principle of justice does formulate a *necessary* condition of the existence of distributive justice. For justice to exist there must be regularities or rules that are followed in the distribution of what is distributed. Yet a land may be without justice even if similar cases are always treated similarly, even if it always distributes according to rules which are known. A society may have and act without fail on rules, laws, and conventions, and yet be an epitome of injustice. It depends on what the rules and conventions are. In other words, rules, laws, and conventions may themselves be unjust or incorporate injustice. They all take the form, "Treat every case of kind X in manner Y," as is required by the formal principle, but the manner specified may in fact be an unjust way of treating things of the kind in question.

Any set of rules that may prevail in a given society is a selection from among all possible rules. They classify people in terms of certain similarities and neglect others; they also neglect certain dissimilarities. They likewise select, from among the possible ways of treating people, certain ones, and they assign these ways of treatment to the different classes they define. But human beings are alike and unlike in all sorts of respects. Not all of their similarities and differences are important or even relevant to the question how they are to be treated, and not just any manner of treatment may be assigned to just any class of cases. Consistency is a requirement of justice, not merely "a hobgoblin of little minds"; but it is not enough, it is not the whole of justice.

In other words, the formal principle of justice does not give us a *sufficient* condition for the existence of justice. As Perelman insists,[4] we must also have some *material* principles of distribution, principles that tell us something more about the content of our rules, more about the similarities and differences that are to be regarded as relevant, more about what Jesus called the measures with which we are to mete and be measured to. This is what we must look for. I shall, however, not seek to give a complete and systematic account of the material principles of justice. I shall limit my discussion almost entirely to a review of some views about the nature of the most *basic* material principles of justice, and to a defense of one of them.

It is sometimes said that, while the formal principle of justice is certain but empty, any material principle must be arbitrary and uncertain. We must choose one, if we are to have any system of justice at all, but our choice cannot have any rational basis, since equally valid reasons can be given for choosing another.[5] I shall not try to take this metaethical position by frontal attack, but, instead, will seek to bypass it by offering, not indeed a "proof" of any material principle of distributive justice, but what Mill calls "considerations determining the intellect to give its assent" to one view of justice and to withhold it from others.[6] That is, I shall simply try to give a rational case for one principle and against others. After all, as someone once said, the best way to answer a man who says there are no giraffes is to show him one. The only trouble about that is that one may be caught by a skeptical lion while looking for a giraffe, like the drunk who saw double and tried to climb the wrong tree.

II

Aristotle's discussions of distributive justice in the *Ethics* and *Politics* will serve as a useful basis for our inquiry.[7] Following his lead we may say that the typical case of distributive justice involves (1) at least two persons , A and B, (2) something to be distributed, P, (3) some basis of distribution, Q, and (4) a geometrical proportion or ratio such that

$$\frac{A\text{'s share of P}}{B\text{'s share of P}} = \frac{A\text{'s share of Q}}{B\text{'s share of Q}}$$

Then a society is distributively just or has distributive justice in so far as it distributes P among its members in proportion to their shares of Q. Not all theories of distributive justice accept this model quite literally, as we shall see, but we can nevertheless use it in order to state the problems involved and the main ways in which they may be answered. Clearly, there are two questions:

(a) What is P? That is, what is to be distributed?
(b) What is Q? What is to be taken as the basis of distribution?

Different theories about the material principles of distributive justice give different answers to these two questions, especially to the second.

Actually, P, or what is to be distributed, may be almost anything, and will vary from context to context; but on all theories of social justice it will consist primarily of such things as offices, privileges, tasks, tax burdens, powers, goods, educational opportunities, vocational opportunities, and the conditions of happiness or of the good life. As for Q, or the basis of distribution, one might, of course, have different theories about the nature of Q depending on what P is; for example, if it is musical instruments that are to be distributed one might take musical aptitude or taste as a basis of distribution, but if it is college credits and grades one might, and presumably should, take performance in college courses as a basis. Even so, we want to know — and this is our main problem — what the most *basic* Q is, if there is one, on the basis of which such P's as have been mentioned are to be distributed.

In his discussion of this question Aristotle indicates that there have been three main theories of social justice: the oligarchical, the aristocratic, and the democratic theories. They agree about what P is: offices, powers, honors, external goods, etc.; what they differ about is Q, the basis of distribution. The oligarchical theory says that Q is wealth or property, i.e., that P is to be distributed to people in proportion to their wealth; the aristocratic theory holds that Q is merit, i.e., that P is to be distributed in accordance with merit; and the democratic theory, as Aristotle conceives of it, claims that Q is simply the fact of free birth, and that P is to be distributed equally among those who are born free, but, of course, he was making allowance for slavery, and a contemporary democrat would prefer to say that Q is simply the fact of being human.

Revising Aristotle's scheme somewhat, we may classify theories of distributive justice as follows: (1) Inequalitarian theories hold that P is to be distributed in proportion to some Q which people have in different amounts, degrees, or forms, i.e., in proportion to some feature in which people are unequal. They are of three sorts: (a) the oligarchical theory, (b) the meritarian or aristocratic theory, (c) other inequalitarian theories, e.g., those that identify Q with blood, sex, color, height, or native intelligence. (2) Equalitarian or democratic theories hold that basically P is to be distributed equally. They are of two kinds:[8] (a) Substantive equalitarianism holds that P is to be distributed in proportion to Q; and it identifies Q with some feature in which all men are alike or equal. It is hard to give a good example of such a theory because it is hard to find any feature in which all men are alike and equal. That is one reason why this kind of equalitarianism finds it so difficult to answer the argument that men are not equal since there is no Q, no property, which they all have in the same amount and form. For example, they all have reason, but they have it in different degrees. They all have color, presumably in the same degree, but they have it in different forms. One might reply that all men are alike or equal in being men or in being human, but it is very difficult to make out just what property "being human" is, or whether it is a property at all, let alone one which everyone has in the same degree and form. (b) Procedural equalitarianism agrees with inequalitarianism in denying that there is any Q which all men have in the same degree and form. But it still maintains a basically equalitarian view of distributive justice. To do this it gives up the

Aristotelian model which holds that P is to be distributed in accordance with some Q. There is, it maintains, no Q of the kind required. It therefore regards equalitarianism as a "procedural" principle: Treat people equally unless and until there is a justification for treating them unequally. This is a procedural principle because it says, not that men are equal in a certain respect and therefore should be treated equally, but only that unequal treatment must be justified or defended, whereas equality of treatment needs no justification.

Before going on, I should like to say something here about the question, "Are Men Equal?" All equalitarians answer "Yes" to this in some sense, and all inequalitarians "No." But we must notice that the question has two senses, a factual sense and a normative one. In the factual sense it asks, "Is there any respect in which all men are in fact equal, any Q which they all have in the same degree and form?" In the normative sense it asks something very different, namely, "*Ought* all men to be treated as equals?" Thus there are really two distinct questions, though this is not always noticed. The real issue between equalitarians and inequalitarians is over the normative question whether all men ought to be treated equally; it is to this question that the former must say "Yes" and the latter "No." But the inequalitarians always say "No" to the factual question too, and, in fact, they rest their negative answer to the normative question at least in part on a negative answer to the factual one; they argue that men should be treated differently because they are different. Equalitarians, on the other hand, though they all say "Yes" to the normative question, may say either "Yes" or "No" to the factual one. Substantive equalitarians say "Yes," and procedural equalitarians say "No." These points are very important to keep in mind in any discussion of distributive justice.

III

Let us now proceed to a discussion of inequalitarian theories of the basic material principle of distributive justice. The oligarchical theory is perhaps not often espoused in so many words, but it does appear to be acted on to a considerable extent in practice, and, in any case, it is a very instructive theory to study. It maintains, it will be remembered, that the Q in proportion to which P is to be distributed is wealth, material possessions. It takes quite literally at least the first part of the saying of Jesus,

> For whosoever hath, to him shall be given,
> and he shall have more abundance; but
> whosoever hath not, from him shall be taken
> away, even that he hath.[9]

But, with all due respect for Jesus' real meaning, it seems reasonable to say that the oligarchical way of favoring the haves over the have-nots is a very paradigm of injustice. Such a theory of distributive justice seems to be mistaken in principle, and it is important to see why. It is mistaken, it seems to me, for this reason: because the Q which it takes as a basis for distribution is itself something that is distributed by human actions and social institutions, and hence something that may itself be or have been distributed justly or unjustly, namely wealth or property. If this point is well taken, then we may argue quite generally that no theory is acceptable which offers as its *basic* principle of distribution the principle that P is to be distributed in proportion to some Q whose distribution is itself dependent on human action and social policy, e.g., wealth, power, or social position. It also follows that even the democratic theory, as Aristotle understood it, is mistaken; for its Q was "free birth," and this, in the sense in which the Greeks took it, was something socially determined, not something one had either by nature or by one's own efforts.

It should be added that, in any case, already possessed wealth is plausible as a basis for distributing other things only if it is a reliable index of the presence of some other Q which is more reasonably taken as a basis of distribution, for example, ability, intelligence, or merit. This is shown by the fact that the defenders of oligarchy have usually argued that the possession of wealth actually is an index of something more fundamental, when they have bothered to give any argument at all.

Putting off the meritarian or aristocratic theory for a moment, let us look at inequalitarian views of our third sort, those taking as a basis for distribution such Q's as blood, sex, color, height, or native intelligence. These views are right in not choosing as the fundamental basis of distribution anything that is directly distributable by man or society. Instead they take as the basis of distribution some Q whose presence is due to nature (though, indirectly, through eugenics, man can do something even about the distribution of color, etc.). It seems apparent, however, that this too is a mistake. For it is reasonable to claim that the use of blood, color, height, etc., as a fundamental basis of distribution is also unjust in itself. It is fair enough to use them as a basis of distribution in certain contexts, e.g., as a basis for distributing costumes or parts in plays. But to take any of them as the most basic Q for the distribution of opportunities, offices, etc. is as unjust as taking wealth as one's basic Q, though for a different reason. The reason (the main reason, not the only one) in this case, I think, is that, if we take color, height, etc., as a basis for distributing P, then we are basing our distribution on a feature which discriminates between individuals but which the individual has done and can do nothing about; we are treating people differently in ways that profoundly affect their lives because of differences for which they have no responsibility.

The most plausible of the natural Q's just mentioned to take as a basis of distribution is native intelligence. Even native intelligence (to be distinguished here from developed intelligence) will not do, however, as our ultimate basis of distribution, though it is certainly in a better case than height or color of skin. For it is something that can be adequately detected and gauged only in the course of some kind of·program of education, formal or informal, so that its use as a basis of distribution presupposes a prior equal distribution of the opportunities for such an education.

In any case, we may also say that blood, sex, color, height, etc., cannot reasonably be taken as important bases of distribution unless they serve as reliable signs of some Q, like ability or merit, which is more justly employed as a touchstone for the treatment of individuals. This again is shown by the fact that when proponents of racial discrimination and slavery have given arguments at all, they have often argued precisely that these features may be taken as signs of such more acceptable Q's.

We have mentioned merit as clearly a more acceptable Q than acquired features like wealth on the one hand or natural ones like color on the other. Shall we then use merit as our most fundamental basis of distribution? That we should is the position of the aristocrats or meritarians, including Aristotle himself and, more recently, Sir David Ross. What do they mean by "merit"? Aristotle meant excellence or virtue, and he distinguished two kinds of excellences or virtues: intellectual ones and moral ones; Sir David, however, means by "merit" simply moral virtue.[10] We may therefore understand the meritarians to hold that, basically at any rate, P is to be distributed to people in proportion to their degree of excellence, intellectual, moral, or both. What shall we say of this conception of social justice?

It certainly has a good deal of plausibility. In particular, its Q does not suffer from the defects of those of the other two kinds of inequalitarianism. For merit or excellence is not something distributed (differentially) by nature without any help from the individual, as color, blood, and height are; nor is it something that can be distributed justly or unjustly by man or his social institutions, as wealth is. Only the potentialities for excellence can be provided by nature, and only the opportunities and accessories for it can be provided by society; excellence or merit itself must be achieved or won by individuals themselves. It looks, therefore, as if merit may be just the Q we are looking for. Nevertheless, I am convinced that it will not do either. I tried to show this once or twice before but now suspect that the argument I then used is fallacious.[11] There is, however, another argument which I hope is better. This argument is that merit cannot be the *basic* Q in matters of distributive justice, since a recognition of merit as the basis of distribution is justified only if every individual has an equal chance of achieving all the merit he is capable of (and it cannot simply be assumed that they have had this chance). If the individuals competing for P have not had an equal chance to achieve all the merit they are capable of, then merit is not a fair basis for distributing shares of P among them. If this is so, then, before merit can reasonably be adopted as a ground of distribution, there must first be a prior *equal* distribution of the conditions for achieving merit, at least so far as this is within the power of human society. This is where such things as equality of opportunity, equality before the law, and equality of access to the means of education come into the picture. In other words, recognition of merit as a criterion of distribution is reasonable only against the background of a recognition of the principle of equality; the primary basis of distribution is not merit but equality, substantive or procedural.

It is worth mentioning, in view of the many recent discussions of "the distribution of education," first, that, strictly speaking, society cannot distribute education but only the means of and opportunities for education, and, second, that it cannot distribute these in accordance with excellence or merit, since the achievement of excellence or merit presupposes a process of education. To this it may be replied that educational means and opportunities are to be distributed, not equally, but according to capacity. But then we may rejoin by pointing out that people's capacities can be determined only by educating them in some way, and that basic educational means and opportunities must therefore be distributed equally, since all must be given an equal chance to show their capacities if their capacities are to be used as a basis for determining their shares of other things. It follows, of course, from such premises, that a program of merit scholarships is fully just only if all of the candidates have had equal educational opportunities of the relevant kinds, though it may be a good thing anyway, as I believe it is.

None of what I have said is meant to imply that merit is not an acceptable basis of distribution in some contexts. I believe, indeed, that it is just to recognize and reward merit or excellence in certain ways; I have been trying to show only that merit cannot reasonably be regarded as our most *basic* criterion of distribution, as meritarians think. Excellence is an excellent thing, but, if it is not taken to be its own sole reward, we must all equally be given the chance to attain it so far as we are able.

In this discussion I have been identifying merit with excellence, intellectual or moral; but there are, of course, other things that it may be taken to mean, e.g., contribution to society or to the welfare of mankind, and it may be proposed that we should employ one of these things as our basis of distribution. What I have just said applies, however, to these further forms of merit also; they may be acceptable as secondary grounds of distributive policy, but they will not do as primary ones. It should be added that at least one of the reasons for rewarding merit in these and other forms is that doing so is useful, i.e., conducive to the public good. But to argue that merit should be rewarded because it is *useful* to do so is not yet to show that *justice* requires us to reward it. What is useful may be right to do, but it is not *ipso facto* a requirement of justice, though it need not be unjust either. This *may* be one of the meanings of the puzzling parable of the workers in the vineyard.

It may be objected that we have been neglecting an important theory of social justice, one which may have more subscribers, if we count both sides of the Iron

Curtain, than any other, namely, that the just society is that which takes from each according to his ability and gives to each according to his need. This theory sounds like a form of inequalitarianism, since it is obvious that people's abilities and needs differ widely. It may, however, be contended that it presupposes a basic equalitarianism, and this contention seems to be supported by the fact that those who accept the theory mean to be equalitarians at least in principle. One of the good things about this ability-need theory, whether one accepts it or not, is its recognition that duties and tasks are to be distributed, as well as opportunities, rights, and goods. But what is involved in the notion that tasks are to be distributed according to ability? Not a belief in inequality, but precisely the reverse. For we do not treat people equally if we ask of them exactly the same performance. To some a given task is easy, to others it is difficult, and hence, to ask the same of everyone is actually to treat them unequally, asking sacrifices from some that others are not required to make. To ask from each according to his ability, then, is to ask the same *proportionate* effort and sacrifice from each, in an effort to leave all as nearly equally well off as possible. In the same way, since needs differ, to give equally to all does not entail giving exactly the same thing to each. Shakespeare is surely mistaken when he tells us in *The Merchant of Venice* not to trust

> The man that hath no music in himself,
> Nor is not moved with concord of sweet sounds,

but it would not be unjust to give such a man a pair of skis when everyone else is being given a violin or a set of the latest Beatles recordings. To give to each according to his need is, again, to make the same *proportionate* contribution to the welfare of each, in an effort to make all as nearly equally well off as possible. The ability-need theory is therefore reasonable only if it presupposes an equalitarian goal or ideal.

IV

If what has been said is correct, then we may reasonably regard inequalitarian views about the basic material principle of distributive justice as unsatisfactory, even if we cannot claim to have "disproved" them. The basic principle is that of equality, as Aristotle's democrats thought. Merit and other Q's which men have unequally may serve acceptably as secondary criteria of distribution, but the basic framework must be the principle of equality. This we may now state. It is the principle that matters are to be so disposed, i.e., P is to be so distributed, that everyone has an equal chance of achieving the best life he is capable of. This is the foundational principle of social justice. Of course, to apply this principle we must have some defensible conception of what the good life is, and which lives are better than others, and these are not easy matters; but they must be left for another occasion.

For what it is worth, it may be pointed out that at least one leading meritarian, Aristotle, sometimes seems to presuppose the principle of equality just stated. For example, he regards slavery as justified because he believes that there are people who can enjoy the best lives they are capable of only if they are slaves of some master. In fact, more generally, he seems at his best to define the ideal state as one in which each member enjoys the highest happiness — the most excellent activity — he is capable of attaining.

To avoid misunderstanding, I should add that I do not mean to suggest that no extra attention should be given either to handicapped persons on the one hand, or to gifted individuals on the other. I have no wish to attack enterprises like Project Head Start, fellowship programs, etc. All that the principle of equal justice requires is that everyone be given an equal chance to enjoy the best life he is capable of, but it may be that doing this entails our giving what seems to be extra attention to certain sorts of people. Such attention seems extra only because it involves more effort or money, but it is not really extra (unjust), since it is necessary if we are to make the same *proportionate* contribution to the best life of everyone. Some people simply are by nature harder to help on their way, and others easier, and we are, therefore, not unjust if we put more effort or money into helping some than we do into helping others, as long as all are enabled to make the same *relative* advance toward the good life.

One might object here that social justice consists, not in making possible the same relative advance for everyone, but rather in bringing everyone up to the same absolute level. One might contend, for example, that it is unjust for society to put anything extra into its gifted individuals until all the others, whether handicapped or not, have been brought up to the highest level possible for them, and that even then it is not unjust if it does not do anything extra for them. To deal with this objection we must distinguish two things a society might do for its members: (1) it might provide them with a certain level of material goods, (2) it might promote a certain level of goodness of life for them. These two things may overlap, but they are not the same. I am somewhat inclined to agree that society should try to make available to everyone the same general level of material possessions, at least up to a certain point. But material possessions are only externally connected with goodness of life, and it is the latter that society should be mainly concerned with. Now, some people just *are* capable of leading better lives than others; these are, in fact, the "gifted" ones. Should not society, in justice, do what it can to help these members achieve the best lives they are capable of (provided it also helps the others), at least after and perhaps even before the others have reached their peaks? A few remarks may perhaps serve to guide further thinking on this matter.

(a) It certainly seems only just that they should be helped, if necessary, at least *after* the less gifted have reached their peaks. We must remember, however, that a just society will also be a free one, and that in a free society such individuals can and will do much to help themselves. (b) It is obviously conducive to the good, not only of the gifted individuals, but of others, if the gifted are aided even *before* the others have gone as high as they can. For, like Plato's rulers, they can then put their gifts to the social use of helping the others. (c) It would seem clear, at any rate, that a just society must at least *permit* exceptional individuals to realize themselves, in so far as this is compatible with others' doing so. (d) Since a just society must provide the utmost freedom for each individual consistent with the freedom and welfare of others, it must even run the *risk* that some, in seeking their own best life, will endanger those of others. (e) In practice, perhaps, any society that seeks to be just must work on two fronts all the time: that of making *possible* the achievement by the gifted of the best lives they can attain *and* that of making *sure* that others also are so positioned as to be able to attain the best lives open to them by virtue of their potentialities.

V

Now, having steered the good ship Justice safely through the straits of inequalitarianism into the haven of equalitarianism, we must ask what side of the harbor we are to anchor on, that of substantive or that of procedural equalitarianism. As was indicated earlier, the difficulty in substantive equalitarianism is that there seems to be no factual respect in which all human beings are equal, no Q which they all have in the same degree and form. (There is the further point that, even if there were such a Q, it still might not follow that all men ought to be treated as equals; but this is balanced by the fact that, if there is no such Q, it also does not follow that men ought not to be treated as equals.) As Benn and Peters put it,[12]

> . . . if we strip away [from human nature] all the qualities in respect of which men differ, what is left? . . . we are left with an undifferentiated potentiality. . . . 'Human nature' implies a varying potentiality for a certain limited range of qualities . . . ; it is not another quality that all men possess equally, on account of which they should in some positive way be treated alike.

Benn and Peters conclude that equalitarianism must take a procedural form.[13]

> . . . What we really demand, when we say that all men are equal, is that *none shall be held to have a claim to better treatment than another, in advance of good grounds being produced*. . . . Understood in this way, the principle of equality does not prescribe positively that all human beings be treated alike; it is a presumption against treating them differently, in any respect, until grounds for distinction have been shewn. It does not assume, therefore, a quality which all men have to the same degree, which is the ground of the presumption, for to say that there is a presumption means that no grounds

need be shewn. The onus of justification rests on whoever would make distinctions. To act justly, then, is to treat all men alike except where there are relevant differences between them. . . . Presume equality until there is reason to presume otherwise.

With some qualifications, I am inclined to agree with this view of the matter. It still seems reasonable, however, to ask why we should adopt this procedural principle in the case of *all* the beings who are *human,* if they are not equal in any factual sense. The answer, I think, has two parts. (1) One part is that it seems to be a rule of reason to deal with similar things in similar ways. Thus, inductive reasoning may be thought of as depending on a presumption that we are to make similar assertions about similar things, unless we have evidence to the contrary. To quote Perelman:

> The fact is, the rule of justice results from a tendency, natural to the human mind, to regard as normal and rational, and so as requiring no supplementary justification, a course of behaviour in conformity with precedent.[14]

This view may be substantiated somewhat by reference to the work of Piaget on the moral judgment of children.[15] But it does not suffice as an answer to our question. For, as we saw, and as Perelman recognizes, this rule of reason — treat similar cases similarly — is purely formal. Besides, even though, in our geological inductions, we must presume that what is true of one rock is true of others unless there is evidence to the contrary, we hardly need draw the conclusion that, in our behavior, we ought to *treat* all rocks in the same way unless we can show good reasons for treating them differently. Why then should we treat all *human* beings equally until we have good reasons for not doing so? (2) The reply, it seems to me, must be that human beings are different from rocks, they have desires, emotions, and minds, and are capable, as rocks are not, of having lives that are good or bad. It is this fact that all men are similarly capable of experiencing a good or bad life, not the fact that they are equal in some respect (if they are), that justifies the presumption that they are to be treated as equals. With this, somewhat hesitantly, I drop anchor on the procedural equalitarian side.

VI

Many problems remain, but we can take up only two of them, and then only briefly. (1) An equalitarian might hold, not only that justice requires us to treat all human beings equally (in the sense explained above, in which giving A a violin and B a pair of skis may be treating them equally, not in the sense of treating them exactly alike), but that any departure from equality, any unequal treatment is *ipso facto* unjust and wrong. But few equalitarians have had the temerity to espouse this position, nor have I, though I should point out that it is much more plausible to maintain that it is never just or right to treat people *unequally* than that it is never just or right to treat them differently. If one does not adopt this position, however, one must allow that unequal treatment is sometimes just or right, that the differences between people sometimes justify treating them unequally. And then the question arises: what differences between humans justify treating them unequally? What differences are relevant to questions of distribution? This is not an easy question, and it is sometimes felt that the relevant differences are so many and so various as to render the principle of equality of no effect. An inequalitarian must answer the question, too; but he *could* say that all differences are relevant, if not, prove why not; whereas the equalitarian must claim that the relevant differences can be limited in some way. Now, I have already intimated that in various kinds of context various kinds of considerations are relevant to questions of distribution, e.g., that differences in height or color of skin may be relevant to decisions about the distribution of costumes and roles in plays. In a sense, then, if we abstract from context, the variety of relevant considerations, like that of evil spirits, is indeed legion. In another sense, however, each context determines what considerations are relevant and limits them; not all considerations are relevant in all contexts. Differences in sex, color, height, or dramatic ability may be relevant to decisions about casting players, but they are not always relevant; indeed they seem obviously irrelevant to most questions of social policy of the kind that a theory of distributive justice is primarily concerned to provide for. For such questions, I suggest, the relevant features of people are not such things as color, height, and the like, but only those features that bear, directly or indirectly, on the goodness or badness of the lives of which they are capable, for example, differences in ability or need.

(2) The last question is somewhat different, and may be put roughly by asking, "Why should we be just?" More accurately put, it is this: why is justice, conceived as treating people equally in the sense explained, right? [16] One traditional answer is that of the deontologist in ethics, namely, that justice or equality of treatment is right in itself, as keeping promises is, or telling the truth. Another standard answer is that of the utilitarian, that justice or equal treatment is right because it is necessary for or at least conducive to the greatest general good or the greatest general happiness. As between these two views I should say that the first is essentially correct and the second mistaken. I should like, however, to propose a third mediating possibility. If we ask what the Ideal state of affairs would be, then, as far as I can see, the deontologist and the utilitarian can both accept the following statement:

The Ideal is that state of affairs in which *every person* (or perhaps every sentient being) has the best life he is capable of.

If this formulation of the Ideal is correct, as I believe it is, then we can plausibly argue that justice in the sense of equal treatment is right because it is a constitutive condition of the Ideal. For then, as Bentham declared, it is an essential aspect of the Ideal that everybody be counted as one and nobody as more than one. In the Ideal, as thus formulated, everyone is equally well off in the sense that everyone has the best life he is capable of, which is all that can reasonably be asked for. An even more ideal equality would be realized, it is true, in a state of affairs in which everyone had the ideally best life or at least the best life that any human being is capable of; but such a state of affairs would be wholly impractical and Utopian as an ideal. It could only be wished, not worked, for. Logically, of course, one could reject even the more practical Ideal sketched in my statement, since "questions of ultimate ends do not admit of proof";[17] but it is hard to believe that anybody would in fact reject it if he were fully informed and completely reasonable,

> . . . whose even-balanced soul
> From first youth tested up to extreme old age,
> Business could not make dull, nor passion wild;
> Who saw life steadily, and saw it whole. . . .[18]

9: On Saying the Ethical Thing

Morality could not become a science without a radical reconstruction of the very uses of such terms as "good" and "right"; but such a reconstitution would no longer enable us to say (or do) "the ethical thing."[1]

I

AT THIS MOMENT I CANNOT HELP WISHING THAT WE WERE ALL SITTING around a banquet table as we did in times past. In defence of banqueting, Kant once wrote,

> Although a banquet is a formal invitation to intemperance in both food and drink, there is still something in it that aims at a moral end, beyond mere physical well-being: it keeps a lot of people together for a long time so that they may exchange their ideas.[2]

We, however, have rejected this transcendental deduction, just as we have rejected the others, and so have brought to an end the old association of philosophy with feasting. The Platonic archetype was a dinner plus a panel of several speakers. This was changed to a dinner with one speaker, or, alternatively, to a symposium of three speakers without dinner. Now we have no dinner and only one speaker. As the speaker, I must hope that this is the end of the line, for only one more step remains: no dinner and no speaker. I shudder to think that this speech may result in that step's being taken.

For this address will be an essay in metaethics, and I know that some have complained that moral philosophers today do too much metaethics and too little normative ethics. But, whatever may be said about my analytical friends and relations, I think I have done enough normative ethics lately to deserve at least one more metaethical fling. There are also some who have attacked the distinction itself that I and my sisters and my cousins and my aunts have made

Reprinted from *Proceedings and Addresses of the American Philosophical Association,* Vol. 39 (1966), pp. 21-42, by permission of the American Philosophical Association.

between normative ethics and metaethics. Perhaps both groups of critics will be placated if I tell them that what I am going to do is *normative metaethics,* that is, "betta" metaethics. I take this occasion as an invitation to say something more about what I think than I have so far. What I shall have to say is not new in any of its parts, but I believe that it has some novelty of form and that the resulting whole is of some interest. In any case, it needs saying, now more than ever, even if I shall not do so with the rigor that would be called for at another time.

II

Let me explain the phrase "normative metaethics." By a *normative* inquiry, I mean one that aims at and results in conclusions to the effect that something is desirable, good, bad, right, wrong, or ought to be done. By a *metaethical* inquiry, I mean one that asks about the meaning and justification of such conclusions. Now, a metaethical inquiry may and usually does take a descriptive, elucidatory, or reportive form, that is, it may seek simply to lay bare what we actually mean when we judge that something is good or right or what our actual logic is for justifying such judgments. But it may also be normative, telling us what our meanings and our logic should be; and then it may be either *conservative,* bidding us to go on using our normative terms and justifying our normative judgments as we have, or *revisionary,* proposing that we reconstruct our meanings or our logic, more or less radically. This last possibility was suggested by P. F. Strawson some years ago in a very interesting passage:

> There is another kind of thinking which might be called the creative or constructive work of the philosophical imagination. To engage in this kind of thinking is to consider how . . . we . . . might conduct our discourse . . . in forms different from, though related to, those which we actually use.[3]

I am not against purely elucidatory metaethics, and I believe that such neutral inquiry is in principle possible. Some form of intuitionism, emotivism, or even naturalism *might* be true as an account of our actual judgments and reasoning when we use terms like "right" and "good." However, I think that, in fact, metaethics has always been normative, for even those who are or claim to be elucidating the rules of our normative discourse have implied that we should go on following those rules — in short, they have been conservatively normative. Some of them have actually been more revisionary than they pretended to be. This is not said in criticism, as others have said it, for I see nothing wrong in being normative in metaethics, even if there are those who tell us to leave our language alone, and I propose to be normative, though not in any drastically revisionary way. If one is going to be normative, let him be so openly!

It does not follow at once that the distinction between normative ethics and metaethics breaks down. Non-normative metaethics still may be possible, and, moreover, an inquiry into the meaning and logic of moral discourse may be normative without being moral. Normative judgments and proposals are not necessarily moral; they may be aesthetic, prudential, technical, methodological, and what not. Hence, the findings of metaethics need not be construed as moral judgments even if they are normative. There might be a normative meta-science or a normative meta-history, telling us how to do science or history, and its conclusions would not necessarily be moral, or even scientific or historical. Meta-disciplines are not *ipso facto* parts of the disciplines they are meta to; and they are not parts of morality simply because they are normative. G. H. von Wright may be right in maintaining that conceptual analysis in the area of practical philosophy must be normative,[4] though I myself doubt that it must be; but, even if he is, it does not follow that such conceptual analysis must make *moral* commitments. It may still be that it will turn out to be committed to some moral judgment or other, but this must be shown and not assumed. *Prima facie,* it is at least possible that there are two levels of normative judgments — the first level ones occurring in normative ethics, aesthetics, etc., and the second level ones occurring in metaethics, meta-aesthetics, etc.

In truth, there is at least an air of paradox in the notion of a normative metaethics. For it will purport to tell us that we ought to use our normative discourse in certain ways (for example, in the same ways in which we have been using it), but then it is itself using the normative term "ought," and it may seem that this is somehow illegitimate. But *is* there really some kind of legerdemain going on here, because one is making normative statements about normative discourse? After all, one can, without any logical inconsistency, advocate the use of Esperanto in English or order silence in a loud voice. One would come closer to paradox if one were to say, as some views to be mentioned later do, that we *ought* to stop using normative discourse altogether, but even then one could appeal to a theory of types of normative judgment. One could also cite a famous text about throwing away one's ladder after having climbed up it.

What, then, is it that normative metaethics would be doing? Two questions have traditionally been central in metaethics:

1. What are the meanings, uses, or functions of words like "good" and "right" or of sentences in which they occur?
2. What are the principles of ethical reasoning? What is the logic of moral reasoning? How can statements using "good" and "right" be justified, if at all?

These questions, however, are ambiguous. The first may mean either:

1a. What are the *actual* meanings, uses, or functions of sentences using words like "good" and "ought"? Or:
1b. What meanings, uses, or functions *should* we assign to such sentences?

The second, likewise, may mean either:

2a. What is the *actual* logic by which we conduct our reasoning about normative matters? Or:

2b. What conception *should* we have of the justification of normative statements?

1a and 2a are for present purposes the main questions of descriptive or elucidatory metaethics, and I see no reason why the answers to them must be any more normative than the answers to similar questions involving history or science. 1b and 2b, on the other hand, will be the main questions of normative metaethics and will require normative answers.

Since the questions and conclusions of normative metaethics are not descriptive, it follows that its methods and arguments must be different from those of descriptive metaethics. For example, the open question argument is stated by R. M. Hare as follows:

> .. if "right" meant the same as "in accordance with the will of God," then, "whatever is in accordance with the will of God is right" would mean the same as "whatever is in accordance with the will of God is in accordance with the will of God"; but according to our actual use of the words, it seems to mean more than this mere tautology.[5]

Taken in this form, if the argument is good at all, it is good only against a definist metaethics that purports to be elucidating our "actual use" of words; it will have little or no cogency against one that proposes to redefine our words in a certain way — as R. B. Perry, for example, proposes to do. In order to operate in the field of normative metaethics, the open question argument must run as follows (using Hare's example):

> If we take "right" as meaning the same as "in accordance with the will of God," then we must take "whatever is in accordance with the will of God is right" as meaning the same as "whatever is in accordance with the will of God is in accordance with the will of God," but surely this is not a desirable use of words.

But then the argument is not obviously and immediately decisive, as it is usually taken to be; it simply begs the question. In general, answers to questions of normative metaethics cannot be established wholly by the methods of descriptive elucidation. No metaethical Ought can be logically inferred from any metaethical Is alone.

Even though this is true, it must be allowed that the descriptive finding that we do use our normative words in certain ways may be used as *an* argument (and a good one) for the (conservative) normative conclusion that we should go on using them in that way. Even then, however, this normative conclusion will not follow from the descriptive premise alone, but only from that taken together with a desire to communicate, with a belief that nothing important is to be gained by revising our language. No doubt we should in normative metaethics presume that revisions are not to be advocated unless necessary (notice, this is a normative judgment, but is it a moral one?), but some revisions may be necessary if we are to avoid the ambiguity, looseness, and vagueness of our actual discourse.

III

Consider now question 1b, namely, "What meanings, uses, or functions *should* we assign to such terms as 'good' and 'right' or to sentences in which they occur?" Several types of answers are possible, paralleling the usual types of answers to question 1a. (1) A normative ethical intuitionist would answer that we ought to use "good" or "right" or both as standing for simple non-natural properties and sentences involving them as ascribing such properties to certain objects. (2) A normative ethical definist, naturalistic or metaphysical, would argue that we should use the terms in question, if we use them at all, to mean "being in accordance with the will of God," "being an object of interest," etc., and sentences involving them as ascribing such empirical or metaphysical properties to things. (3) A normative ethical non-cognitivist or non-descriptivist would hold that we should assign some other use to ethical expressions than that of standing for or ascribing properties.

It may be worth mentioning that one might give one type of answer to question 1a and a different type of answer to question 1b. For example, one might contend that we *actually* use our ethical terms as if they stood for simple non-natural properties, but *ought* to use them simply to express our attitudes or emotions or to evoke similar ones in others. This position was virtually put forward at one time by Richard Robinson.[6] It would combine intuitionism in descriptive metaethics and emotivism in normative metaethics.

However this may be, just what is at issue between the various types of normative metaethics? Is it merely the question whether the noises "right," "good," and the like, should be used in certain ways rather than others? Even if it were in this sense verbal or terminological, it would not necessarily be trivial, since the noises in question are already in use. But the issue is not so simple as all that. For it involves a question, not only about the use of "right" and "good," but also about many other forms of expression in English, as well as about corresponding expressions in other languages — not to mention gestures, inflections, and other linguistic or non-linguistic devices for doing what "good" and "right" do or might be used to do. No, I suggest that the issue is not just one about the use of certain sounds or printed shapes; it is, rather, one about the status, function, or desirability of a whole "symbolic form," "type of discourse," or "realm of meaning."

This is vague, and we must now try to see more fully just what the issue is. In doing so, we may adapt an image borrowed from Michael Oakeshott.[7] He has a very interesting conception of "human activity and intercourse" as "a conversation which goes on both in public and within each of ourselves" and is made up of a number of "voices," namely, those of poetry, history, science, practical activity, and philosophy. Let us likewise conceive of human discourse as a conversation involving at least the following three voices:

Voice A: This is the language of so-called descriptive or factual assertions or statements, or of what J. L. Austin prefers to call "constatives," for example, such sentences as:

> The book is red.
> Lord Raglan won the battle of Alma.
> All snow geese migrate to Labrador.
> The hose burst because of the pressure.
> Many people enjoy skiing.
> The Greeks approved of courage.
> Love of parents is commanded by God.

Perhaps we should include here also such interrogative utterances as "Is the cat on the mat?" since they can be answered by constative ones. I can no more define this voice accurately than Austin could, and must hope that the illustrations given will indicate which one I mean.

Voice B is more varied, for it consists of such utterances as:

> Ouch!
> Shut the door!
> Be careful!
> Hello!
> Hurrah for Michigan!
> Let's go to a movie!
> Would that we were all sitting around a banquet table!
> I promise to return the book.
> You make me sick! I hate you!
> How white the wall is!
> Oh, how love I thy law! It is my meditation all the day.

And many more — all imperatives, expressions of emotion, attitude, or commitment, most, if not all, of Austin's various kinds of performatives,[8] etc., and, of course, interrogatives if they do not belong to Voice A or C.

Voice C I must describe even more vaguely, partly to avoid begging questions. It includes linguistic acts that are at least *prima facie* different from those of the first two Voices, namely, acts of grading, commending, recommending, appraising, approving, evaluating, or criticizing. Many would list acts of prescribing here also, and some of these certainly belong to Voice C, but others seem to belong to Voice B. Estimating and assessing may also be of two kinds, as Austin pointed out, but at least some such acts would belong to Voice C. Perhaps the same thing is true of acts of advising, praising, blaming, enjoining, and the like.

Four remarks are apposite at this point. (a) Roughly speaking, but only roughly, each Voice involves a vocabulary and a syntax, if we use these terms in a broad sense. (b) It seems possible that two of these Voices may be blended in a single utterance. "I hate you!" for example, may be a blending of Voices A and B. (c) It may be that there are still more Voices to be recognized. Where, for instance, are we to put modal utterances, epistemic statements, the statements of logic and mathematics, analytic sentences, etc.? On the other hand, it has at least been suggested that such statements are basically normative and so belong to the kind of discourse we are discussing the status of. (d) It might be argued, of course, that this normative discourse, ethical or non-ethical, should itself be regarded as a fourth Voice distinct from the three described. However, since it is precisely the status of normative discourse that we are discussing, we cannot begin by assuming that it represents a separate Voice. In fact, since Voices are surely not to be multiplied beyond necessity, there may even be a presumption that it does not (actually, in what follows, I shall place it with Voice C).

It will, no doubt, have been observed that Voice A will include all of the sentences regarded by ethical definists as equivalent to sentences of normative discourse, for example, "Skiing is an object of positive interest" or "Love of parents is in accordance with the will of God"; that Voice B will contain all of the sentences or utterances held by emotivists and imperativists, to be equivalent to sentences of normative discourse, for example, "Do not kill!" and "Stealing! Bah!"; and, finally, that Voice C will cover the various other kinds of speech acts to which less reductionistically-minded philosophers have sought to assimilate moral and other kinds of normative judgments. This is, of course, not an accident but a bit of beneficence aforethought. For we are now in a position to say more adequately what the issue under debate in normative metaethics is (or would be if people were actually to debate it).

Let us see, in the terms that are before us, just what each of the parties to that debate would say. Consider first the ethical naturalist.[9] It is sometimes alleged by his opponents that he simply assumes that the conversation of mankind is and is to be carried on in Voice A alone — that he is deaf to the multi-functionality or multi-vocality of language. However, while this may have been true of some naturalists, it need not be true of them all. A naturalist may perfectly well admit the existence and desirability of Voice B and possibly even of Voice C. What he cannot allow is that normative discourse (that is, discourse using words like "good," "right," "ought," "should," their opposites, or their equivalents) should belong anywhere but with Voice A. Actually, the normative ethical naturalist could take *either* of two positions. (a) He might maintain that we should simply drop our normative discourse entirely and use instead only such sentences as are already contained in Voice A, for example, "Skiing is an object of interest" or "Love of parents is commanded by God." (b) He might take the more moderate view naturalists in fact always take, namely, that we should keep our normative vocabulary but use it simply as an alternative way of asserting and describing facts for which we already have another vocabulary. For example, we should use "Skiing is good" as merely another way of saying "Skiing is an object of positive interest" or "The people who do it enjoy it." In this case, he will not object to our using normative expressions like "right" and "good" to guide choice and action, but must insist that the guidance-potential of sentences in which they appear should be thought of as exactly equivalent to that of sentences like "*x* is an object of interest" or "*y* is commanded by God."

The normative intuitionist agrees with the second kind of naturalist in retaining our normative vocabulary and assigning it to Voice A. But he believes that there are brave non-natural properties and facts of a very special kind, that we are aware of them, and that we do and should use our normative discourse as a way of ascribing such properties and asserting and communicating such facts. Like the naturalist, he may allow Voices B and C a role in the conversation of mankind. He may also allow that sentences like "*x* is good" and "*y* is right" may be used to guide action, but must insist that they are action-guiding in their capacity of reporting a fact, albeit a fact of a very special kind. And, to explain this, he may hold either that an apprehension of such a fact is directly "practical" or that it is so only in conjunction with a desire awakened by it.

In opposition to both definists and intuitionists, some non-cognitivists or non-descriptivists would maintain that, if we are to keep our normative discourse at all, we should assimilate it, not to Voice A, but to Voice B. In fact, like the naturalist, such a non-cognitivist may hold *either* (a) that we should simply drop our normative discourse entirely and use instead only such sentences as are already contained in Voice B, for example, "Do not kill!" "Hurrah for promise-keeping!" "How wonderful!" "Would that more people were benevolent!" *or* (b) that we should retain our normative vocabulary but use it simply as an alternative way of expressing our sentiments and uttering commands, that is, use (say) "Killing is wrong" as merely another way of saying "Do not kill!" "Killing, no!" or "Would that people would stop killing one another!"

Other non-descriptivists will cry a plague on all of these houses, contending that we cannot be satisfied with Voices A and B, but must have Voice C as well, and that our normative utterances should be construed as belonging to Voice C. In Euripides' play, *Alcestis,* King Admetus, stricken with grief, cries,

> What can I say? All language is too poor!

For this second group of non-cognitivists, without Voice C, all language is too poor — too poor, that is, to say the ethical or normative thing. For this, they claim, we must have a vocabulary and a syntax in which we can do something besides reporting, describing, or explaining, something besides uttering commands, ejaculating, or expressing emotions and attitudes; namely, such things as grading, commending, evaluating, and advising.[10]

These being the positions of the parties to the debate in normative metaethics, it becomes clear that the issue in that debate is composed of the following questions: (a) Should we retain our normative vocabulary? (b) What voices should we admit to the conversation of mankind? (c) To which of these voices should normative discourse (saying the ethical thing) be assigned?

Now, in connection with the first of these questions, it will be recalled that, on some of the views just described, our so-called normative discourse is merely an alternative way of saying or doing something we already have an adequate way of saying or doing. It might, then, be argued that if our normative discourse is simply a second language of this sort, then we should dispense with it, even if it is stylistically desirable to have more than one way of saying the same thing. This contention certainly is plausible, but it may be replied that in fact we are hardly likely at this time of day to stop using such words as "good," "right," and the like, and that, if we are going to have them always with us (like the poor), then we had better assign them some profitable or at least innocuous employment. As one naturalist expresses it,

> . . . the terms 'value,' 'good,' 'bad,' and their equivalents . . . could now be dispensed with and nothing of empirical consequence would be lost, though many rich literary connotations would vanish, . . . there is no need to use the terms 'good' and 'value,' and . . . confusions vanish as soon as these terms are eliminated. For without them, we are referred directly to the facts. . . .
> Then why not do without these terms? Because they are convenient. And because it is safer to keep them equated with the various selective systems than floating loose where ingenious men [like Moore] may note their freedom from attachment and proceed to hypostatize facts for them to refer to.[11]

Some such thought as this, no doubt, is the reason why the actual elimination of our normative vocabulary has never (well, hardly ever!) been proposed. Omitting, then, the views that propose its elimination, we may take the following positions as the live options by way of answer to question 1b (taken normatively, of course):

1. Definist theories holding normative discourse to be an alternative mode of saying something already in Voice A,
2. Intuitionism,
3. Emotive and imperativist theories holding normative discourse to be an alternative way of expressing emotion, uttering commands, etc., in short, part of Voice B,
4. Other non-descriptivist views, that is, those denying that normative discourse should be assimilated to Voices A or B.

IV

We must now consider these views and what we should say about the issues between them, namely, which voices should be admitted to the conversation of mankind, and to which of these voices should our normative discourse (that is, the use of ''good,'' ''right,'' their equivalents and opposites) be assigned?

About intuitionism, to which I long subscribed even though I was always suspicious of the naturalistic fallacy charge and the open question argument, I shall say little. I still do not think that the usual arguments against it, for example, those of Hare and Nowell-Smith,[12] are as fatal as they are thought to be. However, the existence of the special properties and facts that intuitionists believe in raises such epistemological and ontological problems that it seems to me we must look for a view that saves the insights of intuitionism but does away with these difficulties.

What about emotivism and other similar views? They strike me as being clearly inadequate as accounts of our actual ethical and value judgments. I do not deny that, when we apply ethical and value terms to things, we are normally taking and putting into words some attitude or other for or against them, nor do I wish to propose that we should stop doing so if we can. But it seems obvious to me that in our actual ethical and value judgments, when we are not frightened out of our normative wits by the relativists, subjectivists, and sceptics, we are not merely exclaiming, commanding, expressing emotion, evoking a response, or committing ourselves; rather, we are claiming some kind of status, justification, or validity for our attitudes or judgments. Others have said this very well before me. To quote:

> Amidst all the reputed vagueness and ambiguity of ethical terms, [emotive theorists] have found one constant element, the expression of the speaker's approval, and have seized upon this as the meaning of ethical statements. But at least one other factor is equally constant; ethical statements are always understood to be supported by reason. They imply the claim made is one that a reasonable man would willingly allow. Ethical statements make claims upon us, but claims advanced as impersonal and rationally justifiable.[13]

Or again:

> . . . the new approach takes seriously, as the emotive theory does not, the fundamental distinction between moral judgments, which profess a certain objectivity and impersonality, and mere expressions of taste or interest which neither have nor claim to have any inter-personal 'authority' over the judgments or conduct of others. . . . The terms of moral discourse, are, in use, not such wildly 'open textured' expressions of emotion as the emotivists contend. Governing the use of ethical terms . . . are rules of application. . . . Such rules . . . set limits to the sort of judgment we are prepared to countenance as 'ethical.' Each time we apply moral rules, we are not simply 'venting' our own passing sentiments or wishes; rather, we are in such a case invoking an impersonal linguistic ritual which serves to keep practical deliberation and disagreement within certain socially acceptable bounds.[14]

If someone rejoins here that normative judgments are not peculiar in this respect, that in all we desire, do, or say, we always claim some kind of justification or validity, then I am not really concerned to confute him. For one who answers thus is not so much assimilating normative judgments to utterances in Voice B as the reverse. In any case, however, what these passages say about ethical judgments is, in my opinion, true in some manner of all utterances in Voice C. This is precisely why it is so plausible to hold that normative discourse is an idiom belonging to that Voice.

If what such passages say is true, then it is clear why we cannot seriously propose to reduce normative judgments to interjections, imperatives, emotional expressions, or even ultimate commitments. For, if we were to do so, we would be debarred from doing something we very much want to do, something it would be less than human not to want to do, namely, to claim for ourselves at least a modicum of inter-personal rationality and validity. All language would be too poor — too poor for distinctively human words!

Again, if what such passages say is true, then normative judgments *are* proper judgments, as A. C. Ewing and other cognitivists have insisted; and terms like "true" and "false," "valid" and "invalid," and perhaps also logical connectives, may be applied to them, as many anti-descriptivists have themselves allowed since the salad days of logical positivism and emotivism. Shall we conclude, then, that such judgments belong to Voice A after all, that some form of definism is true, that perhaps we may now roll away the stone from before the tomb in which naturalism has lain ever since that dread day when the earth trembled under the naturalistic fallacy and rocks were rent by the open question? Actually, I should not be much disturbed if it were to appear that the reports of the death of naturalism have been grossly exaggerated; the view I shall be advocating is, as we shall see, akin to a certain form of naturalism. However, the usual kinds of naturalism criticized by Moore and others do strike me as unsatisfactory, whether they are cast in a descriptive-elucidatory or in a normative form. As R. M. Chisholm puts it,

> . . . these attempted reductions are entirely implausible; the sentences expressing our ostensible ethical knowledge *seem* at least to express considerably more than is expressed by any of their ostensible empirical translations.[15]

For one thing, the proposed translations (constatives in Voice A) express only belief, not such pro or con attitudes as ethical judgments normally give voice to. There is a taking of sides, different from mere belief, in a first hand normative judgment that is not necessarily present in any judgment in Voice A, though one may combine such a taking of sides with a statement in Voice A, as the Thin Woman of Inis McGrath does when she says to her philosopher-husband, returning empty-handed and hungry from a day's contemplation, "Your stir-about is on the hob. I hope there's lumps in it."

One might, of course, contend that, while this is indeed true, we should not build this taking of an attitude for or against into the meaning of "*x* is good" or "*y* is wrong" any more than we should build an act of believing into the meaning of "*z* is square." But, even if this contention is correct, we must remember that attitude-taking is just as closely bound up with "*x* is good" or "*y* is wrong" as believing is with "*z* is square." How close this is is indicated by the paradox involved in my saying, "*z* is square, but I don't believe it." Still, however this may be, there remains a difference between normative judgments and pure constatives in Voice A which should be preserved in our language if we mean to go on saying the ethical thing. The difference may be spelled out as follows. A pure constative like "The table is square" does not merely express the speaker's belief that the table is square; it makes a claim that this belief is true, warranted by the evidence, and rationally justifiable. This claim is explicit in "(The table is square) is true," for saying that something is true is not just endorsing it, as P. F. Strawson once suggested, but the claim is also present in "The table is square." There is, in fact, a kind of equivalence between "S is P" and "(S and P) is true." Constatives in Voice A and normative utterances are thus alike in being status-seekers — in making what Carl Wellman has called the "critical" claim that something is true, valid, or justifiable (or the opposite) in some interpersonal sense.[16] To this extent, the naturalists (and intuitionists) are right. A pure constative, however, makes this claim only for the *belief* that S is P, not for *feelings, attitudes, choices,* or *actions* with respect to S, P, or S's being P. But the question whether feelings, attitudes, choices, and actions are justifiable or rationally defensible may also be asked — human beings apparently cannot help but ask it — and it is in asking and answering *this* question that normative discourse (and in general, Voice C) finds and should continue to find its main function.

What I propose, then, in opposition to naturalism (and intuitionism) is that we construe and employ Voice A to express *beliefs* and claim a certain status for them and Voice C (including normative discourse) to express other states of mind and claim a similar status for them — and I mean this both as an account of our actual use of language and as a recommendation for the future. Naturalism and other forms of definism (and intuitionism), if we read them as proposing that normative judgments shall be construed and used merely as alternative ways of formulating certain constatives, would limit us to claiming justifiability or rationality for such beliefs as "*x* is an object of interest" and "*y* is forbidden by God." They would not allow us, through the use of "good," "right," and the like, to claim justifiability or rationality for actions, decisions, preferences, etc. Indeed, pushed to the hilt, they would seem to allow us no way of commending, recommending, advising, no way of "guiding," as distinct from "goading," except by the use of Voice A — no way of doing any of the things Voice C may be used to do, since all of these things involve an appeal to reason in favor of something that is not just a belief. Speaking of advice, W. D. Falk writes:

> 'Do this' may be used in the sense of 'my advice to you is, do this'; it may express a *recommendation*. . . . As advice, it is not direct pleading [or 'goading'], in spite of its grammatical form. . . . It is . . . logically assured here that none but rational methods will be used in support. Advice . . . is understood to set out . . . purely to 'guide,' to make people act as they would have valid and sufficient reasons for acting. . . . One follows advice when one thinks it sound, believing its claim that there are valid reasons for doing the thing suggested. One can give advice without stating this claim. . . . But, also, one might as well have explicitly made it, as certainly the hearer must take it to have been made. . . .[17]

That is, advice (of this kind) belongs to the form of discourse in which, not beliefs, but actions, attitudes, dispositions (other than beliefs), decisions, emotions, etc., are claimed, at least implicitly, to "have valid and sufficient reasons." And the pure definist, like the pure emotivist, is in effect proposing that we do without this form of discourse, conversing in future only in Voices A and B. Perhaps this is what "the naturalistic fallacy" really comes to: advocating that we drop Voice C and use our normative vocabulary simply as an alternative way of formulating constatives in Voice A. Even then, however, as I once said about that fallacy in an earlier rendering of it, it cannot be assumed to be a fallacy, but must be shown to be one by some independent argument. I shall, however, not use this occasion — or the little that is left of it — to mount such an independent argument (In fact, I am not clear what form such an argument would take;[18] if I were, I should certainly present it, regardless of time). Instead, I shall take it as obvious that the conversation of mankind would be a sorry symphony if only Voices A and B could be heard in it — that, without Voice C, or a voice in which we articulate, not beliefs, but other states of mind, and in which we claim rationality, not for beliefs, but for these other states of mind or for actions and decisions in line with them, all language would, indeed, be too poor to say what we want to say.[19]

V

With this I align myself, except for a point to be mentioned later, with the anti-descriptivists or non-cognitivists of what Aiken calls "the new approach," though I put matters more in a normative and less in a descriptive-elucidatory form than they are wont to do — and, hence, also in a more speculative one. If there were time, I would take up two related features of normative discourse (and perhaps of Voice C in general) which were noticed already by Moore and emphasized more recently by Hare, namely, that marked by the notion of universalizability on the one hand and that marked by the notion of consequentiality or supervenience on the other. Instead, I shall conclude the discussion of question 1b by making one more point. I have, in effect, assimilated normative discourse to Voice C and my main point has been that discourse in this voice is and should be used to perform a special function — that of expressing the speaker's partialities and commitments and especially that of claiming justification or rationality (or the opposite) for attitudes, actions, and decisions, not necessarily the speaker's. That we have a *conatus* toward rationality is shown by our penchant for rationalization, though claiming rationality is not necessarily rationalization. It is also shown, I think, by the very fact that words like "good," "right," and "true" have the emotive meaning some recent philosophers have made so much of, for these words would hardly have the particular expressive and evocative force they have if they made no claim to justification and rational validity.

The point I wish to make is largely borrowed from P. W. Taylor.[20] It is that the reasons (and hence the rationality) claimed by normative judgments may be of various sorts: aesthetic, legal, moral, prudential, perhaps even religious. Each of the terms involved — "good," "ought," etc. — has the same meaning in these various contexts but the grounds or reasons claimed are of different kinds. Whether a judgment is moral or aesthetic, for instance, depends on the kind of reason given for it or suggested by it in its context. In fact, the same sentence, "You ought to go to see your grandmother" will be moral if the reason supporting it is "because you promised to," prudential if it is "because she may remember you in her will if you do."[21] Each type of reason may be conceived of as related to a "point of view," and each type of normative judgment claims that something is justified or rational (or the opposite) from some such point of view. The point of view may be that of a simple desire; or it may be something more complex, like "the farmer's point of view," "the prudential point of view (self-love)," "the aesthetic point of view," or "the moral point of view"; possibly it may even be a point of view that overarches all other interests and positions.[22] In short, in making a normative judgment, besides voicing our partiality, we at least suggest that there are good reasons for a certain action or attitude, and we usually have in mind more or less clearly a certain type of reason, that is, we are taking a certain point of view and claiming that one who is rational from that point of view would or would not have that attitude or perform that action.

Now, however, a possible criticism may be raised. This is that my view is a kind of cognitivism after all, and probably a form of naturalism. For it asserts that a normative judgment entails a claim that one who takes a certain point of view and is rational within that point of view (that is, knows the facts, is clear-headed, etc.) will take a certain attitude, perform a certain action, or at least subscribe to the same judgment. And this claim, if meaningful, is either true or false. In fact, it will be said, my view comes close to saying that "x is good" means "x would be favored (from some point of view) by anyone who is rational." But then one can ask the open question: one can sensibly say, "This is favored (from some point of view) by anyone who is rational, but is it good?"

I answer (1) that, as already indicated, I would not be much troubled if my view turned out to be a form of cognitivism or even of naturalism, as long as it also turned out to be tenable. (2) It would, at least, not be a form of pure cognitivism, since it insists that making a normative judgment involves taking a stand that is not simply a belief (even *if* to believe *p* is to be prepared to act on *p*). (3) This means that a normative judgment is not so much a constative assertion on my view as an *act* of approval *from* a certain point of view. It implies or presupposes that there are reasons for approving (etc.) which would convince anyone who is rational and takes that point of view, but the fact that it "implies" or "presupposes" this does not mean that it "asserts" this. (4) It does follow that there is a great similarity between constative judgments in Voice A and normative ones, and I do wish to stress this, but it is not clear that this commits me to any definist position of the form that ". . ." means ". . . . .". (5) If my view is nevertheless a form of naturalism, then it is a naturalism of a rather special kind, since if it is defining "good," "right," etc., at all, it is defining them by reference to the concept of "rationality," which is also involved in the definition of "true," not by reference to notions like "being an object of interest," "being demanded by society," or even "being in accordance with the will of God."[23] (6) As for the use of the open question against such a form of definism — it would mean arguing that one can sensibly say "This is rational to favor (do) from said point of view, but is it good (right)?" And, of course, one can, for one may be asking if it is rational from some *other* point of view. The question is: Can one sensibly say "This is rational to favor (do) from said point of view, but is it good (right) from that point of view?" But this, I submit, it is not obviously sensible to say. One can, of course, say it; as C. H. Langford used to observe, one can close one's eyes and grit one's teeth and say anything. It does not follow that what one says is sensible.

VI

We come finally to question 2b: what should be our conception of the justification of normative statements? The answer to it depends largely on the answer to question 1b, and may be brief, as indeed it must. On the position taken above, the justification of a normative judgment, in its most general terms, involves taking a certain point of view, actually or at least hypothetically, and trying one's utmost to be rational (informed, clear-headed, and so forth) within it — just as the justification of "The table is square" does. It does not involve a "statistical" enquiry into the reaction of rational observers, as some naturalists and their opponents have supposed — any more than the verification of "The table is square" does. Of course, there may be different views about the nature of the point of view in question — different views about the nature of the moral or of the aesthetic point of view. The details of the process of justification will depend, not only on the point of view in question, but also on the position taken about its nature. These are questions we cannot go into now.

There are, however, two matters about which something must still be said. The first is the business of going from Is to Ought (Good, etc.). On the view sketched above, contrary to the usual dictum, there will be a sense in which one can go from an Is to an Ought. According to it, one cannot make a first-hand normative judgment of any kind unless one is taking, at least hypothetically, some aesthetic or practical point of view (not simply one of belief or disbelief), and is claiming to be rational within it. But, if one does take some such point of view and does claim to be rational within it, then there is a sense in which one may appropriately conclude that something is good, right, or should be done, and claim that this conclusion is justified by the facts (Is) alone. For example, if I am building a bookcase and am concerned that it should be secure, then, if I learn that screws hold more securely than scotch tape or even nails, I may correctly conclude that I should use screws. For, on the view suggested, Ought-talk, Good-talk, and Voice C generally, simply *are* the appropriate mode for expressing oneself when one is taking a conative point of view and meaning to be rational within it. One cannot logically or even reasonably go from Is to Ought (Good, etc.) *simpliciter*, but, in the presence of an aesthetic or practical point of view one may reasonably do so — indeed, it would be unreasonable, perhaps also a misuse of language, not to do so — though even then the "inference" would not be a logically valid one (unless "logical inference" is redefined to include it, as some have suggested). To say, without this qualification, that we must not go from Is to Ought is in effect to say that we must do without Voice C, and, in reply, I am minded to ask simply, "By what compulsion must we?" Or perhaps even more simply, "*Can* we?"

The second matter is the business of relativism. It is a prevailing view that the normative sphere of discourse is infected by a difficulty, namely, that, if two people hold conflicting normative judgments, it may be impossible to determine who is right. In fact, it is sometimes thought that both may be right — that no amount of being rational can decide between them and both judgments may be justified or rational. Some such relativistic position could, I think, be accommodated within the framework of what has been said here. But now I wish to propose that it be regarded as of the essence of a normative judgment to claim that it is justified, rational, or valid (as well as the act or attitude it is about) and that conflicting judgments are not — that normative discourse claims that there is a right answer to a normative question and only one, however hard it may be to determine what it is.

"Well," it may be said, "we have in the past so conceived of our normative discourse, at least implicitly. That is why the relativistic position has always come as a shock. Now, however, we know that attitudes are not all rooted in beliefs, that ultimate disagreements are possible in normative matters, and so on. Hence, if we go on using normative discourse (and Voice C) at all, we should use it without laying claim to any kind of final interpersonal validity. Except for the truth-claims involved in using Voice A, we should either drop all claims to justification or rationality (in effect, limit ourselves to Voices A and B) or at least confine ourselves to making only modest and non-absolutistic ones. This is not a failure of normative nerve but only the better or more rational part of valor.''

Now, there is a sense in which rational men may justifiably or rationally differ in normative matters. It may be rational for Peter to hold that *x* is right when it is also rational for Paul to hold that *x* is wrong, if they have different beliefs or evidence about *x*. Here the rationality is analogous to what is sometimes called subjective or probable rightness. But ''objective rationality'' may be and should continue to be conceived as absolute, not only in the case of constative assertions in Voice A, but also in that of utterances in Voice C and of the acts and attitudes they somehow refer to — so I wish to maintain. This involves the claim that rational men who take the same point of view will agree on normative matters if they are fully informed, clear-headed, etc. (The ''*et cetera*'' here is intentional; I am not sure how it should be filled out, though I am also not ready to grant that it cannot be adequately filled out without making the claim analytically true). It has *not* been established that this claim is false; we do *not* know that disagreements in attitude are not rooted in disagreements in belief or that ultimate normative disagreements, if they exist, will continue to exist as knowledge grows from more to more among rational men who share the same point of view. There is even some rough evidence to the contrary; historically, religious people who have theological beliefs of certain sorts tend to adopt the ethics of love, and, today, it begins to appear that, as the peoples of the world come to share more and more the same points of view and the same factual beliefs, they also come to regard the same things as desirable. At any rate, so long as the case against the absolutist claim is not better established than it is, we may still make that claim; it may take some temerity, but it is not unreasonable. As for me and my house, therefore, we will continue to serve the Lord — or, as others may prefer to say, the Ideal Observer. For Tennyson seems to me to be right in a sense (not his own) when he says,

> The good, the true, the pure, the just —
> Take the charm ''Forever'' from them
> and they crumble into dust.

Take from them the claim to an eventual agreement of all rational beings and they collapse into mere expressions and tools of feeling, desire, and will (Voice B).

VII

I have now said my piece on saying the ethical (normative) thing. Having said it, I know I have no prospect of ending up in the black. But I have no wish to finish in the red either, and so I choose to close in purple. In saying my piece, I have a sense of preaching a counterreformation two hundred years too late. For there seems to be a drift, by no means wholly unconscious, away from the use of Voice C or of any form of discourse claiming interpersonal authority or validity, and, especially, away from the notion that any such authority or validity is somehow final. That is what makes Hannah Arendt's title, "What Was Authority?" so *a propos*.[24] I have in mind cultural relativism, irrationalism, psychoanalysis, existentialism, "the new morality," "the new immorality," "adversary culture," post-modernism, the God-is-dead line, whatever that is, "the end of ideology," and many other things — including even the prevailing position among the moral philosophers of "the new approach" with whom I have associated myself. I cannot help but feel that they all somehow conspire against saying the ethical thing as I have construed it, that is, against the appearance of Voice C in the conversation of mankind, and that the final outcome of the drift they illustrate must be a conversation beyond culture, beyond modernity, beyond morality, beyond everything. Therefore, like the hero of a play set in a century to which I and those who are with me no doubt belong, I cry,

> What's that you say? Hopeless? — Why very well!
> . . . What's that? No! Surrender? No!
> Never — Never! . . .
> No! I fight on! I fight on! I fight on![25]

10: The Concept of Morality

WHAT IS MORALITY?" IS A VAGUE AND AMBIGUOUS QUESTION, MUCH DISCUSSED by the metamoralists of recent years. Here I shall ask only one of the many questions involved, namely, "When is an individual, group, or society to be said to have a morality or a moral action-guide?" or "When is a code or action-guide to be called a moral one, a morality?"

This question may be and has been answered in many different ways, some monistic (one-concept theories), others pluralistic (two-or-more-concept theories), some definist, others anti-definist. We cannot try to describe or discuss them all now. All may be presented either as descriptive-elucidatory accounts or as normative proposals, conservative or revisionary — one may even hold one theory as a descriptive-elucidatory account and advance another as a normative proposal (revisionary), as I shall — but I am here interested primarily in views that are presented as normative proposals, at least implicitly. Then four of them strike me as being of the greatest pith and moment. In order to state these four views we must distinguish between a *wider* formal concept of morality and a *narrower* material and social one. According to the former, an AG (action-guide) is a morality (a moral AG as opposed to a nonmoral AG) if and only if it satisfies such formal criteria as the following, regardless of its content:

(A) *X* takes it as prescriptive.
(B) *X* universalizes it.
(C) *X* regards it as definitive, final, over-riding, or supremely authoritative.

According to the second, narrower concept, *X* has a morality, or moral AG, only if, perhaps in addition to such formal criteria as A and B, his AG also fulfills some such material and social condition as the following:

Reprinted from *The Journal of Philosophy,* Vol. 63 (1966), pp. 688-96, by permission of *The Journal of Philosophy.*

(D)   It includes or consists of judgments (rules, principles, ideals, etc.) that pronounce actions and agents to be right, wrong, good, bad, etc., simply because of the effect they have on the feelings, interests, ideals, etc. of *other* persons or centers of sentient experience, actual or hypothetical (or perhaps simply because of their effects on humanity, whether in his own person *or* in that of another). Here 'other' may mean "some other" or "all other."

On this conception, a morality must embody some kind of social concern or consideration; it cannot be purely prudential or purely aesthetic.

In these terms, view I is the proposal that we conceive of moralities only in the *wider* way, or use the words 'moral' and 'morality' only in the wider sense. It is a monistic view and is favored, if I understand them, by Hare, Ladd, Falk, the existentialists (perhaps, without criterion B), many religious thinkers, and at least some Aristotelians. View II is the proposal that we conceive of moralities only in the *narrower* way, or use 'moral' and 'morality' only in the narrower sense. It too is a monistic view, but one which regards formal conditions like A, B, and C as insufficient to make an AG a morality and insists on the necessity of building in a condition of the kind indicated by D. In fact, recognizing that an AG satisfying criterion D may not be or be taken as rationally definitive or supremely authoritative — a point forcefully made by Falk (64)[1] — view II rejects criterion C in all its forms, not only as a sufficient, but also as a necessary condition of an AG's being a morality. View II is maintained by Toulmin, Baier, Singer, Strawson, and Kemp, among others. I believe that it was once held by Aiken, but was given up by him in favor of view I, perhaps with criterion B left out. View III contends that we ought to employ *both* the wider and the narrower concepts of morality, using 'moral' and 'morality' in both senses, though perhaps in different contexts. It is at least a dualistic view, but may be more pluralistic. Though Falk usually favors view I, as I said, he seems to settle, rather despairingly, for view III in the last paragraph of the essay already referred to (66). In any case, view III is in effect maintained by some of those who insist that 'moral', even in the sense in which it is opposed to 'nonmoral', is ambiguous, but propose to do nothing about it. View IV represents a rather different kind of attempt to have it *both* ways; it too seeks to preserve both "the authoritative and the social associations of 'moral' " (63), but it does so by trying to build into a single concept both criterion C and criterion D. It is, therefore, like view II in being monistic and in espousing the narrower social concept of morality, but like view I in regarding criterion C as necessary — and perhaps A and B also — though not as sufficient. I myself have suggested view IV in a longer paper, also called "The Concept of Morality," which will appear elsewhere.[2] Indeed, it suggests itself to a reader of Falk's last paragraph, referred to a moment ago.

II

About view III I shall not say much. The corresponding descriptive-elucidatory theory seems to me to be true, as it does to Falk, Hare, and others, but view III itself is unsatisfactory because it simply proposes to continue the present state of affairs, in which we use the word 'morality' ambiguously for two or more rather different sorts of AG's. View IV, which I recently proposed myself, I still am not entirely ready to reject. Its most dubious feature, to my mind, is the fact that, although it builds in social criterion D, it also makes it senseless for one to ask, "Why should I be moral?" This is a nice trick if it can be done, but it is bound to seem like a trick, at least to opponents of criterion D.

The remaining issue is between view I and view II. Like Falk (65 f), I think that a historical and semantic case can be made for both of these views, though I am inclined to believe that such evidence favors view II. I shall not argue this now. Instead, I shall first briefly indicate my other reasons for opposing view I, and then try to rebut some objections to view II.

The reasons for my being unhappy with view I are of various sorts. (1) Falk and Hare regard a social definition of morality as "misleading."[3] To me, however, it seems at least as misleading to say that an AG is a moral one provided only that it satisfies such formal conditions as A, B, and C. If saying that an AG is not a morality suggests that it is wicked or at least negligible, saying that it is a morality suggests that it is respectable and ought to be supported by the moral sanctions of society. If saying that an "ought" is nonmoral suggests that it is questionable or unimportant, saying that it is moral suggests that it is socially important and legitimate. And I am somehow more troubled by the latter misleadingness than by the former. (2) Falk insists that we must not "expect morality on all levels to do the same kind of job as the institution of law," and I agree that a morality is and should be a very different kind of AG from law. But I still share Kemp's conviction that, "if by the 'function' of a practice is meant the reason why it exists and is carried on" (Falk's words; 63), then the function of morality is not just to serve as a supreme AG but to make possible "some kind of cooperation or social activity between human beings,"[4] as law does, though not in the same way. Indeed, I do not see how society can recognize as a morality any AG that does not serve such a function to at least a certain extent. (3) We generally think that a man who takes prudential or aesthetic considerations as final is living by a nonmoral AG (and perhaps also by an immoral one). But, on view I, his AG will have to be regarded as a morality. (4) If any AG, no matter what its character may be, can become a morality simply by being taken seriously enough, universalized, etc., it becomes very difficult to discuss questions about the relation of morality to other AGs. This is shown by the fact that, though Hare seems to admit the desirability of distinguishing the moral and the aesthetic, he does not actually give us a way of distinguishing them, and ends by counting as fully moral personal ideals he himself describes as "very like aesthetic ones" (146, 150). (5) On view I, a conscientious objector or social critic could claim his objections or criticisms to be made on moral grounds, even if they are made on purely aesthetic or prudential grounds, provided only that he takes such grounds to be finally authoritative (and perhaps also is willing to universalize his judgments). (6) View I makes nonsense of all talk of religion as an AG that is somehow above or beyond morality — such as Kierkegaard, Tillich, and others go in for. I am not sure I want to go in for this talk, but I am reluctant to rule it out by definition. (7) Falk cites the case of a daughter tied to a demanding mother, and points out that we may say to her, "You owe it to yourself to break away, hard as it may be on your mother" (49). Here personal oughts appear to be given precedence *over* moral ones. But, on view I they would thereby *become* moral. (8) View I makes the question whether morality is socially concerned dependent on what the facts about man and the world are. It seems to me preferable, however, to make this a matter of definition and to make the question whether morality is "the rational and autonomous way of life" contingent upon the nature of man and the universe. In fact, I find it hard to believe that Hare and Falk would favor view I if they were not assuming that all or at least most of us would choose a socially considerate AG to live by "on a nonevasive appreciation of all the reasons in the case." (9) View I also makes nonsense of the question, "Why should I be moral?" For one cannot oneself take an AG as supremely authoritative and still ask, sensibly, "Why should I live by it?" It may, of course, be argued that the question, "Why should I be moral?" is, indeed, nonsense — in fact, this has often been argued — but one may at least reasonably doubt that this is so or should be made so by definition.

Only some of the objections to building criterion D, or any "material" condition, into the definition of a morality can be dealt with here. (1) Hare implies that a social definition of morality builds in "utilitarianism" and begs the question against its opponents (163). But I have stated criterion D in such a way as to allow deontological AGs to be moralities, as well as utilitarian ones. In fact, criterion D allows for nationalistic and class moralities, for Nazism, for inequalitarianism — as far as I can see, for anything that Hare himself is really concerned to allow for. I am not even sure that it rules out sadistic AGs. It does rule out AGs that are basically egoistic or aesthetic, but this at least checks with much actual usage. (2) It is argued that view II reads out of the moral party such AGs as those of the Greeks, Spinoza, Nietzsche, the Navaho, etc. But, first, were their AGs consistently and thoroughly nonsocial in their basis? What, for example, about Aristotle's views on justice or Nietzsche's precept, "Be unto thy neighbor an arrow, and a longing for the Superman"? Second, if they were basically nonsocial, should we call them moralities? (3) It might be thought that view II precludes the possibility of there being moral duties to oneself that are not derivative from one's duties to others. However, criterion D, as I have stated, allows that a moral AG may *include* purely self-referential duties and ideals (though I am in fact inclined to doubt that these are moral); it insists only that it must include duties or ideals that are basically other-regarding. (4) There is a sense in which a social definition of morality does not "build out" even egoism or aestheticism. It might be, for instance, that the most effective way for one to serve the welfare of others is to do always what is most to one's own interest. Then, even though one's basic principle would be social, one might adopt an egoistic AG as one's working guide. In this case, however, one's AG would still be moral on view II.[5]

(5) Falk contends that, if we adopt view II, then we demote morality "from its accustomed place of being the sole and final arbiter of right and wrong choice" (65 f). We do so, however, only in the sense of not making it part of the *definition* of morality that it is the sole and final arbiter. But, even if criterion D is made part of the definition of morality, and not criterion C, it still may be that morality "prescribes what a man would do in his wisdom" — in short, morality might still be the definitive commitment of the honestly reflective person, his sole and final arbiter. Whether this is so or not would then be up to the facts about man and the world. It does follow from view II that morality *may* not be the sole and final arbiter of right and wrong; it does not follow that it *is* not that arbiter. That is, it follows that "Why should I live by a moral AG?" is a sensible question, which is as it should be. (Isn't it?)

(6) Hare implies that any view that includes a material or social criterion in the definition of morality is guilty of "naturalism," i.e., of "making moral questions depend upon conceptual ones" or settling normative questions by definition (163, 187, 195). This raises hackles, specters, and large issues, but I must say a little. I am inclined to think that Hare, MacIntyre, and others who attack view II are too ready to think that 'moral', even in such phrases as 'moral code', 'moral judgment', 'moral rightness', etc., is a normative term like 'right' or 'good', when it is at least prima facie a term of a very different kind; they, rather than Toulmin, may be failing to distinguish sufficiently between 'moral' in the sense in which it is opposed to 'nonmoral' and 'moral' in the sense in which it is opposed to 'immoral'. Be that as it may, it is not clear that my adopting criterion D commits me to any particular normative judgment of a substantive kind, moral or nonmoral (except the judgment that we ought to adopt this criterion). To begin with, asserting that an AG is a moral AG does not commit one to agreeing that acting on it is morally right or good, for one may regard it as a moral AG without accepting it oneself. Does holding that an AG is not a moral AG unless it sometimes judges actions and agents simply on the basis of their effects on the lives of others commit me to saying that not considering effects on others at all is wrong or bad? Certainly it does not commit me to saying that this is wrong or bad in every sense. Does it commit me to regarding it as *morally* bad or wrong? It is tempting to say so, and in the longer paper referred to earlier I did say so. Now I think this was a mistake on my part. For I may agree that an AG is not a moral AG unless it calls for a consideration

of the effects on others as such, without myself accepting any moral AG and, hence, without myself making any judgments about what is right or wrong, good or bad, moral or otherwise. On view II, I simply cannot myself make a moral judgment unless I commit myself to considering the effects of my action on others (at least some of them) as such, and I do not commit myself to this merely by agreeing that an AG is a moral one only if it calls for considering effects on others as such.

The point, I suppose, is that criterion D does not specify *what* effects on others (or on persons as such) are to be avoided or promoted. Only if it did specify these would one be begging any substantive moral issue by building it into the concept of a moral code.

(7) Well, there is always the open-question argument, and "them as likes it" have used it to refute alleged definitions of 'moral'.[6] But, however effective this is in the case of clearly normative terms like 'right' and 'good', one must be cautious about using it in the case of 'moral' (as opposed to 'nonmoral'). It will not do to claim, in objection to view II, that one can sensibly say, "This AG calls for a consideration of effects on others as such; but is it right to act on it?" or even "This AG calls for a consideration of effects on others as such; but is it morally right to act on it?" That this will not do follows from what I have said and also from the fact that our problem is not what 'right' means but what 'moral' means, or should be taken to mean. To use the open-question argument against view II, one must claim that the question, "This AG calls for a consideration of effects on others as such, for universalization, etc.; but is it a moral AG?" is a sensible question. And it does not seem obvious to me that it is, even in terms of our actual use of the word 'moral' (in the sense in which it is contrasted with 'nonmoral'). Even if it is a sensible question in these terms, however, this fact would do little to show that we ought not to accept view II, since this is a proposal about our future use of 'moral'.

III

Having made my case, such as it is, for view II — or, more accurately, for a certain form of view II — I wish to finish with a line of thought about the idea of morality which may have a larger import. (1) Although I have been defending view II, I am inclined to think that it can be plausibly maintained only if it is combined with a postulate to the effect that it is rational to live by an AG that is moral or socially considerate in the sense indicated by criterion D. That is, I agree with Kant that a rational man can adopt a moral AG only under the presupposition that it is ultimately rational for him to live by it, even though, for the reasons given, I am reluctant to build this presupposition into the very concept of a morality (as Kant is). (2) In fact, I believe that views I, III, and IV are also plausible only if they are combined with a postulate to the same effect.

Then there are four live options in this part of moral philosophy, namely: view II with the postulate indicated, view I with the postulate that the AG we will find rational to live by if we know what we are about (i.e., moral by its criteria) will turn out to be one that calls for a consideration of others or of persons as such, view III with the postulate that what we take to be moral in the wider will turn out to be moral also in the narrower sense, and view IV with the postulate that criteria C and D will turn out not to pull apart for "a man in his wisdom." (3) One might contend that, with these postulates, which all come to the same thing, the four views are essentially equivalent, and this does appear to be true in some sense, though it still seems to me that view II is preferable to the others on the grounds mentioned before.

(4) The point, I suggest, is that the idea of morality, as we have known it in our history, is the idea of an AG that is somehow *both* rational and social. The idea of morality represents a wager that man and the world are such that these two desiderata will eventually be found to coincide. That this is so is not something that can be proved in our present state of knowledge, but neither is it something that has been disproved. It may and must be *postulated*. Kant thought that this postulate must take the form of a belief that there is a God who sees to it that a life of moral virtue is rewarded by the happiness it deserves. But it need not take this form. In some form or other it is made by Plato and Aristotle, by Butler and Sidgwick, and by all of the religious and idealistic thinkers who believe that he who loses his life for morality's sake shall gain it. Even John Dewey postulates a coincidence of a kind between the happy life and the socially considerate and interested one, and, though Reinhold Niebuhr labels Dewey's faith naive and touching, he himself similarly believes that love is the true way to self-realization. I have already suggested that Falk and Hare, even when they are most in favor of view I, may themselves be betting that the AG a fully rational, informed, and nonevasive man would choose under its criteria would be a socially considerate one.

I have no wish to sound mystical. It does not seem to me that the postulate is at all plausible if it is understood as saying that an individual is never a loser in prudential terms — i.e., in terms of his own interest or happiness — by doing the socially moral thing. But is the finally rational way of life for the individual to be identified with that which is for his own greatest happiness? Butler and Kant thought that it was, but Falk seems to me to be on a better track when he insists that rational personal oughts need not take a prudential form.[7] The finally rational course, he suggests, is "what a man would do in his wisdom — if he were to consider things widely, looking past the immediate concerns of self and giving essentials due weight before incidentals"; and it must not simply be assumed that this is the course known as egoism. Even if we identify being rational with calm deliberation in the light of full knowledge about what one wants and how to get it, it does not follow that the rational life is that of cool self-love. Whether it is or not depends on what one wants when one is enlightened about himself and his world. One might then want exactly the kind of world that a socially considerate AG would call for, even at the cost of some sacrifice on one's own part. There is some evidence in modern psychology — so Erich Fromm and others have been arguing — that this is in fact the case. At least it may be that, as our insight into man, society, and the universe increases, we shall more and more come to see that the finally rational way of life for the individual is or at least may be precisely the socially considerate one.

11: 'Ought' and 'Is' Once More

To be and ought to be; that is the question: — whether 'tis nobler in the mind to suffer the slings and arrows of autonomous obligation, or to take arms against *that* sea of troubles and by opposing end them? Ay, there's the rub! In Dewey's words.

> The problem of restoring integration and cooperation between man's beliefs about the world in which he lives [Ises] and his beliefs about the values and purposes that should direct his conduct [Oughts] is the deepest problem of modern life. [And] It is the problem of any philosophy that is not isolated from that life.[1]

To some it has seemed axiomatic that judgments of obligation and value both can and must be derived from judgments about what is; to others it has seemed equally certain that they neither can be nor need to be in order to be valid since they are intuitively self-evident; still others have thought that they cannot be and yet must be if they are to have any rational basis, concluding that they are arbitrary and irrational. Each of these positions is said by its opponents to puzzle the will and make our enterprises turn awry and lose the name of action, and in this paper I seek to show that all of them are mistaken, at least if they are taken in certain forms. I begin by describing the three positions more fully.

I

The first position I take to hold that judgments of obligation and value, moral or non-moral, can be inferred *logically* from premises which are *all* factual, whether empirical or non-empirical, and that they cannot be regarded as justified unless they can be so inferred from factual premises. In its favor various lines of argument have been or may be advanced, but I shall state only the two that seem to me most apposite.

(1) One, using the parlance of recent philosophy, may be put as follows.

Reprinted from *Man and World*, Vol. 2 (1969), pp. 515-33, by permission of *Man and World*.

Factual statements about what is, was, or will be are often given as reasons for judgments of obligation or value. Sometimes they are given as *motivating* reasons, as in "You should be nice to your neighbors, because then they will be nice to you" or in "Honor thy father and thy mother, that thy days may be long upon the land which the Lord thy God giveth thee." But, sometimes, and this is what counts for the matter in hand, they are given as *justifying* reasons, as in "You ought to be grateful to your parents, because they have done a great deal for you" or in "Let us love one another, for love is of God." In fact, as is often pointed out, if one says that something is good or ought to be done, then he is in some sense claiming that there are reasons for favoring or for doing it, and it is hard to see how these reasons *could* be anything but some *fact* about it, some proposition about what it is like or will lead to. Thus, if A says "X is good" or "Y is wrong," and B asks "Why?" then A may and must answer with something like "Because it is pleasant" or "Because it will injure someone." In short, an Ought itself virtually claims an Is as its ground. One might even say that to justify a judgment of obligation or value *is* to derive it from some judgment of fact which is true or taken to be true.

(2) Another line of argument to show that an Ought can be derived from an Is involves the familiar dictum that Ought implies Can. This dictum says that if I cannot do something, then I have no obligation to do it, even if I would otherwise have one. But, if this is so, then, although "I can" does not imply "I ought," "I cannot" does imply "I do not have an obligation." In this sense, a fact about what I cannot do implies something about what obligations I have or do not have. To parody Emerson:

> So nigh is Ought-to-Be to Is,
> So near is God to man;
> When youth protests aloud, "I can't,"
> Then Duty says, "You needn't."

In this use the Ought-implies-Can doctrine is employed to show that one does not have a moral obligation in certain cases, but it is assumed that we do have such obligations. But the doctrine also has, since Kant at least, had a more drastic use. It is sometimes argued that moral obligation presupposes that the will is free in a contra-causal sense (and even that there is a God and that the soul is immortal). If this is so, however, then, if the will is not free in that sense (or if there is no God or no immortality), there can be no moral obligations *at all.* Then, from an Is of a certain sort one can infer the falsity or irrelevance of all moral judgments — as has sometimes actually been done. I shall not discuss this line of thought, because I am not convinced that morality does have the particular presuppositions claimed. I suspect, however, that the inference involved would turn out not to be a case of going from an Is alone to a denial of all moral Oughts, i.e., that the notion of moral obligation would appear, not only in its conclusion, but in one of its premises.

The proponents of the *second* position admit that justifying (as well as motivating) reasons may be given and expected in the case of many at least of our judgments of obligation and value, and that such reasons involve an appeal to a factual premise, empirical, metaphysical, or theological. They insist, however, that, since the statement to be justified is a judgment of obligation or value, containing a term like "good" or "ought," it cannot be justified unless the reasoning offered implicitly or explicitly includes, not only the factual premise mentioned, but also a normative premise about what is valuable or ought to be. An Ought, it is held, can be validly inferred from an Is only in the presence of a more basic Ought taken as a premise; if an Ought or Value term appears in the conclusion then it must also appear in one of the premises, when the premises are made explicit. Thus, when a factual reason is given as a justification for a judgment of obligation or value, as in the examples cited earlier, the reasoning is to be construed either as invalid or as an enthymeme; if it is to be valid, it must be filled out. Filled out in this way, the reasoning involved in the above examples will read, respectively, as follows:

(a)   We ought to be grateful to those who benefit us,
(b)   Your parents have benefited you,
(c)   Therefore, you ought to be grateful to them,

and

(d)   We ought to imitate God,
(e)   God is love,
(f)   Therefore, we ought to love.

Such reasoning, then, is possible if and only if there not only is a factual premise like (b) or (e) but also a more basic Ought premise like (a) or (d). These Ought premises themselves may be arrived at by a similar piece of reasoning with a still more basic Ought premise, but ultimately our normative reasoning must end in an appeal to a most basic Ought premise that cannot be established in the same way; it cannot be proved, because it cannot be inferred either from another Ought or from an Is or from a combination of the two — it must, in fact, be regarded as intuitive or self-evident.

Thomists sometimes say that the basic propositions of Natural Law are intuitive or self-evident, as if they were holding this second position, but their critics have often interpreted them as subscribing to the first position and have sometimes taken this second position as a ground for rejecting the doctrine of Natural Law. To my mind the Thomist view is unclear at this point. It is true that Aquinas says that the first precepts of natural law are self-evident, which suggests he is holding the second view. But then he explains this as meaning that anyone who knows the definition of the subject term in such a precept will see that the predicate of the precept is "contained in the notion of the subject."[2] That is, in more modern language, the precept is analytic. And this suggests that he is really maintaining, not the second position, but the first — or, in other words, that he is really not an intuitionist but a naturalist in metaethics, as will be spelled out shortly.

As for the third of the positions indicated at the outset — those who maintain it agree with the proponents of the second that judgments of obligation and value can be justified only by syllogistic reasoning of the sort illustrated, that is, only by appeal to a factual premise plus a more basic judgment of obligation or value. But where the proponents of the second position assert that the most basic judgments of obligation or value are intuitive or self-evident, they deny this to be so, and conclude that such judgments have no rational standing but are simply arbitrary commitments, postulates, or preferences. This third position is nicely illustrated by the opening paragraph of an article by Brian Medlin. He writes,

> I believe that it is now pretty generally accepted by professional philosophers that ultimate ethical principles must be arbitrary. One cannot derive conclusions about what should be merely from accounts of what is the case . . . . To arrive at a conclusion in ethics one must have at least one ethical premise. This premise, if it be in turn a conclusion, must be the conclusion of an argument containing at least one ethical premise. And so we can go back, indefinitely but not forever. Sooner or later, we must come to at least one ethical premise which is not deduced but baldly asserted. Here we must be a-rational; neither rational nor irrational, for here there is no room for reason even to go wrong.[3]

II

It seems clear that, for our purposes, the crucial question in thinking about the above three positions is this: can an Ought be logically inferred from an Is without using another Ought as a premise, at least implicitly?[4] Unless we find a fourth view (as I propose to do), if we say *yes*, we are committed to some form of the first position, and, if we say *no*, we must choose between the second and third. And if we say *no*, we must sooner or later take account of the two arguments given in favor of the first position. Before we can say *yes*, however, we must find some satisfactory reply to the argument based on the "No Ought from an Is" dictum. This argument is a very strong one. Can one who holds the first position meet it in any way? There are three ways in which he might seek to do so. (1) One is by introducing the possibility that Ought may be defined in terms of Is — that "obligation" and "value" can be analyzed into factual or descriptive properties, empirical, metaphysical, or theological. Let us grant that one cannot logically infer "I ought to do A" from "A is commanded by God" or "B is good" from "B is that which all things seek after" *without any further ado*. But, if one can show that "ought" may be defined as meaning "commanded by God" and "good" as meaning "sought after by all things,"

then one can validly make the inferences in question. One *can* go from Is to
Ought *if* one can make out that Good and Ought are to be defined in terms of Is.
Spinoza, in effect, saw this when he used definitions of goodness and virtue as
premises in proving that ''the highest good of the mind is the knowledge of
God, and the highest virtue of the mind is to know God,'' and that ''the highest
effort of the mind and its highest virtue is to understand things by the third kind
of knowledge.''[5] One may quarrel with his definitions in this connection, and
with his other premises, but one cannot question his logic, which is simply that
of geometry. To this extent the ''No Ought from an Is'' dictum, so confidently
assumed by those who take the second and third positions, is false. For the
following argument *is* valid:

(g)   ''I ought to do A'' means ''A is commanded by God''
(h)   A is commanded by God
(i)   Therefore I ought to do A.

If I accept (g) and (h) then I must accept (i), and there is no problem about this
because the term ''ought,'' which appears in the conclusion, is also present
in (g).

It is quite possible that this line is the one St. Thomas would take. At any rate,
he places the definition of ''good'' as meaning ''that which all things seek
after,'' at the foundation of his entire doctrine of Natural Law. He writes,

> Consequently the first principle in the practical reason is one founded on the
> nature of good, viz, that *good is that which all things seek after*. Hence this is
> the first precept of law, that *good is to be done and promoted, and evil is to be
> avoided*. All other precepts of the natural law are based upon this . . . [6]

Here he seems simply to assume that one can go from ''X is what all things seek
after'' to ''X is *to be* done and promoted.'' This, as his critics have often
pointed out, cannot be done logically without further ado. However, if, besides
his definition of ''good,'' he were to define what ''is to be done and promoted''
as what we *do* seek after (or would seek after if we knew what we were about),
then the logic of his view would be clear and could not be faulted, though one
might quarrel with his proposed definitions.

(2) The second line of thought by which one might try to sidestep the ''No
Ought from an Is'' dictum can only be vaguely sketched here. The strength of
the dictum lies in the claim that, if one is validly to infer a conclusion from a
premise, then there must be no terms in the former that are not in the latter. But,
it might be argued, while this may be true of syllogisms and other deductive
arguments, there are many inductive inferences in ordinary life, in history, and
in science of which it is not true. Such arguments marshal evidence for their
conclusions, for which they often claim only probability, and it is not clear that
they are ''valid'' only if there are no terms in their conclusions not already in
their premises or only if they are mediated by definitions.

(3) It has been suggested by some writers dealing with our problem that, besides deductive and inductive logic with their respective canons of inference, there may be a third kind of logic for use in reasoning about normative matters, a logic consisting of *special* rules of inference making it possible for an Is to be a reason for an Ought and enabling us to infer validly from a factual premise alone to a conclusion about what is right or good. In effect, each such rule says that a certain fact is a "good reason" (in a non-evaluative sense) for judging that something is good or right, or that, if a certain fact is the case, then one may infer that something is good or right. For instance, one such rule might say that from "X will injure someone" one may infer "I ought not to do X." Then, at least in a society in which this rule is accepted, one may validly reason as follows:

(m)   X will injure someone.
(n)   Therefore I ought not to do X.

That is, an Ought can be derived from an Is without the help of another Ought *as a premise* because there is a valid *rule of inference* that warrants this derivation in certain cases.

It is not possible to deal adequately with these three lines of thought here. For all their plausibility I am still strongly inclined to think that the "No Ought from an Is" dictum is correct if it is taken as saying that no such inference is *logically* valid. I am not sure line (2) is a sensible one, but even if it is correct, it is hard to see how one can use what it says about inferences about factual matters in everyday life, history, and science to show that it is possible to infer from factual matters to normative ones. Line (3), about which I shall say more later, has had hard going to gain acceptance, and, in fact, no one has yet worked it out satisfactorily (to my mind at least). In any case, there seems to be little difference between taking "if doing X injures someone, then one ought not to do X" as a *premise* and taking it as a *rule of inference*. It seems to be equally substantive either way, and leaves us with the question of its justification. Moreover, if there is a difference between taking it as a premise and taking it as a rule of inference, we may still ask why it is to be taken in the latter rather than in the former way. Line (1) seems to me correct as far as it goes. However, whether it goes far enough to show that one can go logically from Is to Ought depends on whether Ought can be *satisfactorily* defined in terms of Is, and, while I am less impressed than some by the open question argument and the naturalistic fallacy charge so often directed against naturalistic and other definists (metaphysical or theological), I nevertheless doubt that judgments of obligation and value can be translated without serious loss into factual or existential ones of whatever sort. In any case, it seems to me that even if, for example, " 'good' means 'aimed at by all things' " is a correct definition of what we actually mean by "good," one can only accept it as a definition for use in thinking about and deciding what to do if one already accepts the normative judgment that what is aimed at by all things is good. If this is so, then, in effect, what looks like a definition is tantamount to a value principle, and, if this is so, then we are still left with the problem of its justification and, in particular, of its relation to beliefs about what is.[7]

III

Of the three positions originally distinguished, the first says that *all* Oughts can be directly inferred from some Is or other, and that such inferences are *logically* valid. The other two insist that no Ought can be logically inferred from any Is except with the help of another Ought taken as a *premise*, and that the most basic Oughts are therefore logically autonomous with respect to Is (as Plato said, the Good is beyond Being). In these terms, it seems to me, for the reasons indicated, that the second and third positions are correct in maintaining that there is no *logical* error in refusing to go from any Is whatsoever to any Ought — and that the proponents of the first position cannot rescue themselves by any of the three lines of thought just discussed. Does it follow, as so many have thought, that we must regard basic judgments of obligation or value as either self-evident or arbitrary? Discussing this question J. S. Mill wrote,

> Questions of ultimate ends are not amenable to direct proof. . . . we are not, however, to infer that [the] acceptance or rejection [of an ultimate end] must depend on blind impulse, or arbitrary choice. There is a larger meaning of the word, "proof," in which this question is . . . amenable to it . . . . The subject is within the cognizance of the rational faculty; and neither does that faculty deal with it solely in the way of intuition. Considerations may be presented capable of determining the intellect either to give or withhold its assent to the doctrine; and this is equivalent to proof.[8]

Here Mill is claiming that, even if basic normative principles and value judgments cannot be proved by being inferred from true factual premises according to logically valid procedures, and also are not seen to be true by intuition, they are still not arbitrary or irrational; it may still be possible to advance factual considerations which make it rational or reasonable, though not logically necessary, to give one's assent to such a principle or value. That is, even if one cannot *logically* infer an Ought from an Is, one may yet be *rational* and justified in doing so, and *unreasonable* otherwise, at least in certain cases. One such case, I take it, is his famous, much-criticized "proof" of hedonism. Here Mill is not pretending that "Pleasure is the good" follows logically from "We all desire pleasure as an end and (basically) only pleasure" (he explicitly says he is not); he is arguing that, since we do all aim at pleasure in this way, it would be absurd or unreasonable, in a "larger" sense than that defined by logic, to deny that pleasure is the good.[9]

Mill seems to me to be on the right track here in suggesting that there is a sense in which one can go from Is to Ought — a sense in which such a process may be rational, reasonable, or justified, even if it is not logical.[10] Let me try to indicate why by considering two examples. Take first the following bit of conversation:

> Him: You ought to go downtown today.
> Me: Why?
> Him: There is a sale on. You want to buy a new suit, don't you?

In this bit of talk an ought-judgment is made, though not a moral one, and it is defended or justified by the use of two statements of fact, without the use of a normative premise, in a manner that seems entirely natural and reasonable. To state the "practical inference" involved more accurately, it is this:

(a)   You want to buy a new suit at a reasonable price.
(b)   There is a sale on downtown today.
(c)   Therefore you ought to go downtown today.

It might be replied that this inference is justified or reasonable only if another premise is understood, namely,

(d)   If you want to buy a new suit at a reasonable price, you ought to adopt the means suited to accomplish that end.

In other words, one needs a further premise with an Ought in it. But, in return, I am tempted to say that adducing this premise is a work of logical supererogation; the inference is really quite rational without it. It is not like:

> Socrates is a man,
> Therefore Socrates is mortal,

which does clearly need an additional premise. One cannot possibly claim that the meaning of "mortal" is such that, if Socrates is a man, then one may correctly go on to say that he is mortal. One has no language-rule connecting "man" and "mortal" and hence one needs a premise that does so.

Von Wright seems to think that the inference in the case cited is justified only if "You ought to . . ." is taken to *mean* "Unless you do, you will fail to . . ." i.e., only if "You ought . . ." is taken to *be* a kind of factual statement. But this is because he assumes that a practical inference must be logically valid in order to be justified, and this is just what is in question. It may be that it simply is linguistically appropriate to introduce "ought" into the conclusion *even if* it does *not* have von Wright's meaning (viz., you will fail if you don't do . . .) *and* does not appear in any of the premises — just because I am there wanting to buy a new suit cheap (and because the speaker has a pro-attitude toward my doing so).[11]

Consider now a similar example, entirely in the first person: here I am, wanting to buy a new suit at a reasonable price. I read an advertisement of a sale on suits and decide that I should go downtown today if at all possible. One could try to set this practical inference up as follows, as von Wright does:[12]

(a)   I want to buy a new suit at a reasonable price
(b)   There is a suit sale on downtown.
(c)   Therefore I ought to go downtown today.

Now, first of all, what I said about the previous example will all apply to this one. But the point I wish to stress is this. If I am actually concluding that I *should* go downtown today if possible, I must not merely *believe that* I want to buy a new suit reasonably, I must *be wanting* a new suit at a reasonable price, and, if I am wanting this, then I may reasonably pass (and only then) from the fact that there is a sale on suits downtown to the conclusion that I should go downtown if possible — without *any* further ado in the way of definitions, additional Ought premises, rules of inference, etc. — simply because "I should . . ." is the appropriate form of expression to use when one has an interest and apprehends facts that are relevant to it. What makes the judgment that I should go downtown today a rational or justifiable one is just such facts as that there is a sale on, plus my desiring to buy a new suit at a bargain price.

What I suggest is that the sort of thing that is true in this rather simple case is true in all cases: i.e., (a) that always, when a piece of practical reasoning seems reasonable and justified, there is present both a factual premise or reason and something that may be called an attitude, interest, or point of view and involves, not just *believing a proposition,* but *being for or against something* (it may be an ordinary desire, self-love, "the farmer's point of view," etc.; in the case of moral judgment and reasoning it is "the moral point of view," however that may be defined); (b) that if one has an interest or takes a point of view and then finds or believes that certain relevant facts obtain (that is, facts bearing on that interest or point of view), then one may rationally and justifiably, at least in principle, proceed to a normative conclusion, even if the inference is not strictly according to *logical* Hoyle (whether it is justified in practice will depend on what the facts appealed to are, whether other interests or points of view are affected, etc.). In fact, while I am less sure of (a) than of (b), I submit that the use of a statement involving some term like "ought" or "good" in a first-hand normative way is appropriate precisely in such a context and only in such a context. Normative discourse just *is* the appropriate discourse in which to express oneself when one is taking some conative point of view and apprehends facts relevant to it.

What I have said is not intended to deny Mrs. Foot's contention that one cannot well agree that Jones is causing offence by indicating lack of respect and yet deny that Jones is rude — that is, that one may justifiably go from "Jones is causing offence by indicating lack of respect" to "Jones is rude" — even when "Jones is rude" is used evaluatively, as it usually is.[13] I do want to claim, however, that this inference from an Is to an Ought is justified only if it is made

in the presence of a concern that people refrain from doing the sort of thing
Jones is doing — the sort of concern that is normally present when people are
said to be rude. If I am utterly indifferent, I cannot properly say he is rude.

IV

If this view of the matter is correct, then there *is* a sense, though not a strictly
logical one, in which one may go from an Is to an Ought in certain contexts, and
the context need not consist of another Ought taken as a premise (as the second
and third positions allege). So far the first of our original three positions is
well-taken. But the other two positions are also well-taken in so far as they
maintain that going from an Is to an Ought is not warranted by deductive or
inductive logic, nor by the rules of a third logic, nor by the possibility that
Ought may be defined in terms of Is. The truth, if I am right, belongs to a *fourth*
position, which preserves what is viable in the other three but rejects their
common assumption that a rational inference must be a "logically" valid one.
In particular, it should be noticed that this fourth position has most of the virtues
claimed for the "third logic" or "good reasons" view, without being open to
the same criticisms. (It may even represent what the proponents of that view
have been fishing for.)

The similarities and dissimilarities of the three positions I have rejected and
the nature of the fourth position I am proposing may be indicated as follows.
Consider four propositions:

(1)   Judgments of obligation and value (Oughts) are rationally justifi-
        able, objectively valid, etc.

(2)   Judgments of obligation and value (Oughts) cannot be logically
        inferred from factual ones (Ises).

(3)   Judgments of obligation and value (Oughts) cannot be rationally
        justified, objectively valid, etc., unless they can be logically in-
        ferred from factual ones (Ises).

(4)   Basic judgments of obligation and value are intuitive, self-evident,
        self-justifying.

The first position affirms (1) and (3) and denies (2) and (4). The second affirms
(1), (2) and (4) and denies (3). The third affirms (2) and (3) and denies (1) and
(4). The first and second positions agree on (1), the second and third on (2), and
the first and third on (3). Only the second position asserts (4). These three
positions have this in common: they all assume that there is no reasonable or
rationally justified way of going from Is to Ought unless there is a *logically*
valid way of doing so. They all assume, even the third-logic people, that every
rational or justifiable passage of thought must be warranted by some canon of
inference — that the whole business must be captured in the logical machinery

of "premises," "rules of inference," and "conclusions," if it is to be a rational or objectively justified transition of mind. What I am suggesting, by way of contrast, is that these assumptions, which are made even by such perceptive moral philosophers as Hampshire and Aiken, are mistaken — that we both do and should regard some inferences or transitions of thought as rational or justified even though the "conclusion" is an Ought, the only "premise" is an Is, and there is no "rule of inference." The resulting fourth position toward which I have been working, then, asserts (1) and (2) and denies (3) and (4).

In objection to this fourth position it may be argued (a) that we do not actually recognize such inferences as those just described as justified or reasonable, (b) that we *ought* not do so now, even if we have been. The first contention is simply false, as my suit-sale example shows. As for the second — if we *do* recognize such passages of thought as rational, this fact is, so far, a good reason for continuing to do so, and I do not see that there are any over-riding reasons why we should not. As long as we are shaping our attitudes, points of view, and normative judgments clearheadedly in the light of the fullest relevant knowledge and insight, I see no reason for refusing to call the transitions of thought in question justified or rational. Commenting on C. L. Stevenson's views about validity, H. D. Aiken writes,

> Thus, for example, although Professor Charles Stevenson is perhaps more sensitive than any other philosopher to the reality of persuasive definition, he himself falls into it when he refuses, for no reason sanctioned by ordinary language, to accept the possibility that there are any "rational methods" other than those of formal logic and science. Although he freely allows the right of moralists to use, *inter alia*, what he regards as rational methods when they happen to be appropriate for the purpose of "irrigating" ethical judgments, he nevertheless insists there are no criteria of validity with respect to ethical disputation as such. But why should he fear lest the notion of "validity" be extended so as to include forms of inference which are neither demonstrative nor inductive? As he himself wisely says, "When an inference does not purport to comply with the usual rules, any insistence on its failure to do so is gratuitous." And yet he maintains, to my mind quite unconvincingly, that it is "wholly impracticable and injudicious" (sic) to sanction a definition of validity which extends its usage beyond its applications to logic and to science. Apart from a tenacious desire to reserve the emotive meaning of such expressions as "rational" and "valid" for processes of reasoning involved in formal logic and inductive science, what is there to commend Stevenson's position?[14]

Extended to cover the third-logic people as well as Stevenson (and possibly Aiken himself), this seems to me just the right thing to say.

It will help to make the view I am proposing clearer if I comment on another passage from Aiken at this point. Shortly after the one just quoted he goes on to say,

> Now I agree once and for all that there are no formal logical rules by means of which one can deduce the ethical proposition "*x* ought to be done" from any combination of purely factual statements. What I do maintain is that, *according to ordinary usage*, it is entirely permissible to *infer* ethical conclusions from factual premises. I should now like to support this contention with some *examples*. Suppose that it could be shown that a certain act would cause another person unnecessary hardship or suffering; I think that any normal person in our society would regard this as a good, if not sufficient, reason for inferring that, other things remaining equal, the act in question ought not to be performed. Again, suppose it could be shown that the fulfillment of a certain promise would probably cause the person to whom one made it to destroy himself; here also, I think that normal persons would, perhaps reluctantly, conclude from this that the promise ought to be broken. Other examples come to mind.
>
> I conclude from this that, however difficult they may be to specify, there are nevertheless broad principles of relevance or valid inference in moral discourse which enable us, in certain circumstances, to infer ethical conclusions from nonethical premises. But I do not in the least wish to imply by this that the ordinary laws of logic should be amended or broadened. Such laws have no immediate application to the kinds of inference in question. My contention is merely that within the universe of discourse called "moral" or "ethical," certain types of inference are viewed as reasonable, others not. Nor do I wish to say that moral judgments may be "logically derived" from nonethical statements of fact. I think, nothing is gained from such an unnecessary and really misleading extension of the expression "logical derivation." All that needs defending is the thesis that moral reasoning has its own proprieties which, while certainly not written into the starry heavens above, are at least constant and extensive enough to enable the members of a given civilization to distinguish a good reason from a bad one.[15]

Here Aiken is defending the good reasons theory referred to above, though without adopting the notion of a third *logic*. Now, I agree with him, of course, when he says that there are no formal logical rules by which we may pass from nonethical statements of fact to moral judgments, and again when he says that ordinary usage permits us to go from factual premises to ethical conclusions, or that within the universe of discourse called "moral" or "ethical," certain types of inference are viewed as reasonable and others not, and yet again when he argues that we ought not to call such inferences "logical" even in an extended sense. But, while he does not choose to call them rules of a third logic, Aiken does think of these inferences as resting on quasi-logical "proprieties" or "principles of relevance or valid inference" which play a role in moral discourse analogous to that of logical rules of inference rather than to that of premises. This conception he supports with two examples, and I agree that "any normal person in our society" would regard it as reasonable to draw the conclusions indicated in these examples. It is, however, not clear to me that the principles of not causing unnecessary hardship or suffering and of not causing others to commit suicide function in our thinking as *rules of inference* rather than as *premises* (if there is a difference). If they *are* functioning as implicit premises, then these examples are not cases of inferring from factual premises to ethical conclusions, as Aiken thinks they are. But suppose that they are not functioning as premises. It does not follow that they are functioning as "rules of inference." For a third analysis is possible. This is that what carries the "normal member of our society" from the factual premises involved to his ethical conclusion — and does so reasonably — is not necessarily any Ought premise, nor any rule of inference, but simply his moral concern for others, his sympathy, or his commitment to the moral point of view. What I wish to suggest, then, is that, when we go from Is to Ought with a sense of reasonableness or justification, we are doing so because we (or someone we are speaking to or of) have an operative concern or interest — not because we have any hidden Ought premises or any special rules of inference that have a quasi-logical status.[16] I would even like to say that, ultimately, all of our Oughts, even those we sometimes use as premises (or perhaps as rules of inference, *if* we do so use them) are generated by or accepted in the presence of some concern or interest in confrontation with some apprehension of fact, and that this process may be entirely reasonable even if it is not logical (perhaps even logical norms are generated or accepted in the same way!). Just now, however, I want only to contend that some "inferences" from Is to Ought are justified or rational even if they use no rules of inference and no suppressed Ought premises, just because words like "ought" and "good" are linguistically appropriate in such contexts.[17] And, when I say these "inferences" are justified (other things being equal), I am claiming that any rational being who shares the same concern or point of view will accept them.

It should be observed that this fourth view could be accepted, if not by St. Thomas and his followers, then at least by some near-cousins. Suppose that one wishes to associate judgments of obligation and value with man's "natural tendency" to happiness or self-fulfillment, as J. D. Wild does.[18] Then one need not define "X is good" or "I ought to do Y" as meaning "X is conducive to the fulfillment of man's natural tendancy" or "Y is required for that fulfillment." One need not be a naturalist (or ontological definist) of this sort, as Wild seems to be. One might contend instead that a judgment of obligation or value is an *expression* of the *conatus* in question, made in the presence of facts taken to be relevant to it, not an *assertion* to the effect that one has that *conatus* or that those facts are relevant to it. Then one would have a view — a non-cognitive one — which would be much like that of the Thomists, but which would be compatible with the one I have been sketching.

However this may be, one could even, if one wished, combine the view sketched with belief that "good" and "ought" can be satisfactorily defined along such lines as have been variously suggested by St. Thomas, Spinoza, J. D. Wild, S. C. Pepper, R. B. Perry, H. R. Niebuhr, and others. One might then still accept such definitions, but, if I am right, one would have to recognize that underlying one's acceptance of the definitions there is or should be an attitude, interest, or point of view already taken — i.e., that the definition is really a crystallization in a certain mode (formal or material) of an attitude, interest, or point of view. The definition would then not necessarily be vitiated by this fact, but the fact would have to be recognized and kept in mind in a way in which it has not usually been by naturalists and other definists. For what would then really mediate the inference from Is to Ought or from Fact to Value would not be the definition but the underlying commitment.

V

At the opening of Section I, I described two lines of argument for the position that an Ought can and must be derived from an Is. It will be clear at once that the view taken in Section III comports well with the first of them. For it agrees that factual premises (Ises) may be reasons for Oughts, and it explains why this is so (as Hume insisted one must). But something must be said about the second — the one using the "Ought implies Can" dictum. Can its point be provided for? This point is that "I cannot" implies "I have no obligation to." The problem is that the use of the word "implies" suggests that there is a logical connection between a statement about what is (cannot be) and one about what obligations we have or do not have. This suggestion I believe to be misleading. The conviction that, if A is unable to do B, then he has no obligation to do B, and the conviction that if C was unable to do D, then he is to be excused for not doing D — these convictions of moral common sense are, in my opinion, not really logical truths. What they mean is something like this: that if A is unable to do B, then he should not be held to doing it, and that if C was unable to do D, then he should not be blamed or punished for not doing it. In other words, what appear to be logical truths are really normative principles. They do not give us logical warrants for going from Is to Ought — or rather from Cannot-do to Have-No-Obligation-to-do. Instead they tell us that it is not morally permissible to hold people responsible for what they cannot do, at least if it is not their fault that they cannot do it. In a sense they enable us to go from Cannot-do to Have-No-Obligation-to-do, but they do so only because they are expressions of the moral point of view to which we are already committed (if we accept them at all). Hence, a recognition of such principles does not contravene the view proposed.

This line of thought is supported by another to which I am inclined, namely, that the "can" in "Ought implies can" has a normative meaning. "Can" does, of course, have a factual sense, e.g., in the sentence, "I can jump two feet but I cannot jump 26 feet.'' But does it have such a purely factual sense in a typical moral case? J. W. Smith and others have suggested that it does not and I think I agree with them. [19] Suppose that someone is on his way to a meeting that he has an obligation to attend, but breaks his leg on the way (not purposely, of course). He and the rest of us would then regard him as absolved from the obligation to attend the meeting (though possibly not from the obligation to notify us) on the ground that he is unable to make it. But, of course, strictly speaking, as Smith points out, he could make it, even if only by crawling and dragging his leg painfully behind him. When we agree that he ''can't'' make it — or ''couldn't have'' made it — we are not strictly saying he ''can't'' or ''couldn't have'' in the factual sense. We are saying something more like ''It would be unreasonable or wrong to expect him to attend the meeting under the circumstances.'' If this is so, then, in going from ''Can't'' to ''Has no obligation to,'' we are not strictly going from a pure Is to a conclusion about an obligation. We are going from something like ''It would be wrong to expect . . .'' to ''He has no obligation to . . . .''

One might reply that our judgment, ''It would be wrong to expect . . .,'' is based on a purely factual premise, namely, in our example, that our friend would suffer great pain if he were to attend the meeting, so that we are still going from Is to Ought, or rather Ought not. This is true, but this particular inference may be dealt with in the same way as any argument in which a factual premise is given as a reason for a normative judgment, and so has already been covered by our discussion.

VI

One final remark — in approaching the subject as I have, I have been talking as if there were a fairly clear distinction between the Is and the Ought. Actually, as is well-known, there are all sorts of complexities and difficulties in defining that distinction — witness discussions by J. L. Austin, John Searle, Dorothy Emmet, and many others. It seems reasonable to hope, however, that my view would survive even if it were to turn out that no clear or workable distinction between the Is and the Ought can be made. Perhaps it would seem more plausible then.

12: Prichard and the Ethics of Virtue

H. A. PRICHARD'S ARTICLE, "IS MORAL PHILOSOPHY BASED ON A Mistake?" was first published in 1912, but attracted very little attention for a quarter of a century, even though it answered its titular question with the forcefully argued thesis that all of the then prevailing systems were in fact rooted in error. Now it is famous, being perhaps the currently most interesting piece of moral philosophy written by an intuitionist. There are a number of reasons for this interest, but for me one of the main ones is the "sharp distinction" Prichard makes between virtue and moral goodness, together with the things he says in the course of making it. Here, however, my attention will not be centered on this distinction as such, but on a footnote to it that is as exciting as it is unexpected.

At the point at which Prichard introduces this footnote, he is making the distinction referred to, which he regards as following from what he has previously said.[1]

According to Prichard, there are two kinds of "intrinsically good" motives: "a sense of obligation," which is not a desire and has no purpose or end, and certain desires, viz., those "prompted by some [intrinsically] good emotion, such as gratitude, affection, family feeling, or public spirit"; two kinds of intrinsically good actions: those done from a sense of obligation and those done from some intrinsically good desire; and two kinds of intrinsically good dispositions: moral goodness or the disposition to do what one believes to be right because it is right and virtue or a disposition to be activated by some intrinsically good desire. There are thus two different species of intrinsic goodness of motives, actions, and dispositions, one moral and the other nonmoral, depending on the presence or absence of a sense of moral obligation. The one is "morality," the other "virtue." An action or person may have both kinds of motives and so both kinds of intrinsic goodness; in this case it or he is better,

Reprinted from *The Monist,* Vol. 54, No. 1 (1970), pp. 1-17, with the permission of the author and publisher. Copyright by the Open Court Publishing Company.

other things being equal, than it or he would otherwise be. Nevertheless, an action or person that is merely virtuous is not morally good and one that is merely morally good is not virtuous.

On this view moral goodness is one, in the sense that there can be only one morally good disposition, namely that which Kant calls good will, but virtue is many, in the sense that there will be a virtuous disposition corresponding to each intrinsically good desire. Thus the virtue of generosity is a tendency to be moved by "the desire to help another arising from sympathy with that other," and that of courage is a tendency to act from "the desire to conquer one's feelings of terror arising from the sense of shame which they arouse." It is worth noting here that Prichard defines virtues, not as "actional traits" or tendencies to act in certain ways externally, but as "dispositions" to have certain desires and feelings in acting.[2]

Some would balk at what Prichard says on the ground that the concept of virtue is identical with or includes that of moral goodness. As the term "virtue" is often used, this is true. However, Prichard could reply by saying that if we use "virtue" in this way, we must distinguish between two kinds of virtue (and perhaps two kinds of moral goodness), one that consists in being moved by a sense of moral obligation and another that consists in being moved by some intrinsically good desire other than the sense of obligation (if the latter can be called a desire at all, as it is by some). Then the distinction is verbally less paradoxical but substantively no less sharp. It also turns out to be familiar, having in essence been made earlier by Sidgwick and Moore, in a way already by Aristotle and Hume, and in another way even by Kant. In this paper I shall use the terms "moral goodness" and "virtue" as Prichard does.

Prichard has in his essay a complex and unclear argument to establish his distinction, but since, apart from some of his addenda, his distinction is more familiar than he seems to realize and may readily be admitted to be correct, we need not try to formulate his argument on this occasion. I come then to that footnote.

II

The footnote consists of three sentences. In the first Prichard says that his distinction will explain a certain fact, in the second he states this fact, and in the third, though in the form of a question, he gives the explanation.

This sharp distinction of virtue and morality as co-ordinate and independent forms of goodness will explain a fact which otherwise it is difficult to account for. If we turn from books on Moral Philosophy to any vivid account of human life and action such as we find in Shakespeare, nothing strikes us more than the comparative remoteness of the discussions of Moral Philosophy from the facts of actual life. Is not this largely because, while

Moral Philosophy has, quite rightly, concentrated its attention on the fact of obligation, in the case of many of those whom we admire most and whose lives are of the greatest interest, the sense of obligation, though it may be an important, is not a dominating factor in their lives?[3]

I said that this note is unexpected because one would not expect a moral philosopher to have this feeling of the remoteness of his subject from the facts of actual life, and especially not Prichard, who otherwise seems to stay close to the facts and language of ordinary moral experience in his discussions and to have no doubts about their relevance. Actually, when I turn to Prichard's book on moral philosophy from some vivid account of human life and action, I do not have any striking sense of remoteness or irrelevance. Still, we may grant that the fact is substantially what he says it is in his second sentence. If even a Prichard senses that remoteness when he reads novels and plays, there must be something to it.

What then is it that explains the felt remoteness of the discussions of moral philosophy from the facts of actual life? For Prichard the distinction between virtue and moral goodness must be central to the explanation. Indeed, the fact he wants to explain is not just that people do as much wrong as they do or even that a sense of obligation plays little if any part in the lives of many interesting people — not just the remoteness of moral theory from life in *these* senses. Such facts might only show that people are largely wicked, amoral, or at least akratic. What Prichard is concerned to explain is the fact that so many *admirable* people live by something other than a sense of moral obligation or an ideal of moral goodness. And he suggests that what takes primacy in the lives of such people, as recounted in biography and fiction, is not morality but virtue — not a sense of moral duty or a desire to do what is right (if this is a desire) but various other good motives or desires rooted in emotions like gratitude, benevolence, or courage, not an ideal of doing the right or of being morally good but an ideal of being virtuous or of acting courageously, benevolently, or gratefully. In other words, theirs is an ethics, if one may call it that, of virtuousness and the virtues, not one of duty or morality, an ethics of good desires expressed in action, not one of doing what is morally required or of being conscientious. This is how Prichard thinks the sharp distinction between morality and virtue explains the fact that we "admire" men and women whose lives are lived under some other aegis than that of the obligation and moral goodness that moral philosophers discuss in their books. Besides the judgments and standards of moral obligation and goodness, we have others of generosity, courage, family feeling, public spirit, etc.; and some people live, primarily at least, by these other judgments and standards and are admired even though moral philosophy disparages or neglects them.

Now *this,* as I said, is interesting. It is all the more interesting because Prichard sees it but still insists that "moral philosophy has, quite rightly, concentrated its attention on the fact of obligation," and on moral goodness rather than on virtue. Presumably this is at least partly because he thinks of moral philosophy as the philosophy or theory of *morality* and equates morality with a concern for *moral* obligation and goodness. Then other kinds of goodness or rightness, among them virtue or intrinsic goodness of desire and emotion, are automatically excluded from morality and the attention of moral philosophy. I have myself a good deal of sympathy for this view of Prichard's, but it is today being questioned in one way or another by a number of moral philosophers, for instance, Bernard Mayo, R. M. Hare, P. F. Strawson, John Macmurray, and R. W. Hepburn. It is certainly not obviously correct. Keeping Prichard primarily in mind, we may note that the key word here, 'morality', is ambiguous. It may be used as a word for the moral quality of actions, motives, or dispositions, that is, for their moral rightness, goodness, or virtue. Thus Prichard uses it as simply another word for moral goodness. It may also be used to refer to what Butler calls "the moral institution of life," as it is when we compare morality with law or religion or talk about the principles of morality. One may with some plausibility hold that what Prichard calls virtue is not a kind of *moral* quality, as he does, and hence, if one also holds that moral philosophy is the theory of moral qualities or predicates, that it need not consider virtue. But it is a different question whether or not the morality of our culture includes a recognition of courage and other forms of virtue; it may well be thought apparent that it does, and that moral philosophy must therefore take virtue within its purview, along with obligation and moral goodness, even if only in a secondary way.

One might, then, take a different position from Prichard's, as the philosophers just referred to do, and argue that courage and other species of virtue do belong to morality in the second sense and should be studied by moral philosophy (perhaps precisely because it will otherwise remain too remote from life). In that case, moral philosophy would have to recognize virtue, not just as an assistant to or a complication in the morality of obligation and moral goodness, but as a coordinate and independent kind of motive or ideal, moral or nonmoral. It would have to exhibit morality, or at least life, as something involving two standards, possibly supplementing one another, but possibly conflicting — that of moral goodness, which Prichard holds high, and that of virtue, which he takes seriously only in a footnote. It would have to recognize the ethics of virtue as well as that of duty and moral goodness, even if it conceived of them as two parts of morality as a whole and not as rival ways of life.

One might even go so far as to argue that what Prichard sees going on in actual life and in Shakespeare is to be preferred to the lessons of moral philosophy, or, in other words, that the way of virtue is not only more practiced and more interesting than the way of duty and moral goodness, but also superior to it. On such a view, the ethics of virtue would be an alternative to the ethics of duty — an alternative that not only has primacy in actual life but should be accorded primacy in moral theory as well.

In this way, reflection on Prichard's footnote brings us to the question of an ethics of virtue. This question was raised before him by Leslie Stephen and James Martineau, and has been raised again since by some religious moralists as well as by the philosophers referred to earlier. It is also mooted by "the new morality," as it is called, for this is, in some of its aspects and forms, a movement away from the ethics of duty and toward one of virtue — of virtues like honesty, love, and sincerity. In the rest of this paper I wish to look at this question, limiting myself to the perspective provided by Prichard's discussion. For, in the course of his article, he gives us at least some of the terms needed to see what an ethics of virtue is like, and some of the arguments that might be used against it. A study thus limited cannot be regarded as final, of course, but it will do for a start.

III

What, then, would an ethics of virtue be like, as Prichard would conceive of it? It will be convenient to use a distinction borrowed from Maurice Mandelbaum, between two kinds of moral judgments.[4] *Direct* moral judgments are those in which a person as agent judges what actions or kinds of actions it is right, good, or virtuous for him to do in situations that face him. *Removed* moral judgments are those in which a person is judging as a spectator, judging the actions done by others, the character of others, his own past actions, or his own character — judging them as right, good, virtuous, courageous, etc. Talking in these terms, I take it that an ethics of virtue must not only guide a spectator in making removed judgments, but must also guide an agent in making direct ones and thus in determining what *to do*. An ethics of virtue might, perhaps, concern itself only with the making of removed moral judgments, such as a reader of Homer or Shakespeare might make, or such as one might make on looking back over one's own life and action, but then it would not be offering us — or those whom we admire — anything *to live by*. For such guidance we would still have to look to an ethics of duty — or simply follow our desires, passions, and interests, unaided and unmodified by any ideal or principle, moral or nonmoral.

It seems clear, then, that a pure ethics of virtue would not propound, as our *basic* guides to life, any judgments or principles about what is morally right or obligatory to do, since it would then be an ethics of duty or principle. It might try to derive some judgments or rules about what is right, wrong, or obligatory *from* its basic ideals of virtue, but these basic ideals must themselves not be judgments or principles about what is right, wrong, or obligatory. They must be ideals about what is virtuous. Nor can an ethics of virtue guide us by putting before us the ideal of being morally good in Prichard's sense, as Kant *seems* to do when he begins by telling us that a good will alone is unconditionally good. For, in this sense, being morally good means being one who always acts from a sense of obligation, and enjoining or urging us to be morally good is just instructing us to do our duty, giving us, once more, only an ethics of duty to go by.

One might think that an ethics of virtue could proceed by instructing us, first, that we *ought* to act courageously (generously, etc.), and, second, what it is to act courageously (generously, etc.). However, as Prichard points out, if one lives by these instructions one will be acting from a sense of obligation after all, and one's actions will not really be acts of courage (generosity, etc.); they will be morally good but not virtuous.[5]

Again, one might suppose that an ethics of virtue would guide our direct judgments and conduct by giving us a definition of the virtue of courage (for example) and then telling us that we *ought* to *acquire* courage, that is, that we ought "to do such things as will enable us afterwards to act courageously,"[6] doing the same for the other virtues in order to make its guidance complete. Then, if we knew or could find out from experience what things will produce courage and the other virtues in us, it would in a sense be telling us what to do. For it could be presumed that, once a person *had* acquired the virtues — dispositions to act courageously, etc. — he would know what to do, namely, just what those dispositions would enable and motivate him to do. St. Augustine once summarized the ethics of love, conceived as an ethics of virtue, by saying, "Love, and then do as you please." Similarly but more generally, an ethics of virtue might say, "Be virtuous (e.g., courageous, etc.), and then do as you please," or, rather, "*Become* virtuous, and then do as you please" — where "Become virtuous" is understood to mean "You have an *obligation* to do what will produce and maintain virtue in you."

For such an ethics there would be, in some sense, two stages in life: one before and one after the point at which an individual can be said (truly) to *be* virtuous (e.g., courageous, etc.) — if there is such a point. In the first stage, one's actions are to be done from the sense of obligation to be virtuous and are themselves not virtuous but at best morally good; in the second, if the line of division is clear, one's actions will not be morally good but they will be virtuous. I am supposing here that the "ought" in "You ought to be courageous, etc." is a categorical one such as Prichard has in mind when he agrees that "there is an obligation to acquire courage,"[7] not a hypothetical one such as appears in "If you want to be courageous, you ought to practice walking along the sides of precipices." Any ethics of virtue can, of course, recognize hypothetical oughts of this kind; my point now is that if it recognizes even the one categorical obligation just indicated, then it is not a pure ethics of virtue — it is still in a very crucial respect a partial ethics of duty. One might, nevertheless, espouse such a partial ethics of virtue, but it will actually be a kind of mixed ethics. Some forms of the ethics of love, for example that of Emil

Brunner, seem to be a mixed ethics of this kind, telling us that we *ought* to love and that, when we do, we are to do what we please.

What would a more complete or pure ethics of virtue be like? It would be like the partial ethics of virtue just described, except that it would not recognize any categorical imperative to be virtuous. It would in effect advise, counsel, or instruct us — perhaps exhort and urge us — to make ourselves virtuous, and let us do what we then please. It might advocate a system of moral education that would inculcate such ideals as courage, generosity, public spirit, and the rest, perhaps by indoctrination, perhaps by more rational methods; but it would not claim that others have a categorical moral obligation to inculcate those ideals in us or we in them, since, if it did so, it would again be a mixed ethics of virtue and duty.

Actually, a moral philosopher might advocate (or a culture have) an ethics or morality that would combine a pure ethics of virtue for one area (not stage) of life with an ethics of obligation and moral goodness for another area. Thus P. F. Strawson distinguishes "the region of the moral" and "the region of the ethical," the first being the sphere of social obligations and rights and the second that of "personal ideals" or "ideal images of life" such as contribute to "the enormous charm of reading novels, biographies, histories."[8] Such an ethics might be said to include a pure ethics of virtue as a part, but it would not be a *complete* ethics of virtue. I suppose that if one combines a pure ethics of duty and a pure ethics of virtue in this way, one could and would agree with Prichard in regarding "as the really best man the man in whom virtue and morality [moral goodness] are united."[9] It is, however, characteristic of proponents of an ethics of virtue to think that a virtuous man is better than a merely moral one, or even one who is both virtuous and morally good. At any rate, where Kant thinks a man is worse if, besides a sense of duty, he needs a virtuous desire to get him to do what is right, they think he is worse if, besides a good desire, he *needs* a sense of obligation to get him to do what is virtuous.

A complete *and* pure ethics of virtue would tell us, without any categorical imperatives, "Be virtuous, e.g., be courageous, generous, etc., and then do as you please," and insist that this is the whole law and the prophets. It would contain no judgments of obligation or moral goodness in Prichard's (or Kant's) sense — nothing but judgments to the effect that certain actions, dispositions, emotions, habits, motives, persons, or traits are good (in some nonmoral sense), virtuous, courageous, loving, etc., and that certain actions are instrumental in the achieving, maintaining, or manifesting of virtue, or such as the virtuous man would do. It might express judgments of this latter sort by using "deontic" words like 'right', 'should', and 'must', but then such terms would be derivative and secondary. Its basic terms and judgments would be "aretaic." How, then, would it interpret its own most basic formulae, "Be courageous," "Be virtuous," etc.? "Be courageous" might be regarded as meaning, "Being courageous is a virtue," but how would "Be virtuous" be regarded? Possibly as a command, as "Love!" is thought of by St. Augustine and Brunner, or, perhaps better, as some kind of instruction or, in Prichard's terms, as saying that virtue is intrinsically (not morally) good.

Of course, different ethics of virtue will differ in their lists of the virtues that belong to being virtuous. Greeks give more than one list, Christians still others, and Hume yet another. Some would be monistic, holding that there is only one "cardinal" virtue, for example, love or honesty; others would be pluralistic, maintaining that there are two, four, seven, or even more such virtues. For all ethics of virtue, however, the basic guide to life is one or more formulae like "Be V, and then do as you please." Much, in fact, everything depends for them on what V is, how it is defined or described, for only if we know this can we take any "Be V!" as a guide to judgment and action. Now, Prichard clearly thought, as we noted earlier, that the virtues are to be defined in a certain way, namely, as dispositions or tendencies to feel and act from intrinsically good desires arising from intrinsically good emotions. In the case of courage for example, the intrinsically good emotion is "a sense of shame" and the intrinsically good desire arising from it is "the desire to conquer one's feelings of terror," and the virtue is a tendency to feel this desire and to act from it in appropriate circumstances. Let us suppose that the proponent of an ethics of virtue adopts Prichard's way of defining the virtues, and stick to courage as our example. Then, as we shall see, if his ethics is anything like adequate, his "Be courageous" would be equivalent to "Act courageously," and this would mean the same as "Act from a desire to conquer your feelings of terror arising from the sense of shame which they arouse." This in turn, if what was said earlier is correct, would be equivalent to "Do such things as will enable you later to act from a desire to conquer your feelings of terror arising from a sense of shame at having them, and then act from that desire." This shows us what an ethics of virtue, couched in Prichard's terms, would be like, or, in other words, what he would think the ethics of the people we admire in Shakespeare and other writers is. Of course, one might object to Prichard's way of defining the virtues and yet advocate an ethics of virtue; then the general idea would be the same, but the details would be different.

IV

How would Prichard argue against the adoption of such an ethics? He does not do so explicitly, but it is clear that he would be opposed to any ethics of virtue, since he regards "the fact of obligation" as the central feature of the moral life. His opposition to any ethics of virtue is also shown by the dissatisfaction he expresses on reading Aristotle's *Ethics,* for it turns out that, whatever is true of other readers, *he* is disappointed with the *Ethics* because in it Aristotle is only giving us "a systematic account of the virtuous character" or, in other words, because Aristotle is expounding an ethics of virtue, not one of obligation and moral goodness.[10]

Part of Prichard's point in his essay is to show that the rightness or obligatoriness of an action does not rest on the goodness, intrinsic or moral, of anything connected with it — of the action itself, of its motive, or of its consequences, actual or intended. The "mistake" of moral philosophy, according to him, consists partly in the belief that the right is dependent in some way on the good. Would Prichard's point here, assuming it to be correct, count against an ethics of virtue? It would, if an ethics of virtue must recognize the kind of categorical obligation Prichard has in mind. We have already seen, however, that it need not. An ethics of virtue must make the virtue of an action rest on the virtue of the motive or disposition behind it, but this is another matter. It may also recognize hypothetical oughts, which tell us that to acquire, maintain, or manifest a certain virtue we must or should do something, but there is nothing in Prichard's argument (or Kant's) to show that it is a mistake to ground the hypothetical or instrumental rightness of such actions in the intrinsic goodness of the virtue.

One might take Prichard's thesis that "virtue is no basis for morality"[11] to be an argument against an ethics of virtue, and, indeed, it would be, if he meant it to say that virtue is no basis for an ethics or for a moral institution of life, and could prove this. For this is just what an ethics of virtue must deny. But Prichard only means by the thesis in question that virtue is not a basis for moral goodness, which, as he uses these terms, is true, but need not be denied by an ethics of virtue.

Another point made by Prichard in a different connection would have more serious implications for an ethics of virtue. He says,

> . . . it is, I think, . . . unquestionable that our approval [of actions] and our use of the term 'good' [as applied to actions] is always in respect of the motive and refers to actions which have been actually done and of which we think we know the motive.[12]

Here he is claiming in effect that all of our judgments about the goodness or virtuousness of actions are retrospective and removed, rather than prospective and direct, and, if this is so, then it is hard to see how an ethics of virtue can support its claim to be able to guide us in making direct moral judgments and decisions about what to do. But is his claim unquestionable? It is plausible; we do tend to express our direct moral judgments by the use of words like 'ought' and 'right' and to limit our use of words like 'good' and 'virtuous' to removed moral judgments.[13] Still, if I am faced with a situation, asking what to do, I need not ask, "What ought I to do? What would it be my duty to do? What is it right for me to do? What would it be right to do?" I can also, quite naturally, ask, "What is the good or virtuous thing to do? What would it be good or virtuous to do?" And if an ethics of virtue can tell me how to answer this question it will serve to guide my action.

The naturalness of this question — and the ease with which many people confuse it with the others — shows that our use of terms like 'good' and 'virtuous' is not always removed and retrospective and may function in the determination of future conduct as well as in commentary on that of the past. But even if it were basically removed and spectatorial, a proponent of an ethics of virtue might be able to counter this point of Prichard's by contending that, when we ask in a normal way what to do, we mean or should mean to ask what the virtuous (e.g., courageous) man would do, or which action it is, of those open to us, that would be judged by a spectator to be virtuous.[14] Again, if we have a way of answering this question, and really want to know the answer, then it may suffice us to be told, as Gower in *Confessio Amantis* is told by his confessor, to

. . . go where moral virtues dwell.[15]

For then this may, indeed, tell us how to live, even if a judgment of the form "Act A is virtuous" is always spectatorial and retrospective — provided, of course, that we know what the virtues are.

In this connection, we may look at another Prichardian point, which might be taken to show that an ethics of virtue really cannot answer the question what to do or how to act. This is the contention that it does not make sense to say, as a way of guiding our conduct, that we ought to act courageously, because "we can only feel an obligation to *act;* we cannot feel an obligation to *act from* a given desire," and to act courageously is to act from a desire to conquer one's feelings of terror.[16] Presumably Prichard thinks this partly because he believes that our desires are not in the control of our wills in such a way that we can have an obligation to act from a certain desire here and now, though we can have an obligation to take steps now to foster certain desires in ourselves. An advocate of an ethics of virtue may answer by avoiding the concept of obligation, but there remains a point to consider: if he seeks to guide us simply by telling us to act courageously, etc., and defines acting courageously, etc., as Prichard does, then he does imply that one can determine here and now to act from a certain desire, which, if true at all, is true only within limits. He must answer either by defining his virtues on other lines or by complicating his instructions to avoid this implication. But this, we have seen, he can and may do.

Earlier, however, Prichard stated his point a bit differently, as follows:

. . . the rightness or wrongness of an act has nothing to do with any question of motives at all [though its goodness does]. There is, and can be, no question of whether I ought to pay my debts from a particular motive. No doubt . . . if we pay our bills we shall pay them with a motive, but in considering whether we ought to pay them we inevitably think of the act in abstraction from the motive.[17]

This seems to me true, but again an advocate of an ethics of virtue can reply by avoiding the notions of obligation and rightness in any but a hypothetical or instrumental (or perhaps aesthetic) sense. But, once more, Prichard's point can be widened, this time to say that whenever anyone asks what to do, even if he does it by saying, "What would it be virtuous (e.g., courageous) to do?" he is only asking what action to do, not what motive to act from. And it does strike me that, if the only thing an ethics of virtue can tell me is to do the act which, if and when I do it, I will be doing from a certain motive, then it cannot do what is needed. One can hardly go about looking to see what motive he will be acting from, if he does a certain action, as a way of determining what to do.

Or perhaps one can. Perhaps it would make sense for a moralist of virtue to instruct us not to tell lies for fun, not to run because of fear, to return benefits with feelings of gratitude, and so on. This line of reply is not without difficulties, especially in conflict situations, but maybe it could be worked out. In any case, however, an ethics of virtue is not confined to saying simply such things as "Act courageously in Prichard's sense." It can define at least some of the virtues in "actional" terms rather than in terms of desires and feelings. Or, as we saw, it can amplify its instructions to say, "Do what will make you virtuous, and act from the motives you will then have." If it does this it can avoid the difficulties mentioned, even if it adopts Prichard's definitions. For then, before one has developed a strong and lasting desire to conquer one's terror, etc., one has only to do what will develop such desires in one, and when one has acquired such desires, one has only to act from them — one need not look to see what motive one can or will be acting from. In cases of conflict between virtuous desires one might act from the higher or more virtuous of the two, as Martineau suggested.[18]

There is a third possibility, and that is to instruct us, as Aristotle sometimes seems to, to do what the good man does, or rather, what the virtuous man would do. Such an instruction could cover both the period in life before one has acquired the virtues and the period after one has done so. It will, of course, do the job only if we have a way of knowing what the virtuous man would do, but this does not involve looking to see what our own actual or possible motives are; it only involves knowing what courage and the other virtues are, perhaps by way of definitions, perhaps in some other way. Of course, my action will not be virtuous on Prichard's kind of view, unless, when I do it, I do it from a virtuous desire, but it still may be such as a virtuous man would do or have done, even if he would do or have done it from a different motive.

So far, it appears that an ethics of virtue such as one might advocate on reading Prichard's footnote can plausibly answer, even if it is pure and complete, the objections that may be gleaned from the rest of his essay, especially if it does not define its virtues as he defines them. After all, however, as the footnote itself indicates, his strongest objection would be that "the fact [and the sense] of obligation" is and must remain the central fact of both moral experience and moral philosophy, not virtue. In another footnote Prichard seems to express this conviction by saying that, " . . . in the end our obligations are seen to be coextensive with almost the whole of our life," though "even the best men [e.g., those we read about in Shakespeare?] are blind to many of their obligations."[19] As we observed, his own dissatisfaction with Aristotle really is not that Aristotle makes the usual mistake of moral philosophy but that he is concerned wholly with virtue and not with obligation and moral goodness in Prichard's sense. Let us suppose that Prichard is right in his interpretation of Aristotle, which may be questioned, and that Aristotle is faced with this complaint. Then Aristotle might well reply, "Why should I concentrate my attention on your fact of obligation and your moral goodness? I am doing *ethike* and *politike,* not moral philosophy as you conceive it. Why should I do moral philosophy along your lines?" Prichard's only rejoinder finally seems to be something like, "Because obligation is a fact. We do have a sense of obligation." He might add, as Kant would, that moral goodness is better, a higher ideal, than virtue, even though he believes a combination of the two is still better, as Kant might. He might even hold that, when it comes down to it, living entirely by ideals of virtue, and not by respect for the moral law, is downright immoral — as Kant did. To me there is *something* essentially sound in this position. But it is not easy to get clear just what the truth is in this matter — or even just what the issue is. Certainly a mere assertion of the position will not suffice to settle the issue, except for one who is predisposed to agree. For a tough-minded proponent of an ethics of virtue (or are they all necessarily soft-headed?) would retort that the whole concept of categorical obligation is a mistake, as has been argued many times in many ways, a mistake possibly inherited from the theological legalism and voluntarism of medieval Christianity; that Shakespeare's heroes, like Homer's, were right in not allowing the sense of obligation to be "a dominating factor in their lives"; and that what ought (?) to dominate in our lives is love, honesty, and/or other forms of virtue.

V

Such would be the conception that Prichard would have of an ethics of virtue, and the kind of case he would make against it in any pure and complete form. He also has an argument against the kind of partial or mixed ethics of virtue that would posit one and only one obligation, namely, to make ourselves virtuous. Such a view, he says, proceeds as if "our only business in life was self-improvement, which is palpably contrary to fact" since we do have other obligations: to speak the truth, to repay a benefit, to pay a debt and keep a promise, and not to harm others.[20] It would be difficult for his opponent here to answer this convincingly, for, if he recognizes the existence of one categorical obligation, he will find it hard to stop short of admitting these others. But he could stand by his guns (or gun) and insist that our only obligation in life is, indeed, to make ourselves virtuous — honest, grateful, trustworthy, kind, etc. — and that then we are, without any sense of obligation, to do what we please. For then we will please to speak truth, return benefits, pay debts, keep promises, and not harm one another — and what more could be desired from a moral point of view?

Thus, by exploiting a footnote in Prichard, we have seen how the idea of an ethics of virtue may come up, as in fact it has in more recent moral philosophy; how an ethics of virtue might be formulated, whether partial and mixed, partial and pure, or pure and complete, though allowing that some other way of formulating it might be more satisfactory; and what Prichard's rather Kantian case against such an ethics of virtue might be. We have also seen, however, that proponents of such moralities need not regard this case as conclusive. As for myself, while I now have doubts about the simple position I once took,[21] I am inclined to remain on the side of Kant and Prichard. It does seem to me, however, that moral philosophy must do more than hint at an ethics of virtue in a footnote — or in an article or chapter. It must fully explore the possibility of a satisfactory ethics of virtue as an alternative or supplement to one of obligation and moral goodness, not only to explain what the people we admire in biography and literature live by, but to see what there is in our "new morality" and how we ourselves should or at least may live. It may even find, if it does so, that it has been based on a mistake Prichard did not recognize, one he himself made. But mistakes, like truth, must out.

13: Moral Education

IN AN ARTICLE ON THE PHILOSOPHY OF MORAL EDUCATION (HEREAFTER abbreviated as ME) one cannot avoid taking positions with which other philosophers disagree. Unless one is simply expounding and comparing the views of others, writing a philosophical article is not like writing one on Pestalozzi, analytical chemistry, or even progressive education, for such an article can be purely expository or historical. There is, however, no such thing as *the* philosophical view of moral education, which might be expounded here, and this piece must therefore take the form of one man's essay in the philosophy of such education. At the same time, it is not unfair to claim that the positions taken in it have a large basis of support in the thinking of moral philosophers, both classical and recent. Moreover, certain other views will at least be presented and discussed. It should be added that, being philosophical, this article will necessarily remain general and theoretical in character.

The concern of society, parents, and teachers about morality and ME has been perennial and often anxious. Yet today the question arises at once whether education should include any element or part that can be called specifically moral. For some writers, including some philosophers, maintain that, in the education of children, there should be no moral lessons or exercises, no inculcation of moral rules or ideals, no use of moral praise or blame (and, of course, no use of punishment or reward) or of any kind of moral language, argument, or exhortation — only love, sincerity, and sense. In fact, this seems to be the view of ME, if it can be called that, that is implied in "the New Morality." This rather drastic and paradoxical position — that ME should include no *moral* education — may, however, be regarded as a too extreme reaction to an older, more traditional, conception of ME; and perhaps the best answer to it is to describe a less radical position that also avoids the main objections to this older one. It is also in a sense a risky doctrine, since a general adoption of it in practice might eventuate in the disappearance from human life of moral forms of thought and expression and of morality itself as we have

Reprinted from the *Encyclopedia of Education,* Vol. 6, L. C. Deighton, ed. (1971), pp. 394-98, by permission of Macmillan Publishing Company, New York.

known it. To allow that to happen would be to throw the burden of maintaining society entirely on our resources in the way of mutual love, prudence, and law, even though history and experience seem to have shown the first to be in short supply, the second to be uncertain, and the last to be sufficient only if made so ubiquitous as to be intolerable.

The older conception of ME that, until recently a least, has more or less prevailed in practice, though not in philosophical theory, may be briefly described as follows. The task of ME is to inculcate the rules or "values" of prevailing morality and a disposition to live by them, not through the means of the law, but through the means of education; and these include, not only an appeal to reason where necessary, but habituation, indoctrination, punishment and reward, praise and blame, exhortation, example, catechism, etc. The main point about this view is its tendency to regard already achieved insight into the patterns of behavior to be inculcated as essentially complete and final, to think of the content of ME (and of morality itself) as consisting of relatively fixed and concrete rules or virtues like honesty and chastity, and to employ restraints, sanctions, and other non-rational methods in inculcating them. In Freudian terms, this older ME typically created an irrational conscience or superego through the internalization of parental and social rules and ideals; in Riesman's, it characteristically produced individuals who were tradition-directed, inner-directed (those who internalized or "identified with" the tradition), perhaps even other-directed, but not autonomous. There is a classic description of it in the great speech ascribed to Protagoras in Plato's dialogue of that name.

This older ME did include a use of specifically moral discourse, and, in spite of Socrates' doubts, it was not entirely ineffective, as is shown by the mere fact that society has been as stable and tolerable as it has. Criticisms of several sorts, however, have been and may be directed against it. First, as Socrates pointed out, and as every parent-generation has complained, it has not been so success-ful or so certain of success in fostering morality as one would like ME to be. Second, it bases its methods and program on false or inaccurate psychological and sociological views. Third, it uses methods of pursuing its goals that are inappropriate to anything properly called education and also immoral for adults to adopt in bringing up children, at least if their use can be avoided. Finally, it rests on a mistaken or at least inadequate moral philosophy: in using methods that are inappropriate to the moral institution of life, methods that are more appropriate to law than to morality; in regarding our past or present moral insight as essentially correct and our prevailing morality as too nearly final; in overemphasizing relatively concrete rules and virtues; and in underemphasiz-ing autonomy, freedom, and reason.

Even if one does not accept these criticisms without modification, one must agree with the extremists first mentioned that the older ME leaves much to be desired and should be given up if something better can be found. In fact, it has already been very largely given up in practice, if not in theory, by our so-called "permissive" culture, though without being replaced by any generally satisfactory substitute. Both on historical and on reflective grounds, therefore, we must find a conception of ME that falls between the two extremes described — one that differs from the "new" ME in using moral discourse and yet does not take the form of the old ME — much as Socrates, Plato, and Aristotle sought a middle and rational way between the Sophists and the Dogmatists, or between what Aristophanes already in his day called the New and the Old Educations.

What form should this more satisfactory ME take? The task of a program of ME, we may agree, is to bring about and maintain a moral social order in which each individual is, insofar as his native endowment permits, a morally good man and a fully developed moral agent, or achieves, in Maritain's words, "uprightness of the will" and "spiritual freedom," and which permits, so far as possible, each individual to have the best life he is capable of In spelling out what this task involves, however, philosophers would distinguish and discuss a number of possible subordinate aims:

(1) cultivating a grasp of "the moral point of view," or the moral way of judging actions and deciding what one should do, as distinct from, say, the aesthetic, legal, or prudential points of view or ways;

(2) fostering a belief in or an adoption of one or more fundamental general principles, ideals, or values as a final basis of moral judgment and decision;

(3) fostering a belief in or an adoption of a number of more concrete norms, values, or virtues, such as were mentioned in connection with the old ME;

(4) developing a disposition to do what is morally right or good;

(5) promoting the achievement of reflective, personal autonomy, self-government, or spiritual freedom, even if this leads the individual to criticize prevailing ideals, principles, or rules (in a way, this aim has two parts: autonomy and reflectiveness).

Of these several aims the older ME centers on (3) and (4), and the "New" ME on (5). There are, however, other alternatives for a more adequate ME to take.

A. There is a certain logical order in the progression from (1) to (5). Thus, having acquired an understanding of the moral way or point of view, one might take this point of view in one's quest for basic ideals or principles, and then, having found them, adopt a set of more concrete rules or virtues as ways of applying or realizing them, going on in this way to become a morally good person and a fully autonomous moral agent. A program of ME might, then, begin by seeking to foster a grasp of the moral point of view in the young, and continue by helping them through the succeeding steps of moral development as thus conceived. Indeed, to a philosopher such a program, carried out in the right manner, might seem to be ideal. It could, however, not be started on at any early age, for its inception would have to wait at least until the child attains the age of reason, and possibly even longer. One wonders, therefore, what form ME would take before that time comes. Now, it might be argued that, before that time, the child's education should be entirely non-moral, along more or less Rousseauian or Summerhillian lines, including "negative" education in the form of a prevention of bad dispositions and habits, but not including any positive moral instruction; but that, after the time in question, it should be specifically moral and follow the logical order just indicated. There is much to be said for this contention. But it implies that, while the use of moral discourse and reasoning would be a part of adult life, it could be kept out of the lives of children, and it is hard to see how this could be done. For that matter it is hard to see why we should resort to such discourse and reasoning at all, even later, if we can dispense with them for so long.

B. A form of ME more congenial to the spirit of "the new morality" would take as its aim merely the cultivation, with the help of a use of moral discourse, of the moral point of view, i.e., of an understanding of the moral way and a disposition to live within it; beyond that it would leave the young free and unguided, to "choose" their own ideals or principles, to determine their own rules, if any, to "decide" for themselves what is right and wrong, possibly on a purely "situational" basis without any appeal to rules, principles, or ideals. Here the emphasis would be entirely on (1), (4), and (5). About this view of the nature of ME the same comments may be made as about the previous one. About both of them one may add that it is also hard to see how the moral point of view can be cultivated without introducing children to any moral rules or standards. It would be like trying to teach a language without initiating a child into any of its literature, or to foster the scientific point of view without teaching him any science.

C. One might agree to this and admit that to aims (1), (4), and (5) must be added aim (2), namely, a fostering of certain basic, general ideals or principles, like love, equality, or the principle of utility, where this is conceived of as a way of teaching the moral point of view, and where it is understood that an individual may reject the ideals or principles he has been taught, and adopt others, when he comes to reflect on them from the moral point of view. Here the concrete rules or virtues of aim (3) might appear as possible deductions from the basic principles or ideals taught, but no particular set of them would in any way be taught or insisted on. This view of ME is also attractive in theory, but, again, it is not clear that it can be put into practice in the education of young children if they are not to be taught to follow any more concrete rules or models, at least for a time. Even Rousseau has Julie in *The New Héloïse* impose certain rules of conduct on her children during their early education.

D. We come, thus, to the conclusion that the best form of ME will include aim (3), as the older ME does, i.e., it will involve the positive teaching of certain relatively specific rules or virtues, even before any other ends are achieved; but, unlike the old ME, it will teach them in the context of aims (1),

(2), and (5), as well as (4), and hence with more stress on moral reflectiveness and freedom. Let us now look more closely at this sort of ME. Like the old ME it will use non-rational or pre-rational methods, i.e., it will involve the use of moral discourse and the citing of moral ideals and rules even before reason appears in the life of the child or has been sufficiently developed for him to reflect on them. It will, however, refuse to rely entirely on indoctrination and the use of non-rational methods throughout its course, for, like the "new" ME, it is concerned about autonomy and rationality, and not just about "law and order." It may take either of two shapes. In both shapes moral discourse would appear throughout, but the education would fall roughly into two parts, and in both the second part would involve reasoning and an appeal to reason; it is only with respect to the first part that there would be a difference. Both would use non-rational methods in this period of ME. But there are two ways in which such methods can be used. One is the way of indoctrination, i.e., the use of example, habituation, suggestion, exhortation, propaganda, and sanctions like blame and punishment, in such a way as to inculcate certain rules or virtues and with the purpose of ensuring behavior in conformity with them, not of preparing the way for reflection and spiritual freedom. The other is a more properly educational way that should not be thought of as indoctrination; it involves using some non-rational methods, e.g., example, environmental influence, and positive statement of rules or ideals, but keeps in view aims (1) and (5) and avoids the use of methods that are inconsistent with them. This kind of ME would make it more like teaching elementary geography, history, or science. Call them, respectively, D1 and D2.

D1, then, would involve the use of indoctrination during the first part of ME, following it with a period in which there would be an appeal to reason and a certain autonomy. This was approximately Aristotle's picture of ME, and perhaps Plato's too, though they both gave music of certain sorts a greater role in it than anyone would give it now. They also thought that the time for reason and autonomy would come relatively late in life and for most people not at all. More democratic thinkers today would hold that it comes somewhat earlier and to almost everyone. D2, on the other hand, would take the second approach and avoid indoctrination at all times, insofar as this is possible. D1 and D2 might, of course, be combined in a child's education, e.g., if D1 were adopted in church or home and D2 in school, but such a combination would have obvious difficulties.

D1 would presumably have the effect of keeping even the more autonomous and reflective members of society from adopting any very radical moralities, as Aristotle thought, and so of reducing the chances of moral anarchy or pluralism. But, by the same token, it would surely make any very full autonomy difficult to attain without trauma, since there would presumably be no continuity of approach between its two parts. It might even prevent many from attaining a degree of spiritual freedom who would be able to do so in D2.

What has been said points to an ME of form D and, more specifically, of form D2. Many people seem to think that there are only two alternatives in ME, namely, either to teach a closed morality with a definite set of rules or values by the method of indoctrination or to keep ME open and non-directive except where and insofar as reason can be appealed to. But there is another possibility, indicated by D2. A moral education along its lines would not be wholly "permissive," for it would seek to teach certain rules or virtues, principles or ideals, at least for a time, but it would not be authoritarian or impositionist either, since it would respect the child's integrity and approaching rationality at all times, much as his geography teacher might and should. It would accord with the view of recent psychologists who maintain that children need and even want to be provided with a set of rules or values, and cannot achieve a reflective morality of their own later, if they are not taught the rudiments of one earlier. Hopefully it is also a form of ME that will hold moral pluralism among adults within tolerable limits.

Our discussion of the *form* ME is to take has included something about its *methods*. To say more about the latter would involve going into questions of psychology. A little must, however, be said about the *content* of ME. Any program of form D2 will entail teaching some rules, principles, or ideals in connection with aims (2) and (3), but just which ones should be taught? Some answer that one should teach the ideals, principles, or rules regarded as desirable by one's society, others that one should teach those one regards as desirable oneself. Ultimately, it seems clear, we should teach those that we believe on careful reflection would be agreed to by all who reflect on them with similar care from the moral point of view. In practice, however, this may have to be modified somewhat, depending on the situation, e.g., on whether it is in the home, a public school, a church, or a church school that one is teaching. In public schools, of course, one's teaching must not include any specifically religious rules or values or make any appeal to specifically religious reasons or premises. There too it should explicitly follow the lines indicated in D2 rather than D1, being particularly careful to avoid indoctrination even while it is positive in teaching certain norms or standards. It should be added, however, that the main burden of ME, in whatever form, must be borne by the home and the community and not by the school. The school should play its part, and it is an important one, but it must not be asked to do the job alone, or even most of it, for then it will surely fail. And then parents and society will themselves be to blame. Any adequate program of ME necessarily presupposes a commitment to morality and its way in the home and in the general community.

The main question in connection with content has to do with aim (1), for the central point in ME as described above (A, B, C, *or* D) is that what has to be passed on is, finally, not any particular moral rule or virtue, but an understanding of what morality is and a commitment to thinking and acting in the moral way. A good deal could be said here because recent moral philosophers have debated at length about what is involved in understanding what morality is and in thinking morally for oneself. However, most of them would agree that the moral point of view or way of thinking entails (a) deciding for oneself what one should do, (b) deciding this, not by asking what one wants to do, what is to one's own advantage, or what will happen to one if one does this or that, but by some kind of consideration of what one's action will do to other people and of what it would be like if everyone were to act likewise. This means that, though children must be taught some concrete moral rules or virtues to begin with in order to help them get the moral idea, they must also be taught to judge and decide for themselves, to be willing to forego their own advantage if necessary, to be ready to recognize that what is right or wrong for one person to do is right or wrong for another to do in the same circumstances, to be able to imagine vividly what it is like to be someone else and what one's actions are likely to do to him, and, finally, in the light of such thinking, to frame new rules, principles, or ideals, if these seem indicated.

BIBLIOGRAPHY

1. Aristotle, *Ethics, Politics*
2. K. Baier, *The Moral Point of View,* Cornell, 1958
3. J. Dewey, *Moral Principles in Education,* Houghton Mifflin, 1909.
4. W. K. Frankena, *Ethics,* Prentice-Hall, 1963
5. R. M. Hare, *Freedom and Reason,* Oxford, 1963
6. T. H. B. Hollins (ed.), *Aims in Education,* Manchester University Press, 1964
7. J. Maritain, *Education at the Crossroads,* Yale Paperback, 1960
8. A. S. Niell, *Summerhill,* Hart Pub. Co., 1960
9. M. Oakeshott, *Rationalism in Politics,* Methuen and Co., 1962
10. Plato, *Meno, Protagoras, Republic*
11. R. S. Peters, *Ethics and Education,* Scott Foresman, 1966
12. I. Scheffler (ed.), *Philosophy and Education,* 2nd ed., Allyn and Bacon, 1966
13. J. Wilson, *et al., Introduction to Moral Education,* Penguin, 1967
14. F. J. E. Woodbridge, "Education," *The Son of Apollo,* Houghton Mifflin, 1929

14: "the principles of morality"

WE OFTEN SPEAK OF MORALITY AS A HUMAN OR SOCIAL ENTERPRISE OR institution more or less coordinate with art, education, law, and science, for example, when we ask how morality is related to law or to religion, or when we talk about the moral sphere as contrasted with the legal or scientific ones. Here "morality" is not used as the opposite of "immorality" but rather to refer to the moral as distinct from what is non-moral or pertains to other areas of human interest. This is what R. B. Perry had in mind when he said,

> . . . there is something which goes on in the world to which it is appropriate to give the name of 'morality.' Nothing is more familiar; nothing is more obscure in its meaning.[1]

Even when we think of morality in this way, however, we use expressions of two rather different kinds. On the one hand, we use expressions like: "the morality of the Chinese," "ancient morality," "the new morality," "business morality," "his morality," "a moral code." In such phrases "morality" seems to refer to something that is relative to an individual, group, or period, something that is variable and changeable. On the other hand, we also use phrases such as: "the moral law," "the moral ideal," "the morally good man," "the morally right way to act," "what morality requires," "the supreme principle of morality," "the principles (dictates, precepts, rules, demands, etc.) of morality." In these uses "morality" and its cognates appear to refer to something that is not relative and variable, something that is somehow absolute and unchanging — to something like what Ralph Cudworth called "eternal and immutable morality." These expressions imply or presuppose, not only that morality is an enterprise distinct from the others mentioned earlier, with its own ideals, principles, or requirements, but also that it is an enterprise in which only one ideal or principle, or one set of ideals or principles, is recognized as valid. Thus, on the one hand, we speak as if there are or could be many moralities or moral action-guides, and, on the other, as if there is or can be only one.

This distinction between what we may call "relative" and "absolute" uses of "moral" and "morality" has been somewhat neglected in our pluralistically and relativistically-minded culture, even by moral philosophers.[2] But there it is — and no account of morality that ignores it, or fails to give an analysis of both kinds of expressions, can be regarded as complete.

The need for recognizing the difference between these two kinds of expressions and two senses of "morality" can be illustrated by a sentence from P. W. Taylor: " . . . morality is a set of social rules and standards that guide the conduct of people in a culture."[3] This is what *a* morality or moral code is — it is a set of standards that guide the conduct of an individual or group. But "morality" as it is used in phrases of the second sort is, so I shall argue, not just a set of standards actually followed, but something more like the true set of standards.

In some earlier papers I dealt with the problem of defining morality in the sense in which it is something relative and variable, that is, I tried to say something about the criteria for distinguishing moralities from other things like religions, legal systems, etc., or for distinguishing moral action-guides from non-moral (as distinct from *im*moral) ones.[4] In this essay I shall pay attention to expressions in the second group, seeking to show what they mean and to defend their use, partly because their use is not entirely clear, and partly because it is constantly under attack in the century in which we live. Sometimes our culture and especially its sub-cultures seem to be opposed to morality in *any* form, but, in any case, though we continue to use the phrases in question, we seem on all sides to be against recognizing it in any *absolute* form.

I

Let us see then what we do or should take expressions in our second group to mean. I shall first state and consider four views about this and then propose and defend a fifth. Then in continuing my defense of this fifth view I shall present and discuss two more. Finally I shall conclude by commenting on an eighth position.

(1) To a "contemporary" who has gotten "with it," it is tempting to say the following: in the expressions of our second group we mean by "morality" and "moral requirements," etc., the prevailing and generally accepted ideals, rules, etc., of our culture or society (i.e., those that belong to *our* moral action-guide), and, when we say, "The principles of morality are . . ." or "Morality requires . . . ," all we mean is "Our society demands . . ." or "The moral code of our culture includes . . . ," or something of this sort. Students find this view hanging in the air about them like a smog, and breathe it in — and

out — as if it were healthy. It appears to be almost taken for granted in psychology and the social sciences. Philosophers, who ought to know better, sometimes also take it for granted. It is the sort of view Bertrand Russell summed up in the remark, "Conscience is the still small voice that tells you someone else is looking."

I submit, however, that this is not, need not be, and should not be what we mean when we use the expressions in question.[5] When one says firsthand that P is a principle of morality, he is himself espousing, and should be understood as espousing, P as part of his own moral action-guide; he is not just saying that it is part of the prevailing moral code — unless he is in effect using "morality" in quotation marks and gives us some indication that he is doing so.

Perhaps, in order to allow for this "inverted comma" way of speaking, we should distinguish between two ways of using the phrases under discussion.[6] There is an "external," spectator way of speaking, which is used when a psychologist or sociologist says, "The requirements of morality are just internalized parental rules." A legal scientist may make statements about what the law is in a similar sense, without subscribing to the law he is stating. Or, suppose that one of our "uncommitted" ones says, as he tramples on them, "So much for the dictates of morality!" He is not just a spectator or scientist then, of course, but he *is* an outsider of a kind who does not subscribe to what he calls "the dictates of morality," though his society does. There is, however, also an "internal" subscribing way of speaking, "prescriptive" in Hare's sense of prescribing to oneself as well as to others, which I take to be the normal one. Here the speaker assents to what he calls "the principles of morality" or just "morality," at least in his preaching, if not in his practice. He takes the moral point of view; he is not an outsider, a spectator, a scientist, a skeptic, or an "alienated" one — as our first theory implies that he is.

Returning to the consideration of this theory. it should be observed that it does not allow for the possibility of criticizing a prevailing morality on moral grounds — something we often do and presumably desire to go on doing. If by "the principles of morality" we *mean* only "the principles of our prevailing morality," then we cannot even suggest, let alone proclaim, that there are moral principles that ought to be recognized in our culture but are not. We can charge our morality with being unclear or inconsistent and we can accuse ourselves of not living up to it, but we cannot claim to have found any new moral principles or ideals. We also cannot condemn on moral grounds the moral code of another culture; we can only say that its principles are different from ours.

(2) The next "contemporary" move, of course, is to say, "Oh, that's right! When one says 'P is a principle of morality' or 'Morality dictates . . . ,' he does not ordinarily mean merely that others take it to be part of their moral action-guides. He is expressing his own moral convictions. What he means to say is

not 'My *culture* demands . . . ,' but rather, '*My* moral code requires . . . ,' not 'Someone else is looking' but 'I am looking.' More simply, he is saying '*I* approve of . . . ' — that and nothing more is what he means." This view of the matter is also mistaken. When one says "P is a principle of morality," one does not merely *assert* the *fact* that he subscribes to P or approves of action in accordance with P, or the *fact* that his own moral code includes P. He is actually approving or subscribing in his very statement; his utterance is "performative" in J. L. Austin's sense.[7] And this means, as I see it, among other things, that he is claiming in his utterance that acting on P and approving of such action are in some way justified or rational. That is, when one says, "It is a requirement of morality that . . . ," he is not just saying, "The prevailing morality requires that . . . ," *or* "My morality requires that . . . ," *or even,* "The morality I regard as valid requires that . . . ," *but* something like "True morality requires that . . . " This last statement may be construed as just a fancy way of saying, "We are morally required to . . . ," but then *this* does not mean simply "It is a rule of prevailing morality that . . . , " or "It is a rule in my moral code that . . . , " or "On what I regard as moral grounds I favor . . . ."

(3) A third and more sophisticated contemporary doctrine would reply as follows at this point: "Of course, when one says 'Morality requires . . . ,' 'The morally good man does . . . ,' or 'I approve of . . . ,' one is not merely *asserting that* something is the case about oneself, one's moral code, or that of one's society. One does not mean simply *that* one or one's society is in favor of something or regards it as the thing to do; rather, one is *taking* and *expressing* a pro-attitude toward a certain kind of character or conduct. But, either *that* is all one is doing or should be taken as doing, or one is doing that and also trying to evoke a similar pro-attitude in others — and *that* is all he is doing."[8]

The main point to be made in reply to this third view is similar to the one made a moment ago in dealing with the second contemporary move, namely, that when one says, "Morality requires . . . ," etc., one is not merely venting one's emotions or pro-attitudes and/or trying to arouse similar ones in others. In W. D. Falk's terms,[9] one is "guiding," not "goading" or commanding, oneself or others. Certainly one is not simply "expressing" oneself. One is claiming that some action, attitude, disposition, or way of life is justified or rational at least from the moral point of view.[10] One *is* having and expressing a moral sentiment about something, but one is not merely expressing it and seeking to evoke it in others. Rather, one is assuming it in oneself and others and then judging, from this point of view, that some action or way of life or quality of character is desirable, justified, or rational. And, in using the expressions we are studying in the ordinary way, one is subscribing to a certain action-guide and claiming that it is the "true" one from the moral point of view. Once again, "Morality requires . . . " means something like "True morality, which I hereby subscribe to and urge you to subscribe to, requires . . . ," where saying "True morality requires . . . " is not just a way of emphasizing one's pro-attitude or reinforcing one's goading of others, as "Big Brother is watching you" is.

Here I must comment on the phrase "true morality," which I have used once or twice and which crops up every now and then even in this "post-modern" age. It is an ambiguous expression and may have at least the following three meanings. (a) It may mean "true virtue," "true moral goodness," or "the truly right way to live." Then it refers to what is truly moral as opposed to *im*moral. In this sense, "True morality requires . . ." says much the same thing as "We have a moral obligation to do . . ."; the main difference is that it makes more explicit the claim that moral codes which do not require the conduct in question are mistaken (a claim also made by the latter utterance but only implicitly).[11] That is why the use of "true" here is not merely an endorsing or emphasizing use or even a "persuasive" one. (b) It may, for example in "a true morality," be used to refer to any action-guide that meets the "true" requirements for being a *moral* action-guide. Here it stands for what is truly moral as opposed to *non*-moral, not for what is truly moral as opposed to *im*moral. For example, P. F. Strawson seems to use "true morality" to mean any socially accepted action-guide that satisfies the ordinary concept of morality.[12] (c) It may also mean or be taken to mean "the action-guide that both passes the tests for being a moral (as versus non-moral) action-guided *and* the tests for being true, justified, rational, or valid, from the moral point of view." This is the sense in which I am using "true morality," and I believe it is what Kurt Baier means by "absolute morality."[13]

It follows from what was said in (1), (2), and (3) that "P is a principle of morality" does not mean "P is a principle in the code that I (and/or my society) take to be important, overriding, or supreme."[14]

(4) There is a fourth interpretation of expressions like "the principles of morality" and "Morality requires . . ." about which I ought to say a word. An anthropologist like Ralph Linton might argue that all accepted moral action-guides include certain prohibitions or requirements, e.g., not to kill a fellow-tribesman or citizen except in self-defense, and that "morality," in the phrases we are concerned with, should be taken to mean the totality of these universally accepted norms.[15] This interpretation has some advantages over the previous three — it gives our phrases a more objectivistic meaning than they do, as is required — but it will not do all that is wanted. It does not permit us to say that the principles on which all prevailing social moralities agree are not really the principles of morality. It tells us, in effect, that to find out what the principles of morality are we must and need only see what norms are actually accepted by all cultures. But what we mean — and want to mean — when we speak of "the requirements of morality," etc., is not the totality of universally prevailing norms, whatever these are, but rather, to quote a Dutch dictionary definition of the moral law (*zedewet*), *"het geheel van de normen die het zedelijk leven moeten beheersen"* (the totality of the norms that should govern the moral life)

— or, as I would prefer to put it, the totality of rationally justified moral norms, the action-guide that both fulfills the criteria for being a moral action-guide *and* is rationally most justifiable from the moral point of view.

II

(5) Thus I arrive at a fifth view, which has been adumbrated in what has been said, and which I shall now try to clarify and defend. An analogy with enterprises other than morality may help here. I wish to maintain that the expressions "moral requirements," "the principles of morality," etc., are like "science tells us . . . ," "history teaches us . . . ," "the laws of nature," etc. When one says "history tells us" or "science tells us" something, let us say *p*, then one is subscribing to *p*, but one is also taking or purporting to take the historical or scientific point of view and claiming that *p* is true or rationally justified by the evidence from that point of view, or as W. P. Alston might put it,[16] one is "taking responsibility for" its being rationally justified from that point of view. Or, in other words, one is subscribing to *p* from a certain point of view and claiming that everyone who views the evidence carefully from that point of view will eventually also subscribe to *p*. Notice here how different "history tells us" is from "historians tell us" and "science tells us" from "scientists tell us." Now I suggest that "morality tells us" is like "history tells us" and "science tells us" in this respect — and not like "moralists tell us," "society tells us," etc. — when one says "*p* is a principle of morality" one is taking or purporting to take the moral point of view, subscribing to *p* from that point of view, and claiming that *p* is rationally justified by the facts as seen from that point of view or that everyone who views the facts carefully from that point of view will eventually also subscribe to *p*.

A point about this fifth view needs clearing up. Roughly, I am holding that when one says "Morality requires P," he means by "morality" true morality in the sense of "the action-guide that fulfills the criteria for being a moral one and is rationally justified from the moral point of view" or "the moral action-guide to which all those who are fully rational within the moral point of view will eventually agree"; and he is in some way implying that he is both taking the moral point of view and subscribing to P. He is, however, not saying or implying that he actually subscribes to the true morality, since he may not know what this is (he claims that P belongs to it, but he does not now know that it does). Yet he is not speaking as an outsider or spectator either, one who is not subscribing to any moral action-guide but only to some belief or fact about himself or the society around him. He subscribes to true morality in intent or promise, just as in doing science one subscribes in intent or promise to the findings of science, whatever they turn out to be, or much as Socrates subscribed to the "laws" of Athens, whatever they might turn out to be, by the mere fact of his remaining there. In this sense, "the principles of morality" are something to be *discovered* (or possibly "revealed"), not something to be created, invented, or decided on by a sheer act of "decision" or "commitment" on one's own part, as so many seem to think nowadays. Thus I reject the notion that when one refers to "the principles of morality" one is simply referring to principles that one accepts as basic or proposes to adopt by some kind of fiat, though I do want to say that when one uses such phrases one *is* then and there subscribing to the principles one refers to.

Suppose, then, that I ask the question, "What are the principles of morality?" and set out to find the answer. The answer is not to look to see what Ps are accepted by me, my society, or everyone, or to make any sheer decisions, however anxious, authentic, profound, or even to look around for some Ideal Observers or gods and see what Ps they accept. It is to take a certain (the moral) point of view myself as fully and "coolly" as I can, get myself clear-headed, logically rigorous, and fully informed about relevant facts, and see what I cannot but accept under those conditions, much as I do when I ask and try to discover the principles of bookcase-building or the laws of nature and of nature's science. Even then the principles I accept (or "decide on") may not *be* "the principles of morality" but I will justifiably claim that they are and call them by that name.

Thus, in such expressions as "the principles of morality," "morality requires . . . ," "the moral ideal," etc., what is ordinarily referred to may be defined as that moral action-guide which, in Baier's words, "can be seen to be required or acceptable *from the moral point of view*" [17] — or, more fully, as the moral action-guide that everyone who looks at the world clear-headedly and informedly from that point of view will eventually agree on. [18] When one makes a moral judgment, espouses a moral ideal, proposes a moral code, etc., one subscribes to it as required from the moral point of view or claims that it is or is included in or entailed by "true morality" in the sense indicated above. In short, our moral discourse, especially in such expressions as I have been concerned with, involves the concept of an objectively or absolutely valid moral action-guide, and our moral judgments and decisions claim to be parts or applications of such an action-guide. Moreover, I maintain that we may and should go on thinking and speaking in this way.

III

In reply to this fifth view, which I am advocating, an opponent may take at least three lines of attack. (a) He may contend that there is no such thing as the moral point of view in any worthwhile sense — that there is an irreducible plurality of moral points of view such that there will also be an irreducible plurality of "true moralities" or of action-guides that can be seen to be required or acceptable from some genuinely moral point of view, with no rational way of choosing between them (except, perhaps, from some non-moral point of view). Part of the time, it looks as if H. D. Aiken means to mount this line of attack.[19] I am not convinced that it is anything like fatal to my position, but cannot discuss it here. (b) He may argue that, while there is such a thing as *the* moral point of view (as is claimed in every firsthand moral judgment), it is not true that everyone who takes that point of view and is rational within it will eventually find the same action-guide to be required or acceptable. Not all disagreements in attitude or action-guidance, he may say, are rooted in differences in factual belief, concept formation, or logic. Hence we ought to give up claiming any kind of rational or interpersonal justifiability or validity for our moral judgments and decisions, and eschew all talk of a true or absolutely valid morality — or, if we keep the talk for its "emotive" force, we should at least give up the idea that has gone with it. To this line of thought I can only say here that, though one cannot prove its premises to be mistaken, neither can its proponent prove them to be correct, and that I therefore choose to stay with the objectivism I take to be involved in our ordinary concept of morality. More generally, I see nothing in these two lines of attack that requires us to give up our absolutist ways of speaking or thinking, no conclusive reasons for accepting a proposal that we revise our moral thought and expression in a more relativistic or pluralistic direction. (c) But, in his essay on "The Concept of Moral Objectivity,"[20] Aiken advances a third line of thought that seems calculated, partly to show that the ordinary moral discourse we have been reviewing does not actually involve any such absolutism or objectivism as I have been describing, and partly to convince us that, even if it does, we ought to be brave, new, and mature enough to give it up. This line of thought is what I mainly want to discuss in the rest of this paper, in defence of my view as stated earlier.

IV

Before I do so, however, it will be useful to discuss a sixth view of the expressions we are concerned with — that of Roderick Firth[21] — together with Aiken's critique of this view.[22] On Firth's view, when I say "Morality requires . . . ," "The principles of morality are . . . ," etc., I am saying or mean that the conduct or principles in question are or will be approved by an Ideal Observer who is omniscient, omnipercipient, disinterested, dispassionate, and consistent. Against this position, Aiken has two arguments, both in essence familiar: (a) the open question argument, and (b) the argument that "disinterestedness," etc., cannot be defined "without reference to principles antecedently acknowledged as moral." Now, I am by no means convinced that these arguments come off, and, indeed, I still agree with Firth that, when I say "Morality requires . . ." or make any moral judgment, I am claiming that any Ideal

Observer would agree, though I worry about some of the details of his definition of an Ideal Observer, as R. B. Brandt and others have.[23] But I agree with Aiken in thinking that Firth's view — a form of ethical naturalism — cannot be accepted without qualification. For, as I see it, when I say "Morality requires . . . ," etc., I am not merely *asserting that* an Ideal Observer, however he or it may be defined, does or will or would approve or agree. I am not that purely cognitive or spectatorial; I am, as I said before, speaking as an insider, I am taking a pro-attitude myself, I am myself subscribing or approving at least in intention or promise — in short, I am trying to *be* an Ideal Observer taking the moral point of view and I am approving or disapproving on the basis of what I then see. As was intimated earlier, I am not simply looking around at Ideal Observers to see if any or all of them agree, though I am claiming they will if there are any, and profess a readiness to revise what I say if they do not. I also agree with Aiken to the extent of holding that any Ideal Observer appealed to must be taking a point of view antecedently acknowledged as moral, and I am not sure he is doing this simply in being disinterested, dispassionate, and consistent. Thus there is a good deal of force in Aiken's arguments against Firth; they do show Firth's view to be inadequate. But I do not see that they show more than this or that all forms of absolutism are mistaken — and I shall try to explain why.

V

Aiken's "bearings in moral philosophy," new or old, are in many ways much like mine. In particular, he would, I think, agree with my criticisms of the four views discussed and rejected earlier, except for the absolutism broached in them. At any rate, he also rejects those views. However, he resolutely refuses to accept anything like the fifth view I have been advocating, either as a descriptive-elucidatory thesis about our actual moral discourse and reasoning or as a normative proposal about them. He also adopts a more pluralistic position about the moral point of view; "there can be," he says flatly, "no such thing as 'the moral point of view' . . . ."[24] Thus he, in effect, provides us with a seventh view of the meaning of the expressions under investigation.

I cannot deal adequately with all of Aiken's complex but interesting and stimulating paper. For present purposes, the main point is that he offers us a non-absolutistic, quasi-existentialist conception of the objectivity claimed in moral judgments. It is non-descriptivist or non-cognitivistic, like mine, but, while it provides moral judgments with a *kind* of objectivity, as mine does, it denies them even the rather Peircean *claim* to being absolute that I take to be implied in them. Yet Aiken insists that his conception is faithful to "the ordinary notion of moral objectivity." I shall maintain that it is not.

It will be necessary here to quote at some length.[25]

In [the workaday] world the problem of moral objectivity is mainly a problem of piecemeal mutual adjustment of acknowledged commitments within a loose framework of precepts and practices, none of which is ever permanently earmarked as an absolutely first principle and each of which is subject to a list of exceptions that can never be exhaustively stated. . . .

What is wanted is not a better understanding of the hypothetical reactions of a perfectly objective somebody-else, but that conscientious second thought which enables us to take a more general view of our own existing responsibilities. Such a general view provides no definition of moral right and wrong; it does not require us to ignore "our own" when we find that their claims upon us cannot conscientiously be universalized; it does not demand that we treat "everybody," whoever they may be, as moral persons; nor does it commit us to some supposed consensus of moral opinion which all other "competent" moral agents must be presumed to share. In brief, there is and can be no absolute or universal vantage point from which conscientious moralists, regardless of their sentiments, may make an objective appraisal of their particular moral decision and principles. Morally, we are always in the middle of things, confronted with eternally exceptionable precepts which, until such exceptions have been made, still lay presumptive claims upon us that we cannot in conscience disavow. What provides the basis for such exceptions? Nothing save other particular principles which, in turn, we are forever driven to qualify in the light of still other principles. And when we come temporarily to the end of a line of qualifications what do we find? To our dismay, nothing but the very "first-level" duties with which we began.

The ordinary principle of moral objectivity thus prescribes, not that we look beyond the moral life itself for a ground of criticism, but only that we search within it for the soberest and steadiest judgment of which, in the light of all relevant obligations, we are capable. When a question arises concerning the objectivity of a particular moral judgment or principle, our task is always and only to look beyond *it* to the other relevant commitments which we ourselves acknowledge. And if this answer seems inadequate, then the reply must be that there is, in conscience, nothing else to go on. In the moral sphere it is always, finally, up to us; nor is there anyone to whose steadier shoulders our burden of moral judgment can be shifted. That is the agony of the moral life; it is also its peculiar glory.

The only principle of objectivity in morals is, then, essentially a principle of reconsideration. What it demands, when a question about the objectivity of a particular judgment or principle arises, is that we consider whether such a judgment or principle, as it stands, can be consistently upheld in the face of whatever other moral considerations might be thought, in conscience, to defeat it. . . .

In summary, there is and can be no definitive criterion of moral objectivity and, hence, no definitive principle of moral right and wrong. When a serious question about the objectivity of a particular moral judgment or principle arises, there is simply the further *moral* obligation to reexamine it in the light of the other obligations and duties that have a bearing upon it. If it should be

replied that objective reconsideration requires, also, an endless search for
new facts which, if known, might alter our notions of our obligations and
duties themselves, the answer must be that such a search would defeat the
very purpose of moral reflection, which is *judgment*. The principle of
objectivity requires only that we take account of any hitherto unconsidered
facts to which we may reasonably be expected to have access. But in that
case what is reasonable? There is no formula for answering such a question:
our judgment can be formed only by weighing the obligation to look for
relevant facts against other obligations. In a word, the principle of moral
objectivity can neither supply the materials for moral judgment nor tell us
where to go in search of them. If we have no time to search for further
possibly relevant facts, the principle of objectivity will provide us with not
one moment more; if we are otherwise lacking in moral sensibility, it will not
make good our deficiency by so much as a single obligation. What it can do
— and it can do no more — is to dispose us to review our decisions so that we
may neglect no pertinent fact that, in the time we have, is available to us and
that we may neglect no obligation which deserves to be considered. Primarily, therefore, it functions as a principle of falsification, and what consistently survives the general scrutiny which it demands may pass as objectively valid or true.

There is a great deal in these and in the supporting paragraphs that one must
agree with. I am ready to agree that it is in general correct as a description
(phenomenological?) of what we *do* when we are trying to solve a moral
problem or reach a moral conclusion either about a particular case or about a
general principle — even the bit about the agony and the ecstasy of the moral
life. What then is there in what Aiken writes here that a would-be absolutist of
my kind cannot accept? It is not "the principle of reconsideration," which
Aiken says is "the only principle of objectivity in morals." The necessity and
possibility of reconsideration is precisely what I regard as recognized in the
claim of a moral judgment that it will hold up through any further reconsideration. If Aiken is saying anything I must disagree with, as he certainly means to
be doing, it must be the following two things. (a) One is the contention that we
do *not* in fact claim in our moral judgments — not even when we use expressions of the second sort listed at the beginning — that they will be sustained by
all further reconsideration of them (and of any principles they involve) in the
light of "possibly relevant facts." This contention seems to be implied when
Aiken writes that the objectivity called for in "the world of workaday moral
problems and judgments" does not "commit us to some supposed consensus of
moral opinion which all other 'competent' moral agents must be supposed to
share."

(b) The other is the thesis that we claim *only* that our moral judgments will
hold up through a certain *kind* of rather *limited* reconsideration — that, while
we do claim a certain objective validity for our moral judgments, it is only a
limited one with no absolutism whatsoever in it. It should be noted here that, if

Aiken is saying only that all we ever *do* in our moral deliberations is to go through a limited and not an "endless" reconsideration, he is, of course, right. But any absolutist can admit this. After all, life is short and *tempus* does *fugit*. Again, if he is asserting only that it is sometimes reasonable and right to cut off our search for possibly relevant facts and to come to a moral "judgment," then he is right too. But, once more, no absolutist denies this; admitting it is quite compatible with holding that when we do come to make the judgment, we are claiming that it will be sustained by all possible reconsideration and not merely that it is the best we can do or reasonably be expected to do under the circumstances. Therefore, Aiken must be asserting (b). And, since (b) entails (a), we may concentrate on (b). What, then, is the limited kind of reconsideration that he regards as necessary and sufficient in morals?

Aiken describes it as follows in the paragraphs quoted: (1) as "a piecemeal mutual adjustment of acknowledged commitments within a loose framework of precepts and practices, none of which is ever permanently earmarked as an absolutely first principle and each of which is subject to a list of exceptions that can never be exhaustively stated"; (2) as a "search . . . for the soberest and steadiest judgment of which, in the light of all relevant obligations [and facts?], we are capable . . . our task [being] always and only to look beyond *it* to the other relevant commitments which we ourselves acknowledge"; (3) as considering "whether [our] judgment or principle, as it stands, can be consistently upheld in the face of whatever other moral considerations might be thought, in conscience, to defeat it"; (4) as taking facts into account as well as moral principles, but only such facts as "we may reasonably be expected to have access" to in the time available to us.

As I said, I believe that these descriptions add up to a very good account of all that we *do* or can be required to *do* in deciding moral questions — except that I would like to bring in the business of taking "the moral point of view," especially when it comes to reconsidering our moral principles (and Aiken comes close to doing this when he says "relevant" and "in conscience"). What bothers me here is the fact that Aiken is by implication reducing the *claim* of moral judgments to objectivity to a claim that they will be upheld by a reconsideration in the light of moral principles one acknowledges oneself and of such facts as one may reasonably be expected to have access to. What, it may be asked, is wrong with doing this? The trouble is that there is an ambiguity. Aiken must, it seems to me, assert one of two things: (1) that, when I make a moral judgment, I am claiming only that it is or would be upheld by a careful review of the matter in the light of the moral principles I *already* acknowledge and of the facts that I can reasonably be expected to have access to *at* or *before* the moment of judging, or (2) that, when I make a moral judgment, I am claiming that it is or will be upheld by a careful review of the matter in the light of the moral principles I *may come* to acknowledge "in conscience" and of the facts I *may come* to have access to and be reasonably expected to make use of in such a review.

Suppose that Aiken affirms the former, as his anti-absolutism suggests he must. Then I have three comments. (a) What he says strikes me as false — just as false as if one were to say the parallel thing about the making of factual judgments. It seems, especially, to be inadequate as an account of what we are to do when we reconsider our moral principles themselves — it does not even provide for the possibility of doing this. (b) Suppose that I did not make my moral judgment or decision carelessly — that before I made it, I did in fact make a careful review of the matter in the light of all the principles I then acknowledged and of all the facts I could then reasonably be expected to pay attention to. Then my claim to objective validity would be impeccable; I could in no sense say on the next day, if I came to acknowledge other principles and have access to further facts, that my judgment was mistaken. I could, if Aiken's view is that represented by (1), only change my mind, and would need to feel no anxiety about this, existential or otherwise. (c) According to (1), in reconsidering my judgment or decision the next day, I need (and may) only rethink the matter in the light of the principles I acknowledged *the day before* and of the facts I could *then* reasonably have been expected to consider. This is possible, but it seems clearly not to be what we should do when we are really reconsidering.

Suppose, on the other hand, that Aiken subscribes to (2), as he seems to when he writes that "the principle of objectivity may require reconsideration of any judgment [or principle?]." Then he is coming very close to the kind of absolutism about the objectivity claimed by a moral judgment that I have advocated. It may be that he would (in the interest of "autonomy") underline the "I"'s in the formulation of (2), so as not to bring in any claim to a possible consensus with *others*. But then I am not sure there really is a difference between us, especially if the individual making a moral judgment is not assumed to be in some special position with regard to the facts or particularly susceptible to certain kinds of principles, for then he can always be replaced by others. If, however, he is assumed to be peculiar or in some unique position, then, again, I think that (2) is plainly false — that Hume (who is not unadmired by Aiken) had things right when he said that in making a moral judgment I choose a point of view common to myself and others and express sentiments in which I expect all my audience are to concur with me.

At this point, Aiken would probably contend that there is no such thing as *the* moral point of view, so that there must always remain an irreducible pluralism in the moral enterprise. He does say this at least twice.[26] This contention is, however, not established by the discussion we are reviewing, and, I have already intimated, Aiken seems to recognize something like the moral point of view when he speaks of "conscience" and "moral commitments."

In this connection Aiken might make some play with the open question argument.[27] (a) It looks as if he would use it against all attempts to define the moral point of view and the distinction between moral and non-moral action-guides. That is, he would insist that one can say of any point of view or action-guide, "Yes, it fulfills your criteria, but is it moral?" And, of course, one can, if by "moral" one means the opposite of "immoral." To allege, however, that one can always say it when one clearheadedly means by "moral" the opposite of "non-moral" is to beg the question, which is precisely whether the definition is satisfactory or not.[28] (b) More to the point here is the fact that it appears as if Aiken would also use a kind of open question argument against all kinds of absolutism, and not only against that of Firth. Then, against me, for example, he would have to argue that one can always say of something, "Yes, it would be approved by all those who are fully rational within the moral point of view, but is it morally right (or good)?" or "X might be approved by all those who are fully rational from the moral point of view and yet not be morally right (or good)." My reply comes in two parts. First, I grant that one can agree that X is or would be approved by all who are fully rational within the moral point of view and not agree that it is morally right or good. For one might be what I earlier called an outsider or spectator and not be ready to make any moral judgment whatsoever. As I said before, when one says "Morality requires . . ." or makes any moral judgment, one is not merely asserting that it is or would be agreed to by all who are fully rational from the moral point of view; one is oneself taking that point of view and judging from it. But, secondly, if anyone is to get mileage out of the open question argument at this point, he must claim that an *insider* who speaks from the moral point of view or "in conscience" can sensibly ask the open question. And this I doubt. An insider could say, "X may be approved by all . . . and yet *be* wrong or bad." But can he sensibly say that it would be approved by *anyone* who . . . and then *himself* go on to *judge* that it is not right or good? Perhaps he can if he is himself not clearheaded or fully cognizant of relevant facts or not taking the moral point of view (as he claims to be), though I am not sure that he could in that case know that X is or would be approved by those who take the moral point of view, are clearheaded, etc. Suppose, however, that he is himself fully cognizant of relevant facts, etc., and actually taking the moral point of view. Then, surely, there *is* at least a "pragmatic paradox" in his saying that X would be approved by all who . . . and then going on to disapprove of it. For then his own moral judgment constitutes an exception to the statement he has just made and presumably has not yet forgotten.

It does not appear, then, that an open question argument is fatal to the form of absolutism I have advanced, and we may conclude that we both do give and may go on giving an absolutist sense of the kind indicated to such expressions as "the principles of morality," "morality requires . . . ," etc., and, for that matter, to all our firsthand moral judgments. *Should* we continue to do so? One could at this point reply simply by asking, "Why not?" But, it is worth suggesting that it may be man is fully human only insofar as he asserts in himself "the image of God," as people used to call it, and bravely claims for his enterprises — science, history, art, and morality — some kind of final and rational validity.

VI

There is an eighth position about which something may now be said against the above background, namely the view that "the moral law," etc., refer to the commands of God. This position makes "the principles of morality" stand for something that is or is claimed to be absolute, and so is like the fifth and sixth positions discussed above (mine and Firth's), and opposed to the others, including Aiken's. But it may take either an intellectualistic or a voluntaristic form, depending on its answer to the question, "Is P commanded by God because it is a principle of morality or is it a principle of morality because it is commanded by God?" If it gives the first answer, we may interpret it as holding that God commands what he commands because he takes the moral point of view and is fully rational within it (clearheaded, fully-informed, etc.). Then it is essentially a form of either the fifth or the sixth of the above positions and stands or falls with them. If it answers that P is a principle of morality simply because it is commanded by God, then and only then does it really constitute a seventh position — one that is absolutistic and yet conceives of the principles of morality as being ultimately (not for us but for God) matters of arbitrary choice or decision. God might then have made not-P a principle of morality simply by deciding to; his choice between P and not-P would not be dictated by his nature, by his reason, or by anything whatsoever. No claim would be made that he is taking the moral point of view or that his choice will be sustained by the consideration of rational beings. When I say "P is a principle of morality" I would be claiming that God wills that we act on P, but not that P will be agreed to eventually by all who take the moral point of view and are rational within it.

Now, I doubt that, when we say, "P is a principle of morality," we *mean* only that P is commanded by God. For, once more, when we say this, we are also indicating that we ourselves accept P as a part of our own moral action-guide (perhaps *because* we believe it to be commanded by God). This point, of course, can be accepted by the theological voluntarist with only a slight emendation of his position. It also still seems to me, however, that, when we accept P as a principle of morality, we are claiming more than simply that it is commanded by God. For (a) we do most naturally give the intellectualistic answer to the above question, as is shown by Socrates' conversation with Euthyphro, (b) if we give it up, this is not on the basis of a study of moral concepts or discourse, but on the basis of theological considerations, and (c) we really believe that God commands P (as a "moral" principle, as distinct from a "positive" duty like keeping the sacraments) only if we believe that P is rational or justifiable from the moral point of view. Else we have a sense of utter paradox, as we do if we take seriously the case of Abraham's being commanded by God to sacrifice Isaac. In fact, I suggest that what makes the equation of the principles of morality with the law of God plausible is precisely an implicit assumption that God *is* fully rational and *does* take the moral point of view. With this assumption it makes perfectly good sense to say that the principles of morality are those that would be sustained by the judgment of God, and even an atheist may agree.[29]

VII

There is a poem by Wallace Stevens that I cannot refrain from using in conclusion. It is entitled ''Sketch of the Ultimate Politician,'' but, with what precedes in mind, I could wish it had been called ''Sketch of the Ultimate Moralist.''

> He is the final builder of the total building,
> The final dreamer of the total dream,
> Or will be. Building and dream are one.
>
> There is a total building and there is
> A total dream. There are words of this,
> Words, in a storm, that beat around the shapes.
>
> There is a storm much like the crying of the wind,
> Words that come out of us like words within,
> That have rankled for many lives and made no sound.
>
> He can hear them, like people on the walls,
> Running in the rises of common speech,
> Crying as that speech falls as if to fail.
>
> There is a building stands in a ruinous storm,
> A dream interrupted out of the past,
> From beside us, from where we have yet to live.

If I am right, then we are all would-be ultimate moralists, whether we know it or not, when we use expressions like ''the principles of morality.'' For then there is a total building of which we are all dreaming. And there are words of this that come out of us and beat about the shapes and run in the rises of common speech — words like ''the requirements of morality,'' ''the right thing to do,'' and ''the moral ideal.'' These words have rankled for many lives and made no sound, but today, when that speech falls as if to fail in the ruinous storm of our time (the new morality, God-is-dead-ism, and all that), they remain like people on the walls crying to us from where we have yet to live.

15: On Defining Moral Judgments, Principles, and Codes

WE MAY DISTINGUISH THREE METAETHICAL PROBLEMS ABOUT MORAL judgments: (a) that of defining the distinction between them and other kinds of normative (or evaluative) judgments, (b) that of analyzing moral judgments, concepts, or terms (e.g., explaining the meaning or use of "good" and "right" in their moral senses), and (c) that of justifying moral judgments. Of these, (b) and (c) are the standard problems of twentieth-century British and American metaethics, but (a) is the problem most discussed recently. This paper will deal only with (a), in the conviction that, if we can answer that problem, and if we can provide a satisfactory account of the analysis and justification of normative judgments in general, then we can also answer the other two problems.

Two further remarks are necessary by way of introduction. (1) I shall discuss the problems of defining, not only moral judgments, but also moral principles and moral codes (or moral value-systems). These three kinds of moral entities are closely related. A moral principle is a general moral judgment like "We ought to treat people equally" or "Love is a virtue," and a moral code is a set of one or more moral principles taken as forming a complete moral guide (in conjunction, of course, with relevant factual premises). But a moral judgment may be particular, and, if it is, it may be thought of as an application or consequence of a moral principle or code. On the other hand, it need not be thought of in this way; one can regard moral principles and codes as inductive generalizations from particular moral judgments, or one may even hold that morality consists entirely of particular or situational judgments and has no place for principles or codes.

(2) I shall be trying to define the distinction between moral and *non-moral* normative judgments, principles, and codes, not the distinction between moral judgments, principles, and codes and *immoral* ones. The word "moral" has two very different uses: as the opposite of "immoral" and as the opposite of

English version of essay which appeared (in Polish) in *Etycka,* Vol. 11 (1973), pp. 45-56.

184

"non-moral." In the first use, it means "morally good" or "morally right"; in the latter, it is used simply to identify one kind of normative judgment, principle, or code, without making any moral or evaluative judgment about it. Here we shall be concerned with the second use.

I

Something must be said about three views on our topic that have been proposed recently.[1] (1) Some hold that a moral judgment, principle, or code is any normative judgment, principle, or code that is not only accepted by an individual or society, but universalized, i.e., judged to be such as anyone should act on in similar circumstances. This view will not do, however, since every normative judgment is universalizable; if one holds that X is good or right in any sense, then one must hold that anything like X, or like X in relevant respects, is good or right in the same sense, moral or non-moral. (2) Others contend that a judgment, principle, or code is a moral one if, besides being universalized by its holder, it is taken by him to be overriding. This formula is ambiguous. It may mean either that a judgment, etc., is a moral one if it actually takes priority in the life of its holder, or that it is so if he thinks that it ought to take priority in his life. But we do not believe that a man's moral judgments, etc., always in fact control his conduct. Moreover, we often think that one moral judgment or principle should take precedence over another, without thinking that the second thereby loses its status as a moral one. We do not even always think that a moral consideration ought to prevail over all others, as is shown by the fact that we sometimes allow non-moral considerations to count as reasons or at least as excuses for not doing what morality requires. In fact, we even talk sometimes as if the question "Why should I be moral?" is one that can sensibly be asked. For all of these reasons, it appears that the second view cannot be satisfactory either.

(3) Both of these views may be regarded as seeking to define moral judgments, etc., wholly in terms of their form as distinct from their matter or content. A third, somewhat different, position is that they can be defined by reference to the feelings, emotions, or attitudes with which they are characteristically associated. The difficulty in this position is that it is not easy to see how moral feelings, etc., can be distinguished from non-moral ones, independently of any consideration of the judgments, etc., with which *they* are characteristically linked.[2]

Two other positions strike me as much more promising. One is that moral judgments, etc., may be defined by reference to the "point of view" from which they are made or accepted, viz., the moral point of view, just as aesthetic judgments, etc., or scientific ones, may be defined by reference to the taking of the aesthetic or scientific point of view.[3] The other is that moral judgments, etc., may and must be defined, at least partly, in terms of their content or matter. Since the former raises the difficult problem of defining the moral point of view, let us consider the latter first.

II

It is not always possible to tell whether a judgment or principle is moral or not by its content. It is sometimes said that a moral judgment or principle is one that tells an individual how to act in relation to others. Actually, however, a reference to others is not always included in a moral judgment or principle. "One ought to restrain one's appetites" is not necessarily a moral principle, but it may be one even though it makes no mention of others. On the other hand, "You ought to visit your aunt in the hospital" may not be a moral judgment even though it does mention both you and your aunt. In both cases, whether the judgment or principle is a moral one or not seems to depend, not on its content — so far those who favor formal definitions of morality are correct — but on something else, namely, the grounds on which it rests or the reasons the speaker would give to justify it. Thus, either of our examples may be aesthetic, prudential, or moral, depending, not on what it says, but on what is or would be said in favor of it. To this extent the view we are considering is on the right track. Incidentally, it would also, if it turns out to be tenable, give us a way of defining moral feelings, attitudes, and emotions, viz., as those to the assessment of which certain kinds of consideration are relevant.

If, then, one rejects "formal" and "affective" definitions of morality, as I have, and means to espouse a "material" concept instead, as I do, then one should characterize the moral in terms of the justification given. Now, however, it may be asked, "What makes a reason for a normative judgment a moral reason rather than an aesthetic or prudential one?" Sometimes, of course, the reply is obvious. If the justification given of a certain normative judgment, J, includes another normative judgment or principle, K, that is a moral one, as is often the case (for example, when the second judgment cited above is justified by appeal to the principle of keeping promises), then the reason for J will be a moral reason and J will be a moral judgment. This, however, presupposes that we know when K is a moral judgment, which is our question over again. If J is a moral judgment because K is one, and K is one because of the reason given for it, and if we are not to be involved in a circle or an infinite regress, then we must hold that K is sometimes moral just because of the kind of fact adduced in its defense. What makes normative judgments, etc., moral ones, if our present line of thought is correct, must be the fact that a certain kind of factual reason is given in its support when it is challenged.

It might be objected here that no factual premise can by itself be a reason for a normative judgment, and that, therefore, what makes a basic normative judgment a moral one is just the fact that no reason can be given for it — the fact that it is arbitrary or at least autonomous. On this line of thought, however, all normative judgments will turn out to be moral ones in the end, which hardly seems plausible.

Three problems now loom up for the view we are exploring. (1) What kind of fact is it that must be cited as a reason for a moral judgment, principle, or code? (2) If one builds into the definition of a moral reason any restriction on the kind of fact that can count as such a reason, is one not taking a normative moral position rather than a neutral metaethical one? (3) How can a fact of the kind in question be a reason for any moral judgment? We must consider these three problems, however briefly.

III

Some religious people seem to define the moral law as the law of God, and to think that a "law" is a moral one if and only if the reason given for it is a fact about the will of God.[4] In my opinion, however, while it may be possible to erect a normative system of some kind upon a foundation of such facts about God, something different, or at least something more, is needed to make it a moral system. John Gay, a theological utilitarian who makes the will of God central in his ethics, implies as much when he says,

> . . . virtue generally does imply some relation to *others:* where *self* is only concerned, a man is called *prudent* (not virtuous), and an action which relates immediately to *God,* is styled *religious.*[5]

Today, those who define morality by reference to the kind of fact given as reasons for its judgments and principles usually specify facts about the interests, needs, or desires of people or sentient beings, about what benefits, harms, or affects welfare.[6] Both proponents and opponents of this view tend to think that it implies that morality is essentially utilitarian, i.e., that utilitarianism of some sort is by definition the only adequate morality. It seems to me, however, as it does to the opponents, that, if this is so, then the view must be rejected as taking sides on an issue in normative ethics, viz., the question of deontological versus utilitarian ethics. However, if the view can be stated so as not to do this, it seems to me to be moving in the right direction.

I think it can be so stated, if it is put more generically, i.e., if it is taken to say that X gives a moral reason for A (and makes a moral judgment) if and only if X seeks to justify A by citing facts about what A does to the sentient life of those affected, including facts about what it does to *other* sentient beings as such, if such facts obtain or are thought by X to obtain. Such a formulation will obviously cover utilitarian conceptions of morality, but it will also cover those of deontologists like Kant and W. D. Ross. Indeed, it is suggested by Ross's remark that "when we think of an act as [morally] right we think that either something good or some pleasure for another will be brought into being."[7] It covers considerations of justice, however these are conceived, as well as considerations of welfare. The only received position excluded from morality by it is that of ethical egoism, but this does not disturb me, for while it does seem natural for philosophers to call this an ethics, it does not seem natural for anyone to call it a morality. It would, of course, also exclude ethical aestheticism, i.e., the view that takes aesthetic "facts" as the reasons to be given for normative judgments about conduct, if this were seriously proposed as an answer to our question. But, again, it would seem that any definition of morality ought to exclude such a view.[8]

IV

This discussion of our first problem has already touched on the second, which has been nicely posed by W. P. Alston. He asks if any analysis of the concept of a moral reason or judgment which "supposes that it is inherent in the concept of morality that certain kinds of facts and not others are relevant to moral issues . . . can be justified." Then he says,

I am rather inclined to doubt that it can. It seems to me that when one proposes any such restriction on what will count as a moral reason, he is in effect presenting a certain moral position (on, e.g., what makes an action morally right or wrong) rather than elucidating the metaethical concept *moral,* a concept that applies to every substantive moral position.[9]

Now, I have suggested that the restriction I have stated does not rule out any "substantive moral position" that can plausibly be regarded as a morality. Several other remarks may be added to take away the force of this widely used objection to any material definition of morality such as we are discussing.
   (a) It must be remembered that a substantive normative judgment or principle is not necessarily a moral one. When a normative judgment, etc., is a moral one is precisely the question at issue here, and it must not be begged. (b) It is true that a metaethical theory about the meaning of "moral" (as opposed to "non-moral") may be normative; if it is not purely reportive or descriptive of ordinary use, it will embody at least a modicum of conceptual legislation or revision. It does not follow, however, that it is morally normative or embodies a substantive moral position. Whether it does so or not depends, on the view here in question, on the kind of reason it gives for its proposal, and these reasons need not be moral. They may consist, for example, of considerations like simplicity and the avoidance of ambiguity or vagueness. (c) What makes an action morally right or wrong is a substantive normative question, because any issue about what makes an action *right* or *wrong* is such a question. But, by the hypothesis in question, to say that A is morally right is to say that it is right on

moral grounds or for moral reasons. And saying that A is right on any grounds is a normative judgment, though not necessarily a moral one. However, to say that the grounds on which A is right are moral grounds rather than non-moral ones is not to make a substantive normative judgment (let alone a moral one), for to say *this* is not to say that anything is good or right. If this is so, then restricting the range of what will count as a moral reason does not necessarily entail taking a substantive moral position or even a normative one, at least not if the proposed restriction accurately reflects the ordinary use of words like "moral."

(d) To hold that what makes actions morally right or wrong is facts about what they do to the sentient life of those affected is not to say *which* facts of that sort make actions morally right and *which* facts of that sort make them morally wrong. It is only to say what makes an action morally right *or* wrong, i.e., what *kinds* of facts are relevant to moral judgments, pro *or* con. It is not to give a criterion for determining what is morally right and what is morally wrong — as any "substantive moral position" does. (e) As far as I can see, one may accept a certain definition of morality (of moral reasons, judgments, etc.), even if it contains a "material" clause restricting the range of facts that count as moral reasons, and yet not accept or make any moral judgment or principle whatever. In other words, one can accept any definition of morality that contains such a clause and still refuse to accept any substantive moral position.

I believe, therefore, that satisfactory answers can be given to our first two problems. What about the third? How can a fact of the kind in question — or a fact of any kind — be a reason for any moral judgment? Can an Is be a reason for a moral Ought? If so, how?[10] It looks as if the position here in question must say that facts of the kind indicated are reasons for moral judgments, etc., because morality is by definition the enterprise of making normative judgments about what is right or good on the basis of facts of that kind rather than on the basis of facts of other kinds. Philippa Foot seems to imply just this about the "practice" of morality when she writes:

> Anyone who uses moral terms at all . . . must abide by the rules for their use, including the rules about what shall count as evidence for or against the moral judgment concerned. For anything that has yet been shown to the contrary those rules could be entailment rules, forbidding the assertion of factual propositions in conjunction with the denial of moral propositions. The only recourse of the man who refused to accept the things which counted in favour of a moral proposition as giving him a reason to do certain things or to take up a particular attitude, would be to leave the moral discussion and abjure altogether the use of moral terms.[11]

Such an answer to the third question may not seem convincing to those who doubt that a fact can be a reason for a normative judgment. In fact, it may be plausibly argued that, even if one agrees that the use of certain kinds of facts is definitive of the practice of morality, one cannot actually use such facts as reasons for normative judgments and actions unless one espouses the practice — which one may refuse to do — and then it is one's espousal of the practice and the conative attitude involved that carries one from the facts to the normative conclusion, as Mrs. Foot herself recognizes in the last sentence quoted as well as earlier when she admits that one can agree X caused offence by indicating lack of respect and yet deny X was rude, if one rejects "the whole practice of praising and blaming embodied in such terms as 'polite' and 'rude'."[12] Here, however, we are raising questions that apply to all normative judgments — problems (b) and (c) of our opening paragraph — not issues that are peculiar to the kind of definition of moral judgments under discussion.

V

Even so, one is still tempted to ask, in connection with definitions of that kind, what it is that makes facts of the sort they refer us to reasons for moral judgments, and this question brings us to the other line of thought mentioned at the end of Section I, for that approach has at least a verbal answer, viz., that what makes a certain fact a reason for a moral judgment (and so makes both the reason and the judgment moral) is the adoption of a certain point of view. This line of thought, which I find attractive, implies that there is something that may be called a point of view — something corresponding to the aesthetic or scientific point of view, something like "the farmers' point of view" or "the agricultural point of view" but more abstract than either of them — that is taken when one makes a moral judgment or adopts a moral principle or code; and it argues that one's judgment, principle, or code is, directly or indirectly, a moral one if and only if one takes this point of view in making or adopting it.

As was indicated earlier, the central problem about this alternative is that of defining the moral point of view (MPV), and, directly or indirectly, there has been much discussion of this topic in recent moral philosophy. Some apparently would seek to define the MPV in formal or affective terms such as are used in the views dealt with in Section I, e.g., one might define it as a disposition to universalize one's judgments and principles, or at least some of them, to take them as overriding, etc. Then the present alternative would coincide with one or another of the positions dismissed earlier.[13] Three other possibilities remain. One is to identify taking the MPV with taking facts of a certain kind, e.g., facts about what actions do to the sentient life of those affected, as reasons for at least some of one's normative judgments. If one does this, one's view is essentially that discussed in Sections III and IV. A second is to hold that adopting the MPV includes taking such facts as reasons for normative judgments but also includes something more, viz., a disposition to be for or against something (presumably not just a disposition to make normative judgments on the basis of such facts). Thus, Jon Moline defines a point of view (PV), or rather taking a PV, as including a tendency to have and pursue certain aims and interests, as well as a tendency to use only certain criteria in the evaluation of actions, traits of character, etc.[14] The third is to try to define the MPV without reference to any concern with any particular kind of fact (and without falling back into one of the views reviewed in Section I) — and without building in any substantive moral principle or position.

For all three of these views, adopting the MPV involves a tendency to make normative judgments from a PV, and it is the fact that a normative judgment is made from that PV that identifies it as a moral one. On all three positions one can, as seems to me desirable, say both (a) that X makes a moral judgment about O if and only if X takes the MPV in making a normative judgment about O, and (b) that X makes a moral judgment about O if and only if X makes a normative judgment about O on the basis of facts of a certain kind. For on all of them one may hold (c) that X takes the MPV in making a normative judgment about O if and only if X makes a normative judgment about O on the basis of facts of a certain kind, if not as a necessary truth, then at least as a contingent one. The first two have the advantage of being clearly able to claim that the MPV can be identified without presupposing any independent ability to tell which normative judgments are *moral* and which are not. The third has the advantage, if it can be worked out, of putting one in a position to maintain that moral judgments, etc., are those for which we give reasons consisting of facts of a certain sort, and that what makes facts of that sort moral reasons is the fact that they are seen to be relevant from the MPV. The last two have the advantage of making it possible to give a more satisfactory answer than the first can provide to the question how facts of a certain sort can be reasons for moral judgments, since, for them, taking the MPV entails having a conative disposition of some kind (other than a disposition simply to make normative judgments on certain grounds).

We have, in effect, already studied the first possibility. About the others much could be said, but I must be brief. In fact, I shall content myself with a personal statement. There is to my mind something inadequate about the answer of the first of the three views to the last question raised in Section IV, because it seems to me that one cannot make a first-hand moral judgment unless, besides appealing to facts of a certain kind, he has some conative disposition toward things of which such facts are true, other than a mere disposition to make normative judgments on the basis of such facts and to act on them. The view that appeals to me most, for reasons already indicated, is one of the third sort, such as attracted Hutcheson and Hume, but I see now no clear way to work such a view out in a satisfactory form. For the moment, then, I rest with a position of the second kind. I am inclined to think that a view of this sort may be tenable if one can say both that facts of a certain kind are reasons for a normative judgment (or for an action) only *because* they are relevant or seem to be relevant from a certain PV, and that this PV is *moral* only because it finds facts of the kind in question relevant and decisive; and I see no reason why one cannot say both of these things.

VI

Somewhat tentatively, then, I arrive at the following position: a "material" conception of morality holding: (a) that normative judgments, principles, and codes are *moral* ones if and only if, besides being universalized, they are backed, at least when challenged, by reasons consisting of facts about what actions, traits of character, etc., do to the sentient lives of those affected, including others if others are affected; (b) that such facts constitute *moral* considerations or reasons because they matter from a certain point of view that includes having a certain conative disposition; and (c) that this point of view is the *moral* one just because it includes a conative disposition responsive to such facts (not necessarily because it, in turn, is justified by appeal to such facts or to facts of any other restricted kind). There remain, of course, the problems of describing further the nature of this point of view and of justifying it — as well as that of exploring the possibility of working out the third view referred to earlier.[15]

16: Sidgwick and the Dualism of Practical Reason

It is well-known that Sidgwick finished his examination of "the methods of ethics" in some difficulty. Just what that difficulty was and how he came to be in it, we shall see in due course. This paper is written in the conviction that what he was doing is worth looking at again in the context of contemporary discussion.

I

Sidgwick begins by defining two concepts: that of "ethics" and that of "a method of ethics." Ethics is not morality; it is a "study," namely, the study of "what is right or what ought to be, so far as this depends upon the voluntary action of individuals."[1] A method of ethics is "any rational procedure by which we determine what individual human beings 'ought' — or what it is 'right' for them — to do, or seek to realize by voluntary action."[2] A number of points must be noticed about these definitions. (1) Ethics has to do with questions about what individuals ought to do; questions about what societies ought to do belong to politics. (2) Ethics is concerned primarily with determining what is materially or objectively right, not what is formally or subjectively right. (3) No use is made in these definitions of qualifiers like "moral" or "morally"; ethics and methods of ethics are described as asking what is right *sans phrase*, not what is "moral" or what is "morally" right. This is not accidental, though I doubt that it was consciously done by Sidgwick, and it is interesting. For Sidgwick, the question of ethics is to determine what an individual ultimately ought to do in the situations he faces, not what he ought to do on some special kind of ground or from some special point of view; and a method of ethics is a view about the manner in which an individual is to

Reprinted from *The Monist*, Vol. 58, No. 3 (1974), pp. 449-67, with the permission of the author and publisher. Copyright by the Open Court Publishing Company.

determine what he ultimately ought to do. Sidgwick himself believes that what one ultimately ought to do is what it is ultimately rational or reasonable for one to do, or what is "categorically prescribed by reason," but he twice remarks that, to have an ethics, one need not take some end or principle to be prescribed by reason, one need only adopt it as "ultimate and paramount"; for, if a person takes any end or principle as ultimate and paramount, he will have a method for determining what an individual finally ought to do in particular situations.[3] In saying this Sidgwick associates himself with a view of morality (though he does not use this term here) that is popular but debated today, namely, that a moral principle, end, or ideal is one that is regarded as overriding all others, whatever its content or ground may be.

Here it seems to me that Sigdwick goes too far, and farther than his general position otherwise permits him to go. For he otherwise insists that judgments of right and wrong involve a claim to be reasonable or "prescribed by reason." This strikes me as in some sense correct, but if it is, then judgments based simply on what one takes as "ultimate and paramount" cannot as such be ethical ones. The most Sidgwick can consistently say is that a method of ethics follows from any end or principle recognized as "ultimately reasonable," whatever its content. Even this is going too far to my mind, but at least it has some plausibility. In any case, Sidgwick limits his discussion to such ends and principles as the common sense of mankind appears to accept as ultimately rational, and his aim in discussing them is to help us to see which of them are in fact ultimately rational, or, in other words, to aid us in finding the most reasonable method of ethics. Still, as far as I can see, his assumption is that the ultimate ends or principles of "practical reason," whatever they may be, are *ipso facto* the ultimate ends or principles of ethics or morality.

It is true that Sidgwick often uses the term "morality," and with it "moral," in a somewhat narrower sense. In one place he distinguishes prudential and moral judgments, saying that while "both kinds might, indeed, be termed 'moral' in a wider sense," nevertheless "in ordinary thought we clearly distinguish cognitions or judgments of duty from cognitions or judgments as to what 'is right' or 'ought to be done' in view of the agent's private interest or happiness," and he adds that "the depth of the distinction will not . . . be diminished by [a] closer examination of these judgments."[4] Here I take him to be thinking that all normative or practical judgments may be called moral in a wide sense, and that moral judgments in the narrower sense form a distinct species of them. In a rather unclear discussion he then goes on to distinguish moral judgments in the latter sense from those of law, "Art," and etiquette, as well as from hypothetical and prudential imperatives. It looks as if he thinks that what distinguishes moral judgments in this narrower sense is the property of being categorical — or, in other words, ultimate. He also argues that the notion of "ought" or "moral obligation" involved in such judgments is indefinable; it is "essentially different from all notions representing facts of physical or

psychical experience'' and ''too elementary to admit of any formal definition'';
it ''cannot be resolved into any more simple notions.''[5] This, however, he
believes to be true also of the ''ought'' in prudential and hypothetical imperatives, and hence is not a special feature of the moral ''ought.''[6]

In this connection Sidgwick also says that the word ''ought'' is used in two
senses. In the stricter sense, ''I ought'' implies ''I can,'' in the wider sense it
does not. The latter use, he says, is normal ''in the precepts of Art generally,
and in political judgments'' — he also calls it ''the political 'ought'.'' The
former is the ''ethical'' sense of the term, and ''the sense in which [it] will
always be used in the present treatise, except where the context makes it quite
clear that only the wider meaning . . . is applicable.''[7] It just is the sense of
''ought'' that appears in Sidgwick's opening definitions.

It seems clear, then, that these passages contain nothing inconsistent with our
earlier interpretation of Sidgwick, nothing that gives aid or comfort to those
(like myself) who today hold out against the view I have ascribed to him. This is
confirmed by another passage in which he raises the question ''whether [ethical
egoism] ought to be included among received 'methods of *Ethics*,' since there
are strong grounds for holding that a system of morality, satisfactory to the
moral consciousness of mankind in general, cannot be constructed on the basis
of simple Egoism.''[8] Sidgwick's answer is, in effect, that it is proper to call
ethical egoism an ethics because it is generally regarded as ''reasonable for a
man to act in the manner most conducive to his own happiness'' and because it
is in fact ultimately reasonable for him to do so. Interestingly, although
Sidgwick is willing to call ethical egoism an ethics, he does not, so far as I can
find, call it a morality, though he does call intuitionism and utilitarianism
moralities,[9] and does not even ask whether they are methods of ethics. This
seems to me as it should be.

II

If it is true that Sidgwick equates the questions ''What is ethically right?''
and ''What is ultimately prescribed by practical reason?'' a very interesting
consequence follows. As Lionel Trilling pointed out in his Sidgwick Lecture,[10]
Sidgwick was largely motivated in his moral philosophizing by a worry about
the ''conflict,'' apparent, actual, or possible, between ''duty and self-
interest.'' This comes out very nicely in the autobiographical sketch prefixed to
the seventh edition of Sidgwick's book.

> . . . it is surely the business of Ethical Philosophy to find and make explicit
> the rational ground of such action [the subordination of Self-Interest to
> Duty]. I therefore set myself to examine methodically the relation of Interest
> to Duty . . . . This investigation led me to feel very strongly *this* opposition,
> rather than that . . . between so-called Intuitions . . . and Hedonism . . . .

Hence the arrangement of my book. . . . I put to [Mill] in my mind the dilemma: —Either it is for my own happiness or it is not. If not, why [should I do it]? . . . I must somehow *see* that it was right for me to sacrifice my happiness for the good of the whole of which I am a part.[11]

We shall see later what the upshot of Sidgwick's investigation was. My point now is that, given the assumption mentioned earlier, Sidgwick's concern about the choice between duty and interest was wrong-headed or at least wrongly formulated. For him the terms "right," "ought," "duty" and "should" are all roughly equivalent. But then, if the right or one's duty is whatever it is ultimately rational for one to do, one cannot sensibly ask why one should do it, whether it is to one's interest or not. One may be motivated not to do it and may resist doing it, but one cannot pose the first question Sidgwick does in the passage quoted or the question he puts elsewhere, "Why should I do what I see to be right?" For then one is asking why one should do what he recognizes to be ultimately rational for him to do. Similarly, to use Sidgwick's other way of describing a method of ethics, if what is right is a function of the end or principle one adopts as ultimate and paramount, then one cannot intelligibly ask why one should do what is right, whether it is in one's interest or not. One can ask whether it is right to sacrifice one's happiness for the good of the whole, but only if one has not acknowledged the latter to be, by itself, ultimately prescribed by reason or even ultimate and paramount.

To be fair to Sidgwick, himself the fairest of men, one must admit that he seems implicitly to see this in his own discussion of the question, "Why should I do what I see to be right?" In view of what he writes in his autobiographical sketch, one would expect a long discussion; in fact, it is incidental to his answer to another question (why the topic of the nature of the moral faculty is a part of ethics) and very brief. He points out that we frequently ask, "Why should I do what I see to be right?" but never "Why should I believe what I see to be true?" Then he says,

It is easy to reply that the question is futile, since it could only be answered by a reference to some other recognized principle of right conduct, and the question might just as well be asked as regards that again, and so on. But still we do ask the question widely and continually, and therefore this demonstration of its futility is not completely satisfactory; we require besides some explanation of its persistency.[12]

Notice that Sidgwick does not deny that the question is in some sense futile. I do not believe that he would agree that it is futile for the reason given, namely, that it involves one in an infinite regress. For he does not himself allow that there is an infinite regress of principles of right conduct; he holds, in fact, that there are self-evident principles of this sort, as we shall see. But he may be seeing darkly that when one comes to such an ultimate principle one cannot sensibly ask why one should act on it, at least not if it stands alone.

At any rate, Sidgwick asks only why the question is so persistent, and his answer is not that it persists because it is a sensible question after all. It is that we persist in asking it because we — ordinary people — have different and possibly conflicting principles or methods of ethics in our minds, which are "not brought into clear relation to each other." If this is so,

> . . . it is easy to see that any single answer to the question "why" will not be completely satisfactory, as it will be given only from one of these points of view, and will always leave room to ask the question from some other. I am myself convinced that this is the main explanation of the phenomenon: and it is on this conviction that the plan of the present treatise is based.[13]

The implication seems to be that Sidgwick thinks the question would not persist (except as a request for motivation) if we had a single consistent view about what it is ultimately reasonable to do, since we would then see that it is not a sensible one. At any rate this is what he should have thought. But then his problem about the conflict of duty and interest disappears; the only difficulty is that of determining what one's duty is, and, given a clear head and a knowledge of the relevant facts, this will finally be a problem only if we cannot find a single conflict-free method of ethics to apply.

III

Sidgwick's real trouble is that in the end he finds himself unable to see through to a method of ethics that is clearly conflict-free and also otherwise satisfactory. In this sense, he remains finally in a state of mind much like the one he ascribes to us ordinary people in his explanation of our asking why we should do what is right. In him ontogeny recapitulates phylogeny, as my biology professor used to say. He distinguishes three main methods (or families of methods) among those advocated by philosophers and less clearly present in ordinary thinking: ethical egoism, utilitarianism, and "intuitionism." The first two he generally thinks of as teleological and hedonistic. By "intuitionism" he means deontological intuitionism, the view that "conduct is . . . right when conformed to certain precepts or principles of Duty, intuitively known to be unconditionally binding."[14] The bulk of his book consists of an examination of these three methods. He concludes that, while no one of them has the whole truth and nothing but the truth, each of them has part of the truth. In fact, he finds or thinks he finds three self-evident principles or intuitions corresponding to the three methods: the Principle of Rational Egoism, the Principle of Rational Benevolence, and the Principle of Justice. He also finds "by a more indirect mode of reasoning" that hedonism is correct in holding that happiness or pleasure is the sole ultimate end or good.

It is not necessary for our purposes to quote Sidgwick's most careful statements of the three principles. Roughly, the first says that one should seek his own good or happiness, the second that one should promote the general good or happiness, and the third that similar cases should be treated similarly. The main problem is that of the relations of the three principles to each other. Sidgwick's answer is not entirely clear. On the whole he seems to regard them as independent. He also seems to think that the Principle of Justice can be recognized both by the Egoist and by the Utilitarian.[15] He says both that it "belongs" to or is "required" by Utilitarianism and that it is needed as a supplement to the Principle of Utility: "we have to supplement the principle of seeking the greatest happiness on the whole by some principle of Just or Right distribution of this happiness."[16] The latter statement implies that the Principle of Justice may conflict with the Principle of Rational Benevolence and require a somewhat different course of action from that which simply maximizes the balance of happiness over unhappiness. This does not seem to worry Sidgwick, though it should. What worries him is "the relation of Rational Egoism to Rational Benevolence," which he regards as "the profoundest problem of Ethics."[17] This is the form the problem of duty versus self-interest finally takes for Sidgwick. As he puts it in his autobiographical sketch, "The rationality of self-regard seemed to me as undeniable as the rationality of self-sacrifice."[18] He saw no way of establishing the coincidence in practice of the two principles and

> concluded that no complete solution of the conflict between my happiness and the general happiness was possible on the basis of mundane experience. . . . I could not solve [it] by any method I had yet found trustworthy, without the assumption of the moral government of the world: so far I agreed with both Butler and Kant.[19]

Here it is important to understand that for Sidgwick the two principles in question are not merely intuitive or self-evident, each of them is also an ultimate principle of actual or absolute duty in Ross's sense. Neither of them is a principle that holds only *prima facie,* or *ceteris paribus,* or from a certain point of view. Neither of them admits of any exceptions or of being overriden by the other. It is true that Sidgwick sometimes represents them as if each is reasonable from a different point of view, one from that of the individual and the other from that of the universe. He even speaks in one place of "two kinds of reasonableness," one in which an individual "considers his own existence alone" and another in which "he takes the point of view of a larger whole."[20] But, if this were all he means to maintain, then he would have no more need to postulate "the moral government of the world" than Ross does. He has this problem only if and because he really believes that both principles are seen to be absolute and to be rational from the same point of view. He seems to see this, though somewhat unclearly, in a tangled reply to something Rashdall had said, in which he takes the position that it is "*actually* reasonable for an individual to sacrifice his own Good or happiness for the greater happiness of others" and that it is "no less reasonable for an individual to take his own happiness as his ultimate end."[21]

Now, if this is Sidgwick's view, then, as was intimated before, his problem is not one of a possible conflict between duty and self-interest but one of a possible conflict between two absolute and ultimately rational, even self-evident, principles of actual duty, one telling us to seek our own good and another telling us to promote the general good. He is left, even at the end of his inquiry, with (at least) two different methods of ethics, though he clearly means us to live by that of Utilitarianism as modified by the Principle of Justice. This means that, even if we follow him, we can still ask, if there seems to be a conflict between the Principle of Benevolence and that of Egoism, whether it is right to sacrifice one's own good, though we cannot ask whether we should do what is right. The point is that we cannot then tell what is right, since we have still two methods of doing so that seem to yield different answers — unless we can demonstrate or may postulate a coincidence in practice of the two principles. Unless such a coincidence obtains, we are left, not with an opposition of duty and interest, but with a dualism of practical reason, or, in other words, of ethics.

It should be noted that Sidgwick is not thinking at this point that our duty of self-interest and our duty on other grounds do actually sometimes conflict; if this were so their coincidence could not even be postulated. He is thinking only that the coincidence cannot be demonstrated and seems in our mundane experience not always to obtain. He has then two alternatives. One is "to admit an ultimate and fundamental contradiction in our apparent intuitions of what is Reasonable in conduct," from which admission "it would seem to follow that the apparently intuitive operation of the Practical Reason . . . is after all illusory."[22] It is one of Sidgwick's conditions of self-evidence that "The propositions accepted as self-evident must be mutually consistent" and he takes this to mean that if two intuitions, principles, or methods conflict "one or other of them must be modified or rejected."[23] At this point, however, he thinks we do not know that they conflict, and so, since the two principles seem to him indisputably self-evident (*qua* absolute and ultimate), he drops or seems to drop this first alternative. It seems to me that two ethical principles cannot both be regarded as self-evident if it is in principle possible for them to come into conflict, and that even a postulate of coincidence in practice cannot save them both. For the coincidence might obtain only because of a fortunate accident about the constitution of our world, and not be true of other possible worlds. But this is a hard question and Sidgwick does not consider it.

Commenting on it, C. D. Broad writes as follows:

> Sidgwick's difficulty was that *both* the principle that I ought to be *equally* concerned about equally good states of mind, no matter where they may occur, *and* the principle that I ought to be *more* concerned about a good state in my own mind than about an equally good state in any other mind, seemed to him self-evident when he inspected each separately. And yet they are

plainly inconsistent with each other, so that, in one case at least, an ethical principle which is in fact false must be appearing to be necessarily true.

Broad goes on to say that to him pure egoism seems plainly false and utilitarianism not plainly true. Then he adds that no postulate can free ethics from the inconsistency Sidgwick finds, if it is really there. The two principles are simply "logically incompatible" and no postulate can alter this fact. Sidgwick should have drawn the conclusion that something which seemed self-evident to him must in fact have been false. These remarks are correct for the situation as Broad sees it. It is not clear, however, that the two principles as Sidgwick understands them are actually *logically* inconsistent (as Broad states them, they are). Sidgwick seems rather to think of them merely as possibly and apparently conflicting in practice. The rule of telling the truth and that of keeping promises may conflict in a certain case, i.e., call for different courses of action, but they are not logically incompatible even if conceived as rules of actual, and not just *prima facie*, duty; and it might be the same with Sidgwick's two principles. If so, it would still be open to him to postulate their coincidence in practice, provided there is in our mundane experience no clear case of real conflict between them — and one can always contend that there is not, if one is willing to allow that mundane cases may be reversed by transmundane action.[24]

The other alternative, which Sidgwick does seem to take, is, of course, to postulate the coincidence, or, in his words, "the moral government of the world."[25] In answer to a question put by Georg von Gizycki, Sidgwick says that, if he were convinced that the required coincidence does not obtain, he would not think it necessary or even reasonable "for us to abandon morality altogether," but only that it is necessary "to abandon the idea of rationalizing it completely."[26] Here his remarks are ambiguous. He talks in terms of a conflict between duty and interest again (or still), and hence he may mean by "morality" only the determination of what is right by considerations other than self-interest (as I think he should). Then by the impossibility of rationalizing it he would mean the impossibility of showing that it is completely rational to do what is right on such considerations when it is contrary to self-interest. But he has already said that it is rational *sans phrase* to sacrifice one's own good in the general interest, and also that one has a duty *sans phrase* to seek one's own good. To be consistent, Sidgwick must mean by "morality" simply ethics as defined at the outset, in which case it will include the Principle of Rational Egoism, and the impossibility of rationalizing it will mean the impossibility of "avoiding a fundamental contradiction in one chief department of our thought," namely ethics, or the necessity of recognizing "the dualism of Practical Reason." Rather than admit such a contradiction or dualism Sidgwick seems ready to espouse a theological postulate, though he ends uncertainly on a hypothetical note.

This account of Sidgwick's conclusions is based on the later editions of his book (the sixth, which was the last in which he himself made any corrections, was the first to include his autobiographical sketch). In the first edition his concluding state of mind was more despairing. He was not yet ready to adopt, even tentatively, any Kantian-type postulates of practical reason and ended by writing,

> . . . the Cosmos of Duty is thus really reduced to a chaos: and the prolonged effort of the human intellect to frame a perfect ideal of rational conduct is seen to have been foredoomed to inevitable failure.[27]

IV

I implied a little earlier that Ross and others, like myself, who accept two or more ethical principles that may in principle conflict in particular cases, and who therefore think of them as principles of *prima facie* and not of actual duty (i.e., as *ceteris paribus* principles), need no such postulate as Sidgwick does. Is this so? Ross does not, because he holds that in conflict situations we can still intuit or somehow *see* what it is right to do. Suppose, however, that one does not hold this, as I do not. Existentialists and their friends and relations would say that then, in conflict situations, we must simply make a *decision* about what is right, either a "decision of principle" as Hare calls it or a decision only for the particular case. For them there is no right action in such situations apart from such a decision, and hence also no need for a postulate that enables us to escape the anxiety involved. In fact, it would be cowardly and hence wrong for us to resort to any such postulate. But suppose we also reject this sort of decisionism or voluntarism, as I do. Must one then not posit a preestablished harmony between one's ethical principles? One can avoid this conclusion if one finds that one can convincingly — and not simply by making a decision — assign all of one's principles an order of priority that rules out the possibility of conflict in cases in which we are careful, clear-headed, and know the relevant facts. But suppose again that one believes, as I do, that one cannot do this. Then one can argue that, if one finds two of one's principles conflicting, one is to revise them, restating them in such a way as to eliminate the conflict. But to take this line — or the previous one — is in effect to give up the idea of *prima facie* duties and to try to come out only with principles of actual duty that do not conflict. Suppose, however, that one thinks it desirable to stick to the notion of principles of *prima facie* duty and also thinks that one has found formulations of principles one can plausibly regard as expressing such duties. Even without his intuitionism, Ross might think this.

It is in any case rather implausible to postulate a lack of conflict between any two of Ross's dozen or so principles. But, once more, suppose that one thinks they can be reduced to two, as I do, or to three, as Sidgwick does. Then, finally, we must ask what role a postulate of coincidence in practice between two principles would play. It would, I take it, put one in a position of being free, in the event of a conflict between those principles, to act on either one of them, and yet feel that he was doing the right thing. This would not mean that he would be without anxiety, but it would transfer any anxiety he might feel from the action to the postulate. It would, however, also mean, in effect, that one could treat either one of the principles involved as a principle of actual duty. Indeed, the net practical effect for Sidgwick of his postulate would be to leave him free to advocate Utilitarianism, supplemented by the Principle of Justice, as our working method of ethics. It seems to follow, then, that the idea of a postulate of coincidence between two or more principles is incompatible with their remaining principles of *prima facie* duty. If one means to keep the conception of *prima facie* duty for all of one's basic principles one simply must run the risk of being mistaken in one's judgment of what one should do in conflict situations — unless one is willing to fall back on intuition or resort to decision. If one wishes to eliminate the risk of being mistaken, and rules out intuition and decision, one must seek principles of actual duty. And then, if one believes that one's principles do not fall into a hierarchy and is convinced that no further revision is either desirable or necessary, one must be making some kind of postulate of coincidence even if one does not say so — unless, perhaps, one is willing to make use of the so-called Law of Double Effect.

What about the risk of being mistaken in one's particular moral judgments? Insofar as one runs this risk because one is uncautious, confused, or ignorant of relevant facts in the case in question, no postulate of coincidence can help one to eliminate the risk of doing what is materially or objectively wrong. One must remember, however, that one can be a good man in acting even when he does the wrong thing — especially if he does the wrong thing only because the best method of ethics he can find after the most careful inquiry, does not always tell him what to do even when he is careful, clear, fully informed about the facts, and bent on doing what is right. Being good does not require a postulate of the coincidence of one's principles even if it is not merely a matter of meaning well (Thank goodness!).

V

Returning to Sidgwick and reflecting on his predicament, one might take the following line. One might argue that, whatever is true of ethics, which is a philosophical study, *morality* should be defined in such a way that "intuitionism" and utilitarianism will be moralities or moral action-guides but "ethical egoism" will not. I have on occasion suggested such a definition of morality myself.[28] Then one could accept Sidgwick's three principles as self-evident, but, assuming that the principles of benevolence and justice do not conflict (as Sidgwick seems to), avoid having to admit *moral* dualism. One could then also speak naturally of a conflict between moral duty and interest and ask sensibly why one should be moral or do what is morally right when doing so is contrary to one's self-interest. However, though taking this line while keeping the rest of Sidgwick's set-up fits in better with our ordinary ways of speaking, it would not change the situation much substantively; we would still have to admit a dualism of practical reason, if not one of morality.

One might then take a more drastic view of the matter, arguing that Sidgwick's final position is simply untenable, because intuitionism, taken in its current metaethical sense, is a mistake, and there are no self-evident principles of the sort he thinks he finds. This view seems to me to be correct, and it does change the form of Sidgwick's problem, but I am not sure that it either solves or dissolves it. For a more up-to-date thinker might reply that, although Sidgwick's principles are not intuitively known or self-evident, they still are such as would be acknowledged by one who is fully rational, i.e., clear-headed, logical, cognizant of all that is relevant, and in Butler's sense "cool." Alternatively, he might maintain that they represent three criteria of rationality or, in Sidgwick's own words, three kinds of considerations that "we commonly regard as valid ultimate reasons for acting or abstaining."[29] Either way, he might say, we are still left with a dualism, perhaps even with a trichotomy, of practical reason, though it would be somewhat different in the two cases. Many writers dealing with the question, "Why should I be moral?" have taken some such view of the principle of egoism, assuming that being moral is rational if and only if it is, in words Sidgwick quotes from Butler, "for our happiness, or at least not contrary to it."[30] And Kant and Hare take some such view of the principle of justice, holding that the place of reason, in ethics at least, is an insistence that we universalize our maxims. It is harder to find thinkers who have adopted such a view of the principle of benevolence, but no doubt there are some.

These adaptations of Sidgwick raise very difficult questions, and I hardly know what to say about them. Assuming that they accord the three principles equal status in their respective versions, one might still conclude that the only way out is to postulate an absence of conflict even if mundane experience seems to provide cases of it. I am myself inclined to adapt a line of thought thrown out by Sidgwick but not taken advantage of by him, possibly because he rejects it. He does not hold that "good" is indefinable, as Moore alleges he does, and in the course of his discussion of the meaning of "good," he considers and does not clearly reject the possibility that "a man's future good on the whole is what he would now desire and seek on the whole if all the consequences of all the different lines of conduct open to him were accurately foreseen and adequately realised in imagination at the present point of time."[31] What I suggest is that we regard a line of conduct as rational *sans phrase* for me to engage in if and only if it is a means to or part of the future life I would desire and seek under such conditions, only if it is a means to or part of my future good on the whole understood in this sense. This is not to say that it is rational if and only if it is in my own interest in the long run, for, if psychological egoism is not true, as both Sidgwick and I believe, then the life that I would prefer under the conditions specified might be one that involves a sacrifice of my long-run interest. It might even be a life that gives me a rather shorter run than some of the others open to me and a smaller balance of happiness over unhappiness.

If this suggestion is well-taken, it provides an individual with a way of telling, at least in principle, whether it is rational for him to seek his own greatest happiness in the long run, to seek the general good, to be moral, or whatever. In this sense, though probably only in this sense, it does away with the dualism of practical reason. Perhaps this should be spelled out a little. For Sidgwick and his more modern adapters, all three principles are equally rational, either analytically or synthetically. They are, however, really *apropos* only if they tell *me* what it is rational *for me to do, period*. Now, according to my suggestion, I am to determine what it is rational for me to do, period, by asking what I would choose to do under the conditions indicated. If I ask this, I may well judge that each of them tells me what it is reasonable for me to do, *ceteris paribus;* but I would not, it seems to me, judge all three principles to be rational, period — perhaps not even that any one of them is. I can do so, of course, if I first postulate that they coincide in practice. But then my postulate is prior to my assertion of the principles and not posterior to it, as it must be for Sidgwick's problem to arise, and I am not involved in any dualism or trichotomy that presses such a postulate upon me.

VI

At this point we may notice a method of ethics that is dealt with, somewhat in passing, by Sidgwick. This is Perfectionism, which he elects to consider as a form of "intuitionism." As Sidgwick understands it, it takes an individual's perfection as the ultimate end or good at which he is to aim and either equates perfection with virtue (moral virtue) or regards virtue as "essentially preferable to any other element [of human excellence] that can come into competition with it as an alternative for rational choice."[32] On such a view, obviously, Sidgwick's kind of problem would disappear, since one's good — the life it would be rational for one to choose — would then coincide with the virtuous life, no matter who one was. This view Sidgwick disposes of by arguing that it is logically circular, as Kant did;[33] it holds that the right is to be determined by reference to the good and also that the good is to be determined by reference to the right (if we assume that virtue consists in doing what is right). But perfectionism need not take this form; it may say that the good consists entirely or primarily in acting rightly or virtuously, but deny that the criterion of right or virtuous action is conduciveness to the good. The criterion of right or virtuous conduct, it might claim, is simply conformity to "certain precepts or principles of Duty, intuitively known to be unconditionally binding," as "intuitionists" would hold. Then it would be free of circularity. Sidgwick in effect attacks this form of the view by contending, first, that "intuitionism" is mistaken, since the precepts or principles of duty cannot be determined without reference to what is good, and, second, that virtue is not "the sole Ultimate Good." It seems to me that he is right on both counts. One might reply that excellence, moral or non-moral, is still a good-making property, in addition to pleasantness. But, even if this is so, which Sidgwick denies (wrongly, in my opinion), it would no longer follow that an individual's good entails his always acting rightly or virtuously. Altogether, it would appear that one cannot escape Sidgwick's problem by resorting to perfectionism.[34]

VII

However this may be, it is not clear that the suggestion made in Section V does away with the need of some such postulate as Sidgwick talks about, either as required by morality or as required by practical reason. We have already seen that morality may be conceived of in wider or narrower ways. Among moral philosophers today the favored wider conception is to define a moral action-guide as whatever action-guide anyone takes as "ultimate and paramount." Sometimes it is added that one must also be willing to universalize; in any case, a morality is defined in purely formal terms, without any reference to its content. One of the latest and most persuasive proponents of this conception of morality is Mary Midgley in an article entitled, "Is 'Moral' a Dirty Word?"[35] Better known proponents are W. D. Falk, R. M. Hare, and D. H. Monro. The favored narrower conception rejects the overridingness condition as either necessary or sufficient,[36] and insists that an action-guide is a morality only if it recognizes as reasons for an agent's doing or not doing something facts about what his actions do to other people in the way of good or evil. It has been put forward by, among others, S. E. Toulmin, Ms. Foot, G. J. Warnock, and myself. On the wider view, the question, "Why should I be moral?" is a senseless one; on the narrower view it is natural and sensible. In other words, being moral is necessarily rational on the wider view but not necessarily considerate of others; on the narrower view it is necessarily considerate of others, but not necessarily rational (except from the moral point of view). Now, as I have argued elsewhere,[37] it seems to me that the narrower view is plausible only if it is accompanied by the postulate that living by the principles of morality (or by the action-guide that is most adequate from the moral point of view) is rational or good in the sense defined a moment ago; and the wider conception is plausible only if it is accompanied by the roughly equivalent postulate that the action-guide one will adopt as ultimate and paramount if one is rational will be one that calls for consideration of others. Without such a postulate, it seems to me, either view would leave us with a dualism much like that which Sidgwick so greaty dreaded.

Back of what I have just been saying is the rather vague, but I hope suggestive (though not very sexy), thought that there have been in human history two sustained drives, as they are called in American football, or "secondary principles," as Butler might have called them: one toward rationality in action (and the good life in the sense explained earlier), and another toward rightness and goodness of conduct judged on grounds that essentially include a considera-tion of others as such, treating them as ends, and so on. Sidgwick and others identify morality with the former; yet others, including myself, with the latter. However this issue be resolved, we must, it seems to me, admit that the two drives may conflict in our experience. In this sense, there is or may be a dualism in human practical reasoning, whether one adopts the wider or the narrower conception of morality, as Butler and Sidgwick saw. The question is whether it is nevertheless rational, moral, or both rational and moral to keep both drives going, assuming that it is psychologically possible not to do so, not only in the life of the race or of a society but also in that of an individual.[38] To answer it affirmatively may well require an optimistic postulate of some sort, though it may not need to be a postulate of a complete coincidence of the dictates of the two drives.

I am not convinced that the postulate required to guarantee the coincidence of rationality and consideration for others must be a "theological" one, as Sidgwick seems to think. It may represent a wager about the nature of man rather than about the government of the world. This possibility is at least suggested by Bertrand Russell's account of his conversion to the ethics of love.[39] One may also ask whether we are justified in making such a wager — or adopting any postulate of coincidence — if or because it is required by practical reason, but, as Sidgwick writes in his last paragraph,

> This . . . is a profoundly difficult and controverted question, the discussion of which belongs rather to a treatise on General Philosophy than to a work on the Methods of Ethics . . . .[40]

Like him, I draw back at the boundary of moral philosophy.

In the Sidgwick Lecture mentioned earlier, Trilling describes our new morality of today. In the course of his very interesting account he writes that

> . . . Sidgwick's . . . dilemma . . . between Interest and Duty no longer engages us . . . because the modern morality, in its powerful imagination of the sources of life and the need to obtain control over them, denies the contradiction between Interest and Duty. Typically in our culture, when a person of good will thinks of the control of the sources of life, he conceives of it as assuring the happiness both of the individual and of the generality of mankind. He assumes that there is a continuity between what he desires for

himself and what he desires for others — what he wants for himself in the way of fullness, freedom, and potency is the paradigm of what he wants for others; what he wants for others he thinks of as the guarantee of the fullness, freedom, and potency he wants for himself.[41]

This is more powerful than clear, but, if Trilling is right, then our modern morality can deny Sidgwick's dilemma only because it makes just such an assumption as Sidgwick thought to be needed, though in less theological terms.

17: Concluding More or Less Philosophical Postscript

ONE CAN HARDLY DO ANYTHING BUT ACQUIESCE AND COOPERATE WHEN someone else says he would like to edit a volume of one's previously published papers, even if one has been so doubtful that this should be done as to be unwilling to do it oneself. One is secretly pleased that someone thinks it desirable, hopes that his judgment about this is better than one's own, and acquiesces with only seeming reluctance. One even makes some suggestions about which papers to include and which not, though one leaves the decision to him, and one wonders whether or not to volunteer to write an additional new essay to help (or hinder?) the proposed volume on its way.

In this case, it was decided that I should do something more philosophers should do for volumes of their collected papers (if these come out in time), namely, what St. Augustine did in 427 A.D. in his *Retractiones,* i.e., write a covering postscript of commentary and review that will provide some needed perspective and unity, make at least some of the necessary explanations and corrections, and be otherwise helpful to a reader. This essay, therefore, will not so much restate or summarize the preceding papers, as comment on them in a historical, interpretative, or even critical way. It will also say something about a number of items not reprinted here, mainly to fill out the picture. It will not do much to answer possible objections to what I have written, and, of course, it must remain incomplete in other ways. I apologize in advance for the rather autobiographical form it has assumed. It simply turned out to be hard to do what seemed necessary in any other way. I have, however, sought to limit myself to what is relevant and may be useful. It may even be of interest for some readers to follow for a little while the Odyssey of a not very typical, more or less eighteenth-century-minded, moral philosopher of the twentieth century.

Two remarks should be made here. (a) This essay is not self-sufficient, and can only be understood in conjunction with the preceding papers. (b) Historical remarks made in those papers must be taken with some salt. Some of them are mistaken (and, of these, some will be corrected here), and many of them are relative to the time at which they were written.

I

The first four of the above papers represent a longish period in my writing career, and may be introduced as follows. I entered my graduate work (done at The University of Michigan, Harvard, and Cambridge University) in 1930, with a Calvinistic background and Hegelian sympathies. Paul Henle later remarked that he could see the Calvinism in me but not the Hegelianism, and I suppose this is still true. In my graduate work in ethics I was most influenced by D. H. Parker, R. B. Perry, and C. I. Lewis, who were ethical naturalists (Lewis with a qualification), and by G. E. Moore and C. D. Broad, who were intuitionists; and, roughly speaking, my position during this first period, held very tentatively, was a cognitivistic one combining naturalism about "good" and intuitionism about "ought." It seemed to me, as it perhaps had to Henry Sidgwick, that it was unnecessary to be an intuitionist about both and implausible to be one about "good," but important and plausible to be one about obligation, as Sidgwick and A. C. Ewing thought. Later I found out that Richard Price and other eighteenth century intuitionists had held much the same position. Almost the only contemporary philosopher who did was C. A. Campbell,[1] and I took some encouragement from his doing so. In general philosophical methodology and style I was mainly a follower of Moore and Broad, whom I took as my models, much to the disgust of some of my teachers and colleagues.

I had already then some worries, which grew on me, about the intuitionist epistemology and ontology, but it was at first chiefly the intuitionist arguments against naturalism that troubled me. They all seemed much less conclusive to me than to their users, and, moreover, it seemed to me incongruous that intuitionism should depend so much on argument and so little on intuition. These feelings, together with my tendency to be a naturalist about "good" anyway, led me to write the papers included here from this early period. To be a naturalist about the good I had to regard the intuitionist arguments, which were used in the case of the good as well as of the right, as inconclusive, but it seemed to me that I could and should still be an intuitionist about the right, not because there were arguments to disprove naturalism about the right or because naturalism commits a "fallacy," but simply on the ground that naturalistic definitions of "ought" did not seem to catch its meaning as certain definitions of "good" seemed to do (plus, hopefully, some kind of intuitive awareness of an indefinable non-natural characteristic). In short, I saw no good reason why such a dualistic theory should not be adopted.

"The Naturalistic Fallacy" ("The NF," 1939), my first published paper and still the best known, was an expansion of a passage in my Ph.D. dissertation on intuitionism in recent British ethics, submitted at Harvard in 1937. It was written in a cognitivistic frame of mind; i.e., I tended to assume, as both intuitionists and naturalists did, that ethical terms stand for properties and that ethical judgments ascribe properties to their subjects and are true or false in the corresponding sense. A few parentheses and references show that I also had non-cognitivistic theories like emotivism and postulationism in mind, e.g., the views of Ledger Wood and C. L. Stevenson, but still, the paper would have to be considerably rewritten if it were to be put in such a form as to take explicit account of such views — let alone views developed after World War II. The idea of a "naturalistic fallacy" remained alive in spite of my effort; indeed, while it was dropped by Moore himself after *Principia Ethica* and was not used by any prominent intuitionist after him, at least not explicitly, it was revived after 1939 by some non-intuitionists. (Actually, all along the main weapon used against naturalists and definists was the open question argument, not the NF. For some discussion of this argument, see the three following articles and *Ethics,* 2nd edition, pp. 99f.) Nevertheless, I believe that my main points about the NF still hold, even though I am myself less inclined to be a naturalist or a cognitivist (even about good) than I was then. I must admit, however, that one of the points I now use against naturalism is very like one of the procedures Moore refers to as "the NF," namely, that of confusing a universal synthetic proposition about the good with a definition of goodness. This will be indicated again later.

Similar remarks apply, *mutatis mutandis,* to "Obligation and Value in the Ethics of G. E. Moore" (1942). Again, my terminology was not such as I now would use. Also, my expression of my main theses was somewhat careless, considering the fact that it was Moore I was dealing with. Moore wrote a long reply in which he took me to task, and he was quite right in some of the points he made in his acute and careful way about my use of "normative," "as such," "by nature," etc.[2] Once more, however, I believe that my main contentions were correct and can be restated and maintained. For example, I put one of them by saying that, if intrinsic goodness is either a simple or an intrinsic quality or both, as Moore thinks it is, then it cannot be as such, essentially, or by nature normative. By "normative" here I meant what Moore, in his reply, means by "ought-implying." Moore replied that x's being intrinsically good may synthetically but necessarily imply that x ought to be brought into being, and that, if this is so, then one can say, even if intrinsic goodness is a simple intrinsic quality, that it is as such, essentially, or by nature normative. This is true, if one is willing to admit that there are synthetic a priori connections between properties, as I was at the time. What I meant to say, and should have said more clearly than I did, is that, if intrinsic goodness is a simple and/or an intrinsic quality, then it cannot be analytically or by definition ought-implying, as Moore seemed sometimes to think, and that, if it is not analytically ought-implying, then it is not plausible to define "ought" in terms of "conduciveness to what is intrinsically good," as Moore did in *Principia Ethica.* To answer that intrinsic goodness may still be ought-implying in a synthetic necessary way, however, is to give up that definition of "ought," as I was contending Moore should. It is, in fact, to move to the position he took in *Ethics* and later writings, including his reply to me.

As for this later position, my main contention was that, if it is true, i.e., if intrinsic goodness is not analytically ought-implying, then there is no very good reason for regarding it as indefinable or non-natural. In his reply Moore gave an argument to show that there is good reason for so regarding it after all; this argument I discuss in the fourth paper included in this volume.

I went on to suggest that two intuitionist positions are more plausible than either of Moore's two: (a) one that defines "good" in terms of "ought" or "fitting," and (b) one that combines an intuitionist view of "ought" with a naturalist view of "good." (a) represents the line taken by Ewing, (b) the line I was inclined to favor.

The next two papers belong together. In both I was trying to defend line (b) by rebutting a number of intuitionist arguments against naturalistic theories of value, including Ewing's. In both the sort of naturalistic theory of value I had in mind was that of Lewis in *An Analysis of Knowledge and Valuation*. Actually, I drew some support for my lingering intuitionism about obligation from Lewis too (as well as from Ewing), for, though he was not an intuitionist about it, he seemed not to be a naturalist about it either. Later I dealt with the problem of interpreting Lewis's views in some papers not included here.[3] Among the arguments I discuss is the open question argument, which was used by emotivists and non-cognitivists, as well as by intuitionists. One point must be added to my discussion of Moore's argument in the second of these two papers, viz., that his premise (4) would be denied by most, if not all, deontologists.

In all of the papers included from this period, I talk as if the questions at issue between naturalists and their opponents can be settled by a kind of "inspection" of our meanings. I now believe that this talk is too simple-minded, as some of the later essays will bring out.[4]

II

The next ten years (the fifties) constitute a transitional period. It begins with a fussy paper on "Obligation and Ability" (1950) that still seems to me to make some points, as do two papers on human and natural rights. It includes essays on the metaethics of Francis Hutcheson, R. W. Sellars, and Broad, and two chapters in a book on the philosophy of language. In the course of writing these pieces, I began to see the possibility of a non-cognitivist theory different from those of A. J. Ayer, C. L. Stevenson, or R. M. Hare. None of these papers are included here. Perhaps the most important paper of this period not included is "Moral Philosophy at Mid-Century" (1951). In it I still saw the alternatives in metaethics as intuitionism, naturalism, and non-cognitivism, though I suggested there might be a fourth alternative. I contended that none of the three positions had been shown to be untenable, that all should be taken seriously, and that none can be regarded as a mere elucidation of our ordinary thinking and discourse. I also discerned changing conceptions of analysis, argued that analysis in the old sense is not enough to settle metaethical issues, and made some suggestions about the doing of metaethics — all points that are reflected in other papers appearing in this volume. I even proposed that moral philosophers should do normative ethics — which they have since begun to do in a gratifying way.

During this decade, I became increasingly dubious about the epistemology and ontology of intuitionism as I understood it, and also increasingly concerned about and interested in emotivism and other alternatives to both naturalism and intuitionism. I wanted a single metaethical theory that would cover both the right and the good in place of the dualistic one I had been holding, but one which would retain what seemed to me sound in cognitivism and intuitionism. With this went a growing concern about the definition of the concept of morality. I was also beginning to extend my work in ethical theory to include the philosophy of education, mainly as a result of thinking about the teaching of religion in state universities and, of course, about moral education.

"Ethical Naturalism Renovated" (1957) is a critical review of some aspects of P. B. Rice's *On the Knowledge of Good and Evil*. The movement to renovate naturalism was only beginning then, and this essay serves to call attention to a neglected moral philosopher who was something of a pioneer. Rice was one of the first to try to refurbish naturalism in ethics as an alternative, not only to intuitionism, but also and more especially to emotivism and "informalism," a term he used to cover S. E. Toulmin, P. H. Nowell-Smith, Hare, and other post-emotivistic anti-naturalists. The essay also formulated my reactions to Rice's proposed new form of naturalism about "ought" in its moral use (what he says about "good" I left to one side), which involves giving "x morally ought to do A" both a descriptive and a non-descriptive meaning. I wondered if it was really naturalism, and I questioned his account of the non-descriptive meaning of "ought." But I liked much of what he says about reasoning and justification in ethics, particularly his somewhat vague notion that a kind of moral point of view is central to it. I suggested, however, that all of what he says can be incorporated in a "monistic" form of non-cognitivism which takes the idea of a moral point of view as basic, a line of thought I was then finding in Hutcheson and Hume.[5] Very tentatively, I was considering the merits of such a metaethical theory.[6] This comes out somewhat in another paper, "Toward a Philosophy of Moral Education," written at about the same time. I should add that the business of validation and vindication was made much clearer by P. W. Taylor in *Normative Discourse* (1961).

"Obligation and Motivation in Moral Philosophy" (1958) was written at about this time, but in it my orientation was still rather cognitivistic, if not intuitionistic. I was trying to bring into the open an issue between "internalism'' and ''externalism'' that cuts to some extent across the issues between intuitionists, naturalists, and non-cognitivists, all by way of a discussion of certain arguments about obligation used by a variety of writers, mainly as ways of refuting intuitionism (which is a form of externalism). Today I do not find myself thinking very much in terms of an internalism versus externalism controversy, but I believe that most of my points against such arguments still hold. In fact, I still think that externalism contains an essential truth, namely, that the question whether or not x ought (morally) to do A is not to be answered by looking to see what his motivations are. About this the intuitionists — and Rice too — were right (on another item Rice himself was too close to the internalists, as I pointed out). On the other hand, I have come to believe that the emotivists were correct in thinking that, when one judges that x ought to do A, one is necessarily taking a pro-attitude toward x's doing A, at least *ceteris paribus*. In this sense, one cannot sensibly judge that one morally should do A and be entirely indifferent about doing it. To this extent I have moved toward internalism. Even so, as I try to show in the first three pages of Section XI, two alternatives remain: (a) a form of externalism that makes certain concessions and (b) a form of internalism that is there described. My own drift has been toward the latter position, but I am not sure that it matters greatly which alternative one espouses, as long as one recognizes that the reasons counting as justifying a moral judgment are not facts about the agent's motivation and that the judgment itself claims the agreement of all who are rational and take the moral point of view.

III

My writing during the sixties was rather more varied than before. A good bit of it was historical, including a longish review of ethical theory in America from 1930 to 1960. Even more of it was in the philosophy of education, moral and non-moral, including a small book on Aristotle, Kant, and Dewey that contains accounts of their ethical as well as of their educational theories. In another little book, *Ethics* (1963, second edition in 1973), I finally worked out, in an elementary version, the outlines of an ethical theory, both normative and metaethical. It is still the fullest and only systematic statement there is of my moral philosophy as a whole. In metaethics I am no longer an intuitionist or a naturalist about either ''good'' or ''ought,'' but a non-cognitivist of the post-emotivist sort indicated above. It is here that I use against naturalism the point mentioned earlier in discussing ''The NF.''[7] In normative ethics I argue for a mixed deontological view that takes as basic in morality a principle of beneficence (or, roughly, utility) and a principle of justice (or equal treatment).

Several times during the first half of this decade I wrote pieces about Christian ethics and about the relation of morality to religion, most of them partly sympathetic and partly critical. These include "Public Education and the Good Life" (1961) and "Is Morality Logically Dependent on Religion?" although the latter was not published until 1973. The only one of these essays reprinted here is "Love and Principle in Christian Ethics" (1964), which appeared in a *Festschrift* for my first teacher in philosophy and has had a gratifying reception among moral theologians. It does not seem to me to need further comment on this occasion. In general, in these papers, I was seeking to be helpful to religious "'ethicists" (their label, which I abhor) but at the same time to resist their tendency to make morality dependent on, or even to turn it into, religion.

Three times I tried my hand on the subject of justice, and the last of these attempts (1966) is reprinted in this volume. The position taken in it is the same as that taken in *Ethics* (though it is considerably restated), but it is different from the more complicated view presented in "The Concept of Social Justice" (1962), being limited to distributive justice. One paragraph strikes me now as confused, though no doubt other criticisms may also be made both of this essay and of my other things on justice. In the first paragraph of Section VI I talk as if differences in ability or need between people may sometimes justify treating them *unequally* as well as *differently,* but this is inconsistent with what I argued earlier. I do not want to say that differences between people ever directly justify treating them unequally, though they may so justify treating them differently. But I do hold that treating them unequally is sometimes justified (and perhaps even "justicized," to borrow a concept from my 1962 essay), not by differences between the individuals involved, but by the consequences in terms of the long-run achievement of equality in society. A temporary college policy of preferential admission for minorities may be an example.

One of my preoccupations at this time was with a question that was then coming to the fore in metaethics — the question of the nature of morality. It seemed to me important to define morality, to distinguish between it and other things, and especially to distinguish between moral judgments and other kinds of judgments that use evaluative or normative terms like "good," "right," "should," etc.; and I thought that intuitionists, naturalists, emotivists, and even prescriptivists, had not paid enough attention to such matters. It also seemed to me that the best way to distinguish a moral judgment from a non-moral normative one is not by the normative terms used, by the subject being judged, by the feelings accompanying the judgment, or by any purely "formal" criteria, but by the nature of the reasons that are given for it or would be given for it if it is questioned. One can also put this by saying that moral judgments are to be distinguished from other normative ones by the point of view that is being taken and that the moral point of view (MPV) can be distinguished from other normative points of view by the kinds of considerations it takes account of. This, however, is a view that has been much debated since it was espoused by Toulmin, Kurt Baier, Rice, Philippa Foot, etc. Several of my essays represent contributions to this debate. In 1958 I defended the idea of defining morality against Alasdair MacIntyre's attack on it. In "Recent Conceptions of Morality" (1963) I tried to bring the debate more fully into the open and to say something about its nature and participants. In still other essays I sought to state and defend the "material" kind of definition of morality and the MPV that seems to me most satisfactory.

Two of these later essays unfortunately, because of an unexpected conjunction of circumstances, have the same title, "The Concept of Morality"; what is worse, they embody rather different views, since I changed my mind in the interim; and, what is worst, the later one, which represents my present position, came out first. It is the later one that is reprinted here. The other is included in *The Definition of Morality* (1970), edited by G. Wallace and A. D. M. Walker,[8] except that it is mistaken on the point in which the two papers differ, it represents my thinking somewhat more fully than the present one does. A later article on the same topic is also included here and will be noticed shortly.

"On Saying the Ethical Thing" (also 1966) was a presidential address to the Western Division of the American Philosophical Association, and it contains some of the rhetoric and attempted humor that used to grace such occasions. In it I plump for a normative conception of metaethics and seek to restate the controversy between intuitionism, naturalism, and non-cognitivism accordingly, using the idea that human discourse contains three Voices. Talking in those terms, I try to formulate a fourth kind of theory of the sort indicated earlier, which may be a kind of naturalism but which I prefer to think of as a somewhat novel kind of non-descriptivism variously anticipated by Hume, Ewing, J. N. Findlay, and Taylor, one which combines what is true in internalism and externalism. I also touch on topics dealt with in earlier and later essays: the NF, the MPV, the relation of Is and Ought, and relativism.

One of these topics, also dealt with in "The NF," in *Ethics*, and in other papers not included here, is taken up in " 'Ought' and 'Is' Once More" (1969). I was tempted to entitle it " 'Ought' and 'Is' Once More and for the Last Time," but decided that neither others nor even I myself were likely to leave that delicious subject alone. This was fortunate, for W. D. Hudson's *The Is/Ought Question* came out soon afterwards — and I returned to the topic recently in an essay on Spinoza. In any event, in the present paper, against the background of the general metaethical theory I had arrived at, I state the three usual views about the business of going from Is to Ought (roughly, naturalism or descriptivism, intuitionism, and the usual kind of non-cognitivism), and then argue for a fourth, viz., that, although one cannot in strict logic go from Ises to an Ought in any important sense, it may still sometimes be rational to do so and irrational not to. This position I later illustrated and, I hope, reinforced in the paper on Spinoza just referred to. Incidentally, I should note that I here again correct the interpretation of Hume and Mill used in "The NF," as I already had in *Ethics*.

IV

Some pieces in the philosophy of education, all written in the late sixties, have appeared in the present decade. My main concern, however, has been with questions about the nature of morality and, especially, about the forms it may or should take — what I call metamoral problems (rather than metaethical ones). The latter interest comes out in "The Principles and Categories of Morality" (1970) in which, partly by way of a defence of my principles of beneficence and justice, I argue that morality should recognize five deontic categories instead of the usual three (obligatory, permitted, and wrong). It also shows up in the next essay reprinted here, "Prichard and the Ethics of Virtue" (1970), where I raise a related question: whether aretaic or deontic concepts and judgments are or should be basic in morality? In particular, I am there exploring the question of an ethics of virtue, which has intrigued me ever since I wrote *Ethics* in 1963, where I dismissed it rather cavalierly (I do somewhat better by it in the second edition). The same interest led me to write "The Ethics of Love Conceived as an Ethics of Virtue" (1973, but not here), which also reflects my continuing attention to Christian ethics. My latest thoughts on the ethics of virtue — and on the relations of morality as I conceive of it to religion — may be found in "Conversations with Carney and Hauerwas" (1975, and also not here).

With an interest in the forms of morality naturally goes an interest in the forms of moral education; as Michael Oakeshott says, "Every form of the moral life . . . depends upon [a form of moral] education."[9] In an encyclopedia article here reprinted, "Moral Education" (1971), I describe and discuss some views about the form moral education should take. Other discussions of moral education occur in an earlier article already referred to, in "Public Education and the Good Life" (1961), and in "Moral Authority, Moral Autonomy, and Moral Education," which will appear in the near future.

In "On Defining Moral Judgments, Principles, and Codes" (1973) I am again on the problem of distinguishing moral judgments, etc., from non-moral ones. Besides reviewing alternative answers to this problem, I endeavor here to explain, complete, and defend the answer given earlier in "The Concept of Morality."

The next essay, "the principles of morality" (1973), was written about 1966. By way of a discussion of a number of views about what is or should be meant when we say "P is a principle of morality" or "The principles of morality require . . .," I expound and support the kind of objectivism in ethics that is part of the metaethical theory the evolution of which I have been trying to sketch. In a way, it represents an attempt to preserve what now still seems to me correct in intuitionism, without the epistemology and ontology that went with it in Price, Sidgwick, Moore, H. A. Prichard, or W. D. Ross — in fact, within a non-cognitivist framework of sorts. This attempt has close affinities with the views of Hutcheson, Hume, Adam Smith, Findlay (in 1944), and Baier, and perhaps some with those of Ewing (in his *Second Thoughts*), Kai Nielsen, and John Rawls.

Another metamoral problem is that raised by asking, ''Why should one be moral, take the MPV, etc.?'' In ''Sidgwick and the Dualism of Practical Reason'' (1974), I show how Sidgwick wrestled with this problem and assess his solution. I myself take the same line adopted at the end of *Ethics*, but here, as also in ''Conversations with Carney and Hauerwas,'' I follow Sidgwick in thinking that such an answer involves a postulate about man and the world — essentially the same postulate I make use of earlier in a somewhat different connection in ''The Concept of Morality'' (both versions).

Most recently, for those who are interested, I have been occupied with these and other metamoral questions, e.g., whether morality has or should have an object, whether it is or should be a system of hypothetical imperatives, whether it may or should take the form of a positive social morality or be regarded as a wholly private, personal matter, whether the basic principles of morality should be taken as action-guides for individuals or as principles for institutions, and whether morality should subscribe to the so-called doctrine of double effect. Like many other recent moral philosophers, however, I have also been reflecting on some of the current problems of normative ethics: the ethics of respect for life, the problem of world hunger, etc. Some fruits of these reflections have appeared and, hopefully, more will appear shortly.

William K. Frankena
Roy Wood Sellars Professor of Philosophy
The University of Michigan

Notes

INTRODUCTION

1. Highly relevant also is Frankena's "Hutcheson's Moral Sense Theory" (1955).

2. See "Recent Conceptions of Morality" (1963), "The Concept of Morality" (1966), " 'The Principles of Morality' " (1973), and "On Defining Moral Judgments, Principles and Codes" (1973).

3. But more parsimonious. Frankena himself prefers to call it a "mixed deontological" view.

4. See "Love and Principle in Christian Ethics" and "Some Beliefs About Justice."

5. *Ethics,* second edition, p. 53.

1: THE NATURALISTIC FALLACY

1. A. E. Taylor, *The Faith of a Moralist,* vol. I, p. 104 n.

2. *Value and Ethical Objectivity,* p. 58.

3. *Principia Ethica,* pp. 38, 64.

4. M. E. Clarke, "Cognition and Affection in the Experience of Value," *Journal of Philosophy* (1938).

5. *Principia Ethica,* pp. 73, 77. See also p. xix.

6. "Ethics as Pure Postulate," *Philosophical Review* (1933). See also T. Whittaker, *The Theory of Abstract Ethics,* pp. 19 f.

7. Book III, part ii, section i.

8. See J. Laird, *A Study in Moral Theory,* pp. 16 f.; Whittaker, *op. cit.,* p. 19.

9. See C. D. Broad, *Five Types of Ethical Theory,* ch. iv.

10. *A Study in Moral Theory,* p. 94 n.

11. See *Philosophical Studies,* pp. 259, 273 f.

12. See J. Laird, *op. cit.,* p. 318. Also pp. 12 ff.

13. P. E. Wheelwright, *A Critical Introduction to Ethics,* pp. 40-51, 91 f.; L. Wood, "Cognition and Moral Value," *Journal of Philosophy* (1937), p. 237.

14. See *Principia Ethica,* pp. 114, 57, 43, 49. Whittaker identifies it with the naturalistic fallacy and regards it as a "logical" fallacy, *op. cit.,* pp. 19 f.

15. See *ibid.,* pp. 50, 139; Wheelwright, *loc. cit.*

16. See C. D. Broad, *The Mind and its Place in Nature,* pp. 488 f.; Laird, *loc. cit.*

17. See *op. cit.,* pp. 11 f.; 19, 38, 73, 139.

218

18. See L. Wood, *loc. cit.*
19. P. 10.
20. P. 40.
21. P. 58, *cf.* pp. xiii, 73.
22. *Cf.* pp. 49, 53, 108, 139.
23. P. 13.
24. See pp. 38-40, 110-112.
25. *Five Types of Ethical Theory*, p. 259.
26. P. 14.
27. As Whittaker has, *loc. cit.*
28. See *op. cit.,* pp. 6, 8, 12.
29. See J. Wisdom, *Mind* (1931), p. 213, note 1.
30. See *Principia Ethica*, pp. 10, 16, 38; *The Nature of Existence*, vol. ii, p. 398.
31. Leo Abraham, "The Logic of Intuitionism," *International Journal of Ethics* (1933).
32. As Mr. Abraham points out, *loc. cit.*
33. See R. B. Perry, *General Theory of Value*, p. 30; *cf. Journal of Philosophy* (1931), p. 520.
34. See H. Osborne, *Foundations of the Philosophy of Value*, pp. 15, 19, 70.
35. *Cf.* R. B. Perry, *Journal of Philosophy* (1931), pp. 520 ff.
36. *Principia Ethica*, pp. 17, 38, 59, 61.
37. But see H. Osborne, *op. cit.,* pp. 18 f.
38. For a brief discussion of their arguments, see *ibid.,* p. 67; L. Abraham, *op. cit.* I think they are all inconclusive, but cannot show this here.
39. See *Principia Ethica*, pp. 124 f., 140.

2: OBLIGATION AND VALUE IN THE ETHICS OF G. E. MOORE

1. Cf. *Principia Ethica* (hereafter I shall refer to this work simply as *P.E.*), Pref., and *passim*; "Mr. McTaggart's Ethics," *Int. Journal of Ethics,* Vol. xiii (1902-1903); "Brentano's *Origin of Our Knowledge of Right and Wrong,*" *Int. Journ. of Ethics,* Vol. xiv (1903-1904). The only philosophers whom Moore mentions as recognizing any of his principles are Sidgwick and Brentano.
2. Cf. *P.E.,* viii, 37.
3. *P.E.,* 21-23, 74, 90, 27-30.
4. *P.E.,* 6-17, 21, 41, 110-111; *Philosophical Studies*, chaps. viii, x.
5. *P.E.,* viii-x, 7, 74-76, 118, 143-144; *Ethics,* 223-224; *Phil. Studies,* chap. x; *Intern Journ. of Ethics,* Vol. xiv (1903-4), 116.
6. *P.E.,* xi, 2-3, 5, 21; *Phil. Studies,* 257.
7. *P.E.,* 23-27, and chap. v; *Ethics,* chaps. i, ii. I use "right" and "ought" as interchangeable, though this is not quite the case.
8. *P.E.,* 187, 184; cf. also 27-33, 95, chap. vi; *Ethics,* chap. vii (b) is what Moore calls "the principle of organic unities."
9. *P.E.,* ix-x; cf. 38 and chap. vi, *passim*; *Ethics,* chap. vii. This conclusion is especially directed against hedonism.
10. P. 195. In connection with the rest of this paragraph see *Ethics,* chap. v, and *passim.*
11. *Ethics,* 17. Cf. *Phil. Studies,* chap. x.

12. But see *P.E.*, 25.

13. But cf. Moore's review of H. Rashdall's *Theory of Good and Evil, Hibbert Journal*, Vol. vi (1907-1908), 447-448.

14. *Ethics*, 61, 72-73.

15. What I shall say applies to W. D. Ross, J. Laird, and N. Hartmann, as well as to Moore.

16. Pp. viii, 118. This view of Moore's does support my point, I think; but one cannot make much of it by itself, because Moore does not attach much obligatoriness to the notion of what ought to exist for its own sake. The view, of course, is not to be taken as a definition, since Moore regards intrinsic value as indefinable. It is a mere statement of the synonymity of two expressions. Cf. B. Russell, *Philosophical Essays* (1910), 5-6.

17. Pp. 51-52, 64-66. Cf. 99-100. On p. 17 Moore takes his 'good' as synonymous with Sidgwick's 'ought'. It is true that on pp. 25-26 Moore denies that "X is intrinsically good" is equivalent to "We ought to aim at securing X," but this does not refute my contention.

18. My account here is only partly based on *Principia Ethica*. Nevertheless it describes the view of intrinsic value which he expresses there, as well as that expressed in later works.

19. Cf. *Ethics*, 161; *Proc. of the Arist. Soc.*, Supp. Vol. xi (1932), 117.

20. Cf. *Ethics*, 69-72, 161, 167, 185-188, 250.

21. Cf. *P.E.*, 21; Moore takes these phrases as equivalent.

22. I neglect Moore's distinction between what is intrinsically good and what is ultimately good or good for its own sake. Cf. *Ethics*, 73-76.

23. Cf. *Proc. Arist. Soc.*, Supp. Vol. xi, 126.

24. Cf. *Phil. Stud.*, chap. viii. This can hardly be always true of the property of being good as an end. Often, at least, "X is good as an end" seems to mean "X is good as being someone's end." Then its being good as an end is not intrinsic in Moore's sense.

25. Cf. *Ethics*, 65; *Phil. Studies*, 260; *Proc. Arist. Soc.*, Supp. Vol. xi, 121-124. Moore is inclined to think that all of these expressions have the same meaning, though he confesses that this may not be true, and seems to favor the last as a translation of the first. Cf. the last of the references cited.

26. Here being intrinsic entails being objective and absolute. Cf. *Phil. Studies*, chap. viii.

27. Cf. *P.E.*, 6-10.

28. Cf. *P.E.*, 38-41, 110-112, 123-126; *Phil. Studies*, chaps. viii, x.

29. It is not a tautology to say that intrinsic value is intrinsic in Moore's sense, as many moralists hold that it is not intrinsic in that sense.

30. Cf. C. D. Broad, *Five Types of Ethical Theory* (1930), 165; W. D. Ross, *The Right and the Good* (1930), 105.

31. Here "pleasant" means "containing a balance of pleasure." Cf. *Phil. Studies*, 272-273. D. H. Parker, while defining value as satisfaction, holds it to be intrinsic in Moore's sense. See "The Metaphysics of Value," *Int. Journ. of Ethics*, Vol. 44 (1934).

32. *Proc. Arist. Soc.*, Supp. Vol. xi, 127.

33. Cf., e.g., the paper by C. L. Stevenson in this volume. In *Phil. Studies,* 331, Moore confesses that he is not satisfied that his later arguments are conclusive.

34. Cf. my article, "The Naturalistic Fallacy," *Mind,* Vol. xlviii (1939); Essay 1 of this collection.

35. *Phil. Studies,* 274.

36. See *Proc. Arist. Soc.,* Supp. Vol. xi, 121-126.

37. Here cf. especially *Ethics,* 59-61; the preface to the 1922 edition of *Principia Ethica;* and *Proc. Arist. Soc.,* Supp. Vol. xi, 127.

38. I should add that both of the views just described as alternatives to Moore's can be so formulated that in practice they will be equivalent to his.

39. For suggested definitions of 'good' in terms of 'ought' or 'right' see H. Osborne, *Foundations of the Philosophy of Value* (1933), 22-23, 67, 93-95, 109, 124-126, A. C. Ewing, "A Suggested Non-Naturalistic Analysis of 'Good'," *Mind* (1939).

40. Cf. *P.E.,* 25-26.

41. Cf. Russell, *op. cit.,* 6.

42. Cf. *Phil. Studies,* 319.

43. Cf. Ross, *loc. cit.; P.E.,* 30.

44. P. 66.

45. See *Ethics,* 59-61.

46. See *ibid.,* 61, 173.

47. Cf. A. J. Ayer, *Language, Truth, and Logic* (1936), 160.

48. I do not mean here to be granting that "intrinsic value" *is* clearly intrinsic in Moore's sense.

49. Cf. J. Laird's remark, *A Study in Moral Theory* (1926), 94, note 2.

50. *Proc. Arist. Soc.,* Supp. Vol. xi, 127. Moore may also mean that he is not greatly concerned to hold that intrinsic value is indefinable, so long as it is admitted to be an intrinsic quality in his sense. My contention is that, if he insists that value is an intrinsic quality in that sense, then he must be prepared to regard it as definable in non-ethical terms, and he must hold that it is *not* definable in terms of obligation. Moore goes on to say, "I think perhaps it [intrinsic value] is definable, I do not know. But I also think that very likely it is indefinable." In the first part of this passage he seems to be agreeing with me. If so, then it is only the second part that I wish to deny.

51. I do not myself regard it as important to hold this, at least if obligation is held to be indefinable in non-ethical terms. But it is hard to believe that Moore no longer considers it to be important.

52. If intrinsic value is definable in terms of obligation in the manner just discussed, then principle (5) is false and both parts of principle (6) are analytic. Cf. Ewing, *op. cit.*

3: EWING'S CASE AGAINST NATURALISTIC THEORIES OF VALUE

1. See pp. 3-4, 46-56, 169, 178-183, 200-201.

2. Pp. 54-55.

3. Pp. 46, 50, 52-54.
4. Pp. 50, 51.
5. P. 81. Cf. 109 f.
6. ". . .whatever definition be offered, it may be always asked, with significance, of the complex so defined whether it is itself good," *Principia Ethica,* p. 15.
7. P. 81.
8. P. 42.
9. Pp. 42-43.
10. P. 43.
11. P. 75.
12. P. 75; cf. pp. 56 f., 67, 178.
13. Pp. 64, 67.
14. P. 167.
15. P. 67 f.; cf. pp. 75, 178.
16. P. 178.
17. Pp. 56, 178.
18. P. 57.
19. Ch. iv.
20. Pp. 57, 63.
21. P. 57.
22. Pp. 43-44.
23. P. 44; cf. p. 14.
24. P. 75; cf. p. 58.
25. P. 44.
26. P. 14.
27. Pp. 44-45.
28. *Meno,* 71 E.
29. P. 43.
30. P. 43.

4: ARGUMENTS FOR NON-NATURALISM ABOUT INTRINSIC VALUE

1. I shall use "goodness" to mean "intrinsic goodness."
2. See, e.g., P.A. Schilpp, ed., *The Philosophy of G. E. Moore* (Evanston, Ill.:
Northwestern University Press, 1942), pp. 57-62, 581-92; W. D. Ross, *The Right
and the Good* (Oxford: Clarendon Press, 1930), pp. 87, 114-22.
3. *The Philosophy of G. E. Moore,* pp. 62-65.
4. This is not a tautology. A characteristic may be indefinable (and therefore
indefinable in natural terms) and yet be natural, as yellow is according to Moore.
5. M. E. Clarke, "Valuing and the Quality of Value," *Journal of Philosophy,*
35:10 (1938).
6. See Moore, *Philosophical Studies* (London: Kegan Paul, 1922), pp. 253-75,
and W. D. Ross, *The Right and the Good.*
7. Cf. the example of yellow.
8. *The Philosophy of G. E. Moore,* pp. 591-92, 605-6. He seems also to hold that
goodness is intrinsic, resultant, and nonempirical, pp. 588, 592.
9. For his definition of an ought-implying property, see pp. 603 ff.

10. *The Definition of Good* (New York: Macmillan, 1947), chap. 2, especially pp. 74-75.

11. *Philosophical Review*, 57: 481-92 (1948); Essay 3 of this collection.

12. See pp. 43-44.

13. It should be noted that many metaphysical idealists and theists are naturalists about intrinsic value in the sense of that term which is here in question.

14. *Logic and the Basis of Ethics* (Oxford: Clarendon Press, 1949) p. vii.

5: ETHICAL NATURALISM RENOVATED

1. Philip Blair Rice, *On the Knowledge of Good and Evil*, (New York, 1955).

2. Cf. P. B. Rice, op. cit.; W. D. Lamont, *The Value Judgment* (1955); G. Hourani, *Ethical Value* (1956); B. Blanshard, *The Impasse in Ethics — and a Way Out* (1955). C. I. Lewis, *The Ground and Nature of the Right* (1955), should be listed here, even though he does not run through the various alternative views, and is not unambiguously a naturalist in the present sense. Two articles should also be mentioned, J. Harrison, "Empiricism in Ethics," *Phil. Quart.* (1952); R. B. Brandt, "The Status of Empirical Assertion Theories in Ethics," *Mind* (1952).

3. Much of Rice's criticism of Stevenson does not seem to me to be well-taken, but I like the direction of his effort.

4. "The Emotive Conception of Ethics and its Cognitive Implications," *Phil. Rev.* (1950).

5. *The Place of Reason in Ethics*, Ch. 10, 12; cf. also the articles of H. D. Aiken.

6. Even the view of the Oxford informalists is more monistic than Rice recognizes, for most of them agree with him in accepting a utilitarian theory of the justification of maxims or rules. Cf. P. H. Nowell-Smith, *Ethics*, chs. 15, 16.

7. Cf. D. H. Monro, "Are Moral Problems Genuine?" *Mind* (1956).

8. Op. cit. (Rice himself discusses Lewis' appeal as made in *Analysis of Knowledge and Valuation*.)

6: OBLIGATION AND MOTIVATION IN RECENT MORAL PHILOSOPHY

1. See W. D. Falk, " 'Ought' and Motivation," *Proceedings of the Aristotelian Society*, N.S. XLVIII (1947-48), 137, reprinted in *Readings in Ethical Theory*, ed. W. S. Sellars and J. Hospers (New York: Appleton-Century-Crofts, 1952). The older term "rigorism" would do for externalism, but it has no good opposite for present purposes.

2. I owe this use of the phrase "built into" to my colleague C. L. Stevenson.

3. *Duty and Interest* (Oxford: Oxford University Press, 1928).

4. R. M. Blake, "The Ground of Moral Obligation," *International Journal of Ethics*, XXXVIII (1928), 129-40. Blake was especially concerned about the "internalism," as I call it, of the idealistic ethics of self-realization. See also Falk, " 'Ought' and Motivation," and articles cited below. H. Reiner in *Pflicht und Neigung* (Meisenheim: Westkulturverlag A. Hain, 1951) is dealing with a somewhat different problem.

5. Notice, the question here is about a reference to the interests of the *agent* spoken of, not the interests of the *speaker*.

6. Not all theological theories of obligation are externalistic, for theologians

often hold or imply that "the moral law" is law or is obligatory because it is divinely *sanctioned* (i.e., because it is made to our interest to obey), not merely because it is commanded by God.

7. *Moral Theory* (London: Methuen & Co., 1921), pp. 51, 52, 56 f.

8. Cf. F. Hutcheson, "Illustrations on the Moral Sense" (1728), section 1, in *British Moralists*, ed. L. A. Selby-Bigge (2 vols.; Oxford: Clarendon Press, 1897), I, 403 f.

9. W. T. Stace, *The Concept of Morals* (New York: Macmillan Co., 1937), pp. 41-43.

10. That one may fail to feel any disposition whatsoever to do what is right cannot simply be asserted, for it is to make an important claim about human nature even on an externalist view.

11. *Ethics* (London: Penguin Books, 1954), pp. 36-43. Nowell-Smith is a non-cognitivist, not a cognitivist as Field and Stace are. There are similar arguments in A. J. Ayer, "On the Analysis of Moral Judgments," *Horizon,* IX (1949), 171 ff.; Alf Ross, "The Logical Status of Value Judgments," *Theoria,* XI (1945), 203-8; R. C. Cross, "Virtue and Nature," *Proceedings of the Aristotelian Society,* N.S. L (1949-50), 123-37; H. Reichenbach, *The Rise of Scientific Philosophy* (Berkeley and Los Angeles: University of California Press, 1954), chap. xvii; R. M. Hare, *The Language of Morals* (Oxford: Clarendon Press, 1952), pp. 30, 79-93, 171; and elsewhere. I do not discuss these writers, however, because they may not be advancing quite the same argument; they seem to be insisting not so much that moral judgments are motivating, as that they are prescriptive. Hence they may not be internalists. But, if they are, then what I say will apply to them, too.

12. A. N. Prior says that Hume was but repeating Cudworth! Cf. *Logic and the Basis of Ethics* (Oxford: Clarendon Press, 1949), p. 33.

13. The famous passage in Hume (*Treatise, Bk.* III, Pt. I, section 1), often appealed to lately, can be read as stating either of these arguments, but they must not be confused. He himself seems to distinguish it from the more obviously internalistic argument given a few pages earlier; hence he may intend it only in the first sense.

14. As G. E. Moore pointed out in his reply to me, *The Philosophy of G. E. Moore,* ed. P. A. Schilpp (Evanston and Chicago: Northwestern University, 1942), pp. 567 ff.

15. As H. D. Aiken has pointed out. See below.

16. *Moral Theory,* pp. 56 f.

17. Cf., e.g., W. D. Ross, *The Right and the Good* (Oxford: Clarendon Press, 1930), pp. 157 f.

18. "The Emotive Meaning of Ethical Terms," *Mind,* N.S. XLVI (1937), 16.

19. Cf. Also D. C. Williams, "The Meaning of Good," *Philosophical Review,* XLVI (1937), 416-23.

20. "Evaluation and Obligation," *Journal of Philosophy,* XLVII (1950), 5-22, reprinted in *Readings in Ethical Theory.* See also "The Authority of Moral Judgments," *Philosophy and Phenomenological Research,* XII (1951-52), 513. A similar view is present in A. Moore, "A Categorical Imperative?" *Ethics,* LXIII (1952-53), 235-50, to which my criticisms also apply.

21. Cf. *British Moralists,* II, 16.

22. Or, "It is to my interest to do B," or, "B is conducive to my self-realization."

23. Cf. also H. Reiner, *Pflicht und Neigung.*

24. Cf. "Morals without Faith," *Philosophy,* XIX (1944), 7; "Obligation and Rightness," *Philosophy,* XX (1945), 139.

25. *Hume's Moral and Political Philosophy* (New York: Hafner Publishing Co., 1948), p. xxxi.

26. "A Pluralistic Analysis of the Ethical 'Ought,' " *Journal of Philosophy,* XLVIII (1951), 497.

27. See G. E. Moore, *Principia Ethica* (Cambridge: Cambridge University Press, 1903), pp. 169-70.

28. W. James, "The Moral Philosopher and the Moral Life," in *The Will to Believe* (New York: Longmans, Green & Co., 1897), p. 196. James is inconsistent on this point, for he also says that a man has an obligation as soon as someone else makes a demand on him.

29. "Obligation and Rightness," p. 147.

30. *Ethics,* pp. 210, 320.

31. Cf. *Philosophical Analysis,* ed. M. Black (Ithaca: Cornell University Press, 1950), p. 220.

32. See H. J. N. Horsburgh, "The Criteria of Assent to a Moral Rule," *Mind,* N.S. LXIIII (1954), 345-58; Hare, *The Language of Morals,* pp. 20, 169.

33. Cf. Plato, *Symposium;* R. Price, *Review of the Principal Questions of Morals* (Oxford: Clarendon Press, 1948), chap. iii; W. D. Ross, *The Right and the Good,* pp. 157 f. If the doctrine of total depravity does not imply that we have naturally no disposition *whatsoever* to do what is right, but only that such a disposition as we have to do what is right is always overcome by other desires when it comes into conflict with them, except by the grace of God, then even its proponents can accept (7) as a psychological statement.

34. "Obligation and Rightness," pp. 139-41. Falk also recognizes, however, that externalism "finds some support in common usage" (p. 138).

35. E.g., A. Moore, "A Categorical Imperative?" pp. 237 f.; I discuss a similar claim by S. M. Brown, Jr., in "Natural and Inalienable Rights," *Philosophical Review,* LXIV (1955), 222 f.

36. Cf. Nowell-Smith, *Ethics,* pp. 186 ff., 261; W. S. Sellars, "Obligation and Motivation," in *Readings in Ethical Theory,* p. 516; H. D. Aiken, "Emotive Meanings and Ethical Terms," *Journal of Philosophy,* XLI (1944), 461 ff.; P. B. Rice, *On the Knowledge of Good and Evil* (New York: Random House, 1955), pp. 108 ff., 113, 231 f.

37. *The Right and the Good,* p. 90.

38. Nowell-Smith, *Ethics,* p. 199 (the phrase "contextually implies" is owed to Nowell-Smith); Aiken, "Emotive Meanings and Ethical Terms," pp. 461 ff.

39. Cf. Nowell-Smith, *Ethics,* pp. 146, 152, 178, 261. Note: "I *ought* implies I *shall*" is much stronger than "I *ought* implies I *feel some disposition to*," and an internalist need not hold the former.

40. *Ibid.,* pp. 261-63, 267 f.

41. It seems to me also to refute *egoistic* forms of internalism.

42. In "The Naturalistic Fallacy," *Mind,* N.S. XLVIII (1939), 464-77 (Essay 1 in this collection), I made a similar point about the issue between naturalism and nonnaturalism, but I then had rather simple-minded views about an appeal to "inspection" which was to decide it.

43. " 'Ought' and Motivation."

44. In "Morals without Faith," Falk distinguished four senses of "should" or "ought," one "moral" but all "internal."

45. Suggestions of such "macroscopic" considerations as I describe here may be found in Nowell-Smith, *Ethics,* chap. i and p. 267; C. L. Stevenson, "The Emotive Conception of Ethics and Its Cognitive Implications," *Philosophical Review,* L

(1950), 294 f.; H. D. Aiken, "A Pluralistic Analysis of the Ethical 'Ought' " and "The Authority of Moral Judgments"; and in two less technical works: W. T. Stace, *The Destiny of Western Man* (New York: Reynal & Hitchcock, 1942), and Erich Fromm, *Man for Himself* (New York: Rinehart & Co., 1947). In fact, Field, *Moral Theory*, pp. 51, 52, 56 f., broaches the line of argument sketched in this last section, but in a very incomplete way. Such a macroscopic line of reasoning must also be in W. S. Sellars' mind in "Obligation and Motivation," note 36, as a support for his identification of moral obligation with a certain kind of motivation, though he appears to expound only this conclusion without the supporting argumentation.

7: LOVE AND PRINCIPLE IN CHRISTIAN ETHICS

1. *Morals and Revelation* (New York, 1951), p. 14. In writing this Lewis had in mind the work of the intuitionists before World War II, but the remark holds equally well if one has in mind the work of the non-intuitionists after the war.
2. By "normative ethics" I mean the endeavor to propound and defend ethical judgments, rules, or standards; by "metaethics" I mean a theory about the meaning or nature of such rules and principles or about the method and possibility of justifying them.
3. See von Hildebrand, *True Morality and its Counterfeits* (New York, 1955). The quotation is from p. 135.
4. See C. H. Dodd, *Gospel and Law* (London, 1951), p. 42.
5. There is, for instance, the question of the relation of the love of God to the love of neighbor and mankind (or to the promotion of the general welfare).
6. When I say a theologian may hold a certain position, I mean that it is logically open to him, not that he can hold it and be orthodox.
7. *What I Believe* (London, 1925), Ch. II.
8. G. F. Thomas, *Christian Ethics and Moral Philosophy* (New York, 1955), pp. 381-388.
9. Here and in connection with this entire section, see J. Rawls, "Two Concepts of Rules," *Philosophical Review*, 64 (1955), 3-32; J. D. Mabbott, "Moral Rules," *Proceedings of the British Academy*, XXXIX (1953), 97-118; J. J. C. Smart, "Extreme and Restricted Utilitarianism," *Philosophical Quarterly*, 6 (1956); R. B. Brandt, *Ethical Theory* (New York, 1959), Ch. 15.
10. Baton Rouge, 1958. What Sittler means by "structure" here is hard to make out; as he represents it, Christian ethics has almost none. But he is both for and against principles, and this may mean that he is trying to be a modified act-agapist (or perhaps act-fideist, since he stresses faith rather than love). On the other hand, he may be trying, confusedly, to state one of the forms of rule agapism or even mixed agapism yet to be described.
11. See *War and the Christian Conscience* (New York, 1961), p. 14.
12. A parallel question may be asked in the case of rule-utilitarianism.
13. *Op. cit.*, pp. 119-133.
14. *Utilitarianism*, near the end.
15. Especially, *An Interpretation of Christian Ethics* (New York, 1935), Ch. VII; *Moral Man and Immoral Society* (New York, 1932), Ch. II.
16. One who holds this view may also be an agapist in the sense of holding that the *motive* for fulfilling the moral law is or should be love.
17. See, e.g., Kierkegaard's, *Three Stages on Life's Way;* Brunner as quoted by

H. D. Lewis, *op. cit.*, p. 18. On Brunner see also N. H. G. Robinson, *Christ and Conscience* (New York, 1956), pp. 72ff.

18. See *The Right and the Good* (London, 1930). Ross is an intuitionist, but one need not take an intuitionist view of "independent principles."

19. Pp. 91-92.

20. See Tillich, *Love, Power, and Justice* (New York, 1954), pp. 76-77; Reinhold Niebuhr, *The Nature and Destiny of Man* (New York, 1941), Vol I, Ch. X; H. R. Niebuhr, "The Center of Value," in *Moral Principles of Action,* edited by R. Anshen (New York, 1952).

21. *An Interpretation of Christian Ethics,* p. 51.

22. For (a) see *ibid.,* pp. 46, 49.

23. *Op. cit.,* p. 387.

24. See *A Short Introduction to Moral Theology* (London, 1956), Ch. I. Dewar does not go on to show just how they are related to the "law of love," but he seems to be holding a mixed theory, for he speaks of "natural law" as well as "divine law." C. H. Dodd in *Gospel and Law* also appeals directly to revelation to show that Christian ethics includes certain "ethical precepts."

25. I am not arguing here that moral philosophy is "omnicompetent" or even "sufficient."

26. For parts of the story see my "Public Education and the Good Life," *Harvard Educational Review* (Fall Issue, 1961).

8: SOME BELIEFS ABOUT JUSTICE

1. See W. K. Frankena, "The Concept of Social Justice," in R. B. Brandt (ed.), *Social Justice* (Englewood Cliffs, N.J., 1962); W. K. Frankena, *Ethics* (Englewood Cliffs, N.J., 1963), ch. 3.

2. Cf. J. S. Mill, *Utilitarianism,* Ch. V.

3. *The Idea of Justice and the Problem of Argument* (London, 1963), pp. 15-16.

4. *Ibid.,* pp. 27-28.

5. Cf. *ibid.,* p. 11. But see also pp. ix-x.

6. *Op. cit.,* near end of Ch. I.

7. See *Nicomachean Ethics,* Bk. V; *Politics,* Bk. III, Ch. IX, XII, XIII.

8. See S. I. Benn and R. S. Peters, *Social Principles and the Democratic State* (London, 1959), pp. 108-111.

9. Matt. 13:12.

10. W. D. Ross, *The Right and the Good* (Oxford, 1930), pp. 135-138.

11. Cf. *Ethics,* p. 40.

12. *Op. cit.,* p. 109.

13. *Ibid.,* pp. 110-111; cf. M. Ginsberg, *On Justice in Society* (Pelican Books, 1965), p. 79.

14. *Op. Cit.,* p. 86. For the point I am borrowing, see pp. 79-87. Cf. J. N. Findlay, *Language, Mind and Value* (London, 1963), p. 250.

15. Jean Piaget, *The Moral Judgment of the Child* (New York, 1948). Perelman refers to Piaget's *Apprentissage et connaissance,* p. 42.

16. Meritarians have a corresponding question: why is justice, conceived as treating people according to their merits, right? They too can give either deontological or utilitarian answers.

17. Mill, *op. cit.,* opening sentence of Ch. IV.

18. Matthew Arnold, "To a Friend."

9: ON SAYING THE ETHICAL THING

1. H. D. Aiken, *Reason and Conduct* (New York, 1962), p. 22.
2. I. Kant, *The Doctrine of Virtue* (New York and London, 1964), pp. 91-92.
3. See D. F. Pears, et. al., *The Revolution in Philosophy* (London and New York, 1956), p. 107.
4. See *The Varieties of Goodness* (London, 1963), pp. 3-6.
5. *The Concise Encyclopedia of Western Philosophy and Philosophers*, ed. by J. O. Urmson (London, 1960), p. 139.
6. "The Emotive Theory of Ethics," *Proc. Arist. Soc., Supp. Vol. XXII* (1948), pp. 79-106.
7. See *Rationalism in Politics* (London, 1962), pp. 197ff, 327f.
8. See J. L. Austin, *How to Do Things With Words* (Oxford, 1962), p. 150. His "verdictives" probably combine Voices B and C.
9. The same will, of course, be true of the metaphysical or theological definist.
10. Cf., e.g., P. W. Taylor, *Normative Discourse* (Englewood Cliffs, N.J., 1961), pp. 257-258.
11. S. C. Pepper, *The Sources of Value* (Berkeley and Los Angeles, 1958), pp. 689-690. Cf., p. 269. Pepper's metaethics is really normative in my sense, even though he calls his definitions of ethical terms "descriptive."
12. Cf., Hare, *The Language of Morals* (Oxford, 1952), pp. 29-30; P. H. Nowell-Smith, *Ethics* (London, 1954), pp. 36-43; Carl Wellman, *The Language of Ethics* (Cambridge, Mass., 1961), pp. 81-87.
13. A. Sesonske, *Value and Obligation* (Berkeley and Los Angeles, 1957), p. 16.
14. H. D. Aiken, *op. cit.,* pp. 21-23.
15. *Theory of Knowledge* (Englewood Cliffs, N.J., 1966), p. 60.
16. Cf. *op. cit.,* Ch. X.
17. "Goading and Guiding," *Mind,* LXII (1953). Reprinted in R. Ekman, *Readings in the Problems of Ethics* (New York, 1965). See pp. 226-227.
18. Part of it, perhaps, would be the contention that, if we cast out Voice C, then Voice B will enter and dwell in its place, so that our last state will be worse than our first.
19. I do not mean to deny that sentences like "He is a good man" may have *both* descriptive and evaluative meaning, as Hare thinks (*op. cit.,* pp. 24ff.). But, if they do, then they claim rationality *both* for a belief and for something else.
20. *Op. cit.,* preface, pp. 107-114, 299 ff.
21. Cf., J. Xenakis, "A Mistaken Distinction in Ethical Theory," *Philosophical Studies,* VIII (1957), pp. 69-71.
22. In short, it may be any one of Pepper's "selective systems," *op. cit.,* pp. 663, 673.
23. For such a special kind of naturalism, see R. G. Turnbull, "Imperatives, Logic, and Moral Obligation," *Philosophy of Science,* 27 (1960), pp. 374-390.
24. Cf., C. J. Friedrich (ed.), *Authority* (Cambridge, Mass., 1958), pp. 81-112.
25. Rostand, E., *Cyrano de Bergerac.*

10: THE CONCEPT OF MORALITY

1. W. D. Falk, "Morality, Self, and Others," in H.-N. Castañeda and G. Nakhnikian, eds., *Morality and the Language of Conduct* (Detroit: Wayne State, 1963), pp. 25-67; page references will appear in parentheses in the text.

2. In the *University of Colorado Publications in Philosophy*. Compare also an earlier essay, "Recent Conceptions of Morality," in Castañeda and Nakhnikian, pp. 1-24.

3. Falk, *op. cit.*, pp. 30, 53; R. M. Hare, *Freedom and Reason* (New York: Oxford, 1963), p. 147.

4. J. Kemp, *Reason, Action and Morality* (New York: Humanities, 1964), p. 196.

5. Compare, e.g., the position of R. G. Olson, *The Morality of Self-Interest* (New York: Harcourt, 1965).

6. A. McIntyre, "What Morality Is Not," *Philosophy* 32, no. 123 (October 1957): 325-335; cf. my "MacIntyre on Defining Morality," *ibid.*, 33, no. 125 (April 1958): 158-162. H. D. Aiken makes a similar use of the argument, "The Concept of Moral Objectivity," in Castañeda and Nakhnikian, pp. 69-105.

7. Falk, *op. cit.*, pp. 33-38. I think Aiken would agree; see *op. cit.*

11: 'OUGHT' AND 'IS' ONCE MORE

1. John Dewey, *The Quest for Certainty* (1929), p. 255.

2. See *Summa Theologica*, I-II, Quest. 94, art. 2, or *Basic Writings of Saint Thomas Aquinas*, ed. by A. C. Pegis (1945), II, p. 774.

3. "Ultimate Principles and Ethical Egoism," *Australasian Journal of Philosophy*, 35 (1957), p. 111.

4. Throughout this paper I take Oughts to include judgments about what is desirable, good, or valuable as well as judgments about what is right or obligatory.

5. *Ethics*, Bk. IV, Prop. xxviii; Bk. V, Prop. xxv.

6. *Loc. cit.*

7. Here cf. my *Ethics* (1963), pp. 80-85.

8. *Utilitarianism*, near end of Ch. I.

9. My interpretation of Epicurus and Mill in "The Naturalistic Fallacy," *Mind* XLVIII (1939) (Essay 1 of this collection), was simply mistaken, as was my interpretation of Hume. For Mill's own rejection of such an interpretation, see *loc. cit.* and the opening of Ch. IV.

10. "Not logical" does not mean or imply "illogical"; it includes what is "neither logical nor illogical."

11. Cf. G. H. von Wright, "Practical Inference," *Philosophical Review, LXXII* (1963), pp. 159-179, and Max Black's comments in "The Gap between 'Is' and 'Should'," *ibid., LXXVIII* (1964), pp. 170 f. Black's own view in this article is very close to the view I am proposing here, but, I think, somewhat less clear. About such views R. M. Hare remarks ("The Promising Game" *Revue Internationale de Philosophie, 70* (1964), p. 398n) that they set a lower "moral tone" than that of John Searle. In reply I am tempted to quote the old song: "You take the high road, and I'll take the low road." But, of course, the real point is that not all "shoulds" and "oughts" are moral, and a general theory, which Searle's is not, must apply to them all. For other indications of my general theory see *op. cit.*, pp. 94-96, and "On Saying the Ethical Thing," *Proc. and Addresses of the American Philosophical Association,* XXXIX (1966), 21-42.

12. *Loc. cit.*

13. Philippa Foot, "Moral Arguments," *Mind* LXVII (1958), 502-513.

14. *Reason and Conduct* (1962), p. 62.

15. *Ibid.*, pp. 63f.

16. In the case of institutional Oughts such as Searle discusses in "How to Derive 'Ought' from 'Is'," *Phil. Rev.*, 73 (1964), 43-58, I would say that the inference, if justified at all, is mediated by a commitment to the institution in question and its rules. Cf. A. I. Melden, *Rights and Right Conduct* (1959) and "Reasons for Action and Matters of Fact," *Proc. and Add. of Am. Philos. Assoc.*, XXXV (1961), 45-60; P. Foot, *Theories of Ethics* (1967), pp. 11f; H. Ofstad and L. Bergstrom, "A note on Searle's Derivation of 'Ought' from 'Is'," *Inquiry*, 8 (1965), pp. 309-314.

17. This does not necessarily imply that "ought" and "good" are definable in "non-ethical" terms.

18. Cf. Plato's *Modern Enemies and the Theory of Natural Law* (1953).

19. Cf. J. W. Smith, "Impossibility and Morals," *Mind*, LXX (1961).

12: PRICHARD AND THE ETHICS OF VIRTUE

1. The discussion summarized in this section is found in *Moral Obligation* (New York: Oxford Univ. Press, 1950), pp. 11-14. All references to Prichard will be to this volume, hereinafter cited as MO.

2. Cf. Maurice Mandelbaum, *The Phenomenology of Moral Experience* (Glencoe: Free Press, 1955), pp. 142-5. Hereinafter cited as PME.

3. P. 12n. Prichard's remark about Shakespeare is nicely illustrated by the case of the Trojans in *Troilus and Cressida*. It is nearly reflected in a comment by T. S. Eliot: ". . . we kick against those [like Dante] who wish to guide us, and insist on being guided by those [like Shakespeare] who only aim to show us a vision, a dream if you like, which is beyond good and evil in the common sense." "Introduction" to G. W. Knight, *The Wheel of Fire* (New York: Meridian Books, 1957), p. xx.

4. PME, pp. 45, 95.

5. MO, p. 13.

6. MO, p. 13.

7. MO, p. 13.

8. See "Social Morality and Individual Ideal," *Philosophy* (1961), reprinted in Ian Ramsey (ed.), *Christian Ethics and Contemporary Philosophy*, pp. 280-98.

9. MO, p. 12.

10. See MO, pp. 13-14.

11. MO, p. 13.

12. MO, pp. 5-6.

13. Cf. "That was a good deed."

14. Cf. F. E. Brouwer, "A Restricted Motive Theory of Ethics," in A. C. Plantinga (ed.), *Faith and Philosophy* (1964), pp. 181-200.

15. John Gower, *Confessio amantis*, Penguin Classics (1963) Bk. VIII, line 2925. This book is a good literary example of an ethics of virtue and vice.

16. MO, p. 13.

17. MO, pp. 6-7.

18. Cf. *Types of Ethical Theory* (Oxford: The Clarendon Press, 1901), 3rd ed.; vol. II, p. 270.

19. MO, p. 10n.

20. MO, p. 13.

21. Cf. my *Ethics* (Englewood Cliffs, N.J.: Prentice Hall, 1963), pp. 49, 52-54.

14: "THE PRINCIPLES OF MORALITY"

1. *Realms of Value* (1954), p. 86.
2. For an exposition of the distinction, see J. Kemp, *Reason, Action and Morality* (1964), pp. 183ff. It is half ignored and half recognized by J. H. Hartland-Swann, *An Analysis of Morals* (1960), pp. 62-67. Recognition of it would also have helped in Kurt Baier's discussion in *The Moral Point of View* (rev. ed., 1965) pp. 82ff. Among other things, it is important to recognize that one may agree that a certain code or principle is a moral one in the "relative" sense and deny that it is one in the "absolute" sense.
3. *Problems of Moral Philosophy* (1967), p. 8.
4. See "Recent Conceptions of Morality," *Morality and the Language of Conduct*, ed. by H. Castaneda and G. Nakhnikian (1963); 'The Concept of Morality," two versions, one reprinted in G. Wallace and A. D. M. Walker (eds.), *The Definition of Morality* (1970) and the other in K. Pahel and M. Schiller (eds.), *Readings in Contemporary Ethical Theory* (1970). See also "MacIntyre on Defining Morality," reprinted in Wallace and Walker.
5. Cf. R. F. Atkinson, *Conduct: an Introduction to Moral Philosophy* (1969), pp. 52f.
6. Cf. H. L. A. Hart, *The Concept of Law* (1961), pp. 55f, 86f, 99; J. D. Urmson, *The Emotive Theory of Ethics* (1968), pp. 107f.
7. Cf. Urmson, *op. cit.*, pp. 52ff, on "I approve of . . . ."
8. Cf. A. J. Ayer, *Language Truth and Logic* (1936), Ch. VI; C. L. Stevenson, *Ethics and Language* (1944). For criticism see, e.g., Urmson, *op. cit.*
9. "Goading and Guiding," reprinted in R. Ekman (ed.), *Readings in the Problems of Ethics* (1965).
10. Cf. C. Wellman, *The Language of Ethics* (1961), pp. 258ff, 263ff; Urmson, *op. cit.*, pp. 56, 58, 63.
11. Cf. Wellman, *loc. cit.*
12. "Social Morality and Individual Ideal," reprinted in I. Ramsey (ed.), *Christian Ethics and Contemporary Philosophy* (1966), pp. 284ff.
13. *Op. cit.*, pp. 112ff. What he here means by "true morality" is somewhat different, something more like "true morality" in sense (b). Note: *here* Baier comes close to recognizing the distinction between "relative" and "absolute" senses of "morality."
14. See Hartland-Swann, *op. cit.*, p. 62.
15. Cf. Linton, "Universal Ethical Principles," in R. Anshen (ed.), *Moral Principles* (1952); C. S. Lewis, *The Abolition of Man* (1947).
16. *Philosophy of Language* (1964), p. 41.
17. *Op. cit.*, pp. 90f.
18. It is in this sense that I take myself to be asserting that the principles of benevolence and justice are the basic principles of morality, *Ethics* (1963), pp. 35-42. Cf. pp. 95f.
19. See article to be cited in next note.
20. In Castaneda and Nakhnikian, *op. cit.;* reprinted in his own *Reason and Conduct* (1962). I here use the former.
21. Cf. "Ethical Absolutism and the Ideal Observer," *Philosophy and Phenomenological Research*, XIII (1952).
22. *Loc. cit.*, pp. 87-94.
23. Cf. Brandt, "The Definition of an 'Ideal Observer' Theory in Ethics," *Phil.*

and Phen. Research, XV (1955), 407-423, with subsequent reply by Firth and rejoinder by Brandt.

24. Pp. 74, 79, 95.

25. Pp. 96-100.

26. See note 24.

27. Cf. pp. 80, 85. I take the open question argument to be constantly in Aiken's mind in this essay.

28. Aiken does recognize the difference between the two opposites of "moral" in one reference to the open question, p. 81. But if his "autonomist" can use this point, so can an "objectivist" like myself.

29. In this connection, cf. R. L. Mouw, "The Status of God's Moral Judgments," *Canadian Journal of Theology,* XVI (1970), pp. 61-66.

15: ON DEFINING MORAL JUDGMENTS, PRINCIPLES, AND CODES

1. On these views, see also A. M. Quinton, "The Bounds of Morality," in H. E. Kiefer and M. K. Munitz (eds.), *Ethics and Social Justice,* State University of New York Press, Albany, 1970, pp. 122-141; and G. J. Warnock, *Contemporary Moral Philosophy,* Macmillan and Co., London, 1967, pp. 52-61. In general in connection with the topic of this paper, see G. Wallace and A. D. M. Walker (eds.), *The Definition of Morality,* Methuen and Co., London, 1970; and my articles referred to below.

2. For this point, see W. P. Alston, "Moral Attitudes and Moral Judgments," *Nous,* II, 1968, pp. 1-23. My paper has been much influenced by his article.

3. See, e.g., K. Baier, *The Moral Point of View,* Random House, New York, 1965, pp. 90-109; P. W. Taylor, *Normative Discourse,* Prentice-Hall, Englewood Cliffs, N. J., 1961, *passim;* J. O. Urmson, *The Emotive Theory of Ethics,* Hutchinson University Library, London, 1968, pp. 98-116.

4. More humanistic thinkers might substitute facts about the will of society. Then a similar remark would apply.

5. See D. D. Raphael (ed.), *The British Moralists,* Oxford at the Clarendon Press, 1969, Vol. I, p. 411.

6. Cf. e.g. Quinton and Warnock, *op. cit.*

7. *The Right and the Good,* Oxford at the Clarendon Press, 1930, p. 162.

8. The formula proposed also raises the question whether there are *moral* duties relating to oneself alone, which cannot be treated here.

9. *Op. cit.,* p. 16.

10. On this problem in general, see my "Ought and Is Once More," *Man and World,* 2, 1969, pp. 515-533.

11. See "Moral Arguments," in J. J. Thomson and G. Dworkin (eds.), *Ethics,* Harper and Row, New York, 1968, p. 17.

12. *Loc. cit.,* p. 16.

13. I assume that the MPV includes a disposition to universalize since it entails making normative judgments, and, for the same reason, that it is not identical with "reason," because then it must include conation.

14. "On Philosophical Neutrality," *Metaphilosophy,* I, 1970, p. 36.

15. I have dealt with the subject of this paper in several earlier articles. Two of these are in Wallace and Walker, *op. cit.* Others are "Recent Conceptions of Morality," in G. Nakhnikian and H. Castaneda (eds.), *Morality and the Language of*

Conduct, Wayne State University Press, Detroit, 1963, pp. 1-24; and "The Concept of Morality," *Journal of Philosophy,* LXIII, 1966, pp. 688-696; Essay 10 in this collection.

16: SIDGWICK AND THE DUALISM OF PRACTICAL REASON

1. Henry Sidgwick, *The Methods of Ethics,* London: Macmillan and Co.. Ltd., 7th edition, 1907, p. 4. All references to ME will be to this edition unless otherwise indicated.
2. ME, p. 1.
3. ME, pp. 8, 77n.
4. ME, pp. 25f.
5. ME, pp. 25, 32.
6. ME, pp. 25, 36, 37.
7. ME, p. 34n. Cf. 508.
8. ME, p. 119.
9. ME, p. xx.
10. "The Two Environments," *Beyond Culture,* Penguin Books, Ltd., 1967, pp. 183-202.
11. ME, pp. xvi.
12. ME, p. 5.
13. ME, p. 6.
14. ME, pp. 3, 96.
15. ME, pp. xviif, 386f.
16. ME, pp. 416f, 432.
17. ME, p. 386n.
18. ME, p. xviii.
19. ME, pp. xvi, xx.
20. ME, p. 405.
21. ME, pp. 404, 404n. For the reference to Rashdall see Sidgwick, "Some Fundamental Ethical Controversies," *Mind,* XIV (1889), pp. 486f.
22. ME, p. 508.
23. ME, pp. 341, 6.
24. For Broad's comments see *Five Types of Ethical Theory,* pp. 245, 253.
25. ME, pp. xx, 508.
26. ME, p. 508. For the reference to von Gizycki see the article cited in note 21. He was a hedonist and a utilitarian.
27. Quoted by D. G. James, *Henry Sidgwick,* London: Oxford University Press, 1970, p. 38.
28. See "The Concept of Morality," *The Journal of Philosophy,* LXIII (1966). Reprinted in *Readings in Contemporary Ethical Theory,* ed. by K. Pahel and M. Schiller, Englewood Cliffs, N. J.: Prentice-Hall, Inc., 1970, pp. 391-398.
29. ME, p. 78.
30. ME, pp. 5, 120.
31. ME, pp. 111f.
32. ME, p. 11.
33. ME, pp. 378, 392.
34. For Sidgwick's discussion of perfectionism, see ME, pp. 8f, 78ff, 115, 391-407. Incidentally, perfectionism of the sort Sidgwick was attacking, was maintained in two articles in *Mind,* V (1880), viz. "Perfection as an Ethical End" by

Thomas Thornely and Norman Pearson's reply. Better known perfectionists were Aristotle, Wolff, and Friedrich Paulsen.

35. See *Philosophy,* XLVII (1972), pp. 206-228.

36. It may retain the universalizability requirement.

37. *Op. cit.*

38. See in this connection Ms. Midgley's remarks, *op. cit.,* pp. 226f. Sidgwick touches on this question, ME, pp. 170-174.

39. *Autobiography of Bertrand Russell, 1872-1914,* London: George Allen and Unwin, 1967, pp. 146f.

40. ME, p. 508.

41. *Op. cit.,* p. 220.

17: CONCLUDING MORE OR LESS PHILOSOPHICAL POSTSCRIPT

1. See his "Moral and Non-Moral Values," *Mind,* 44 (1935).

2. For Moore's reply see P. A. Schilpp (ed.), *The Philosophy of G. E. Moore* (Evanston and Chicago: Northwestern University Press, 1942).

3. For these and other papers referred to in this postscript, but not reprinted here, see the bibliography included in this volume.

4. See e.g., note 42, "Obligation and Motivation in Recent Moral Philosophy."

5. See "Hutcheson's Moral Sense Theory," *Journal of the History of Ideas,* 16 (1955).

6. See "Ethics, 1949-1955," in R. Klibansky (ed.), *Philosophy in the Mid-Century* (Florence: Nuova Italia, 1958), pp. 67f.

7. See second edition (1973), pp. 100f.

8. So is my reply to MacIntyre, referred to earlier.

9. *Rationalism in Politics* (London: Methuen and Co., 1962), p. 62.

Bibliography of the Published Work of W. K. Frankena

1939   "The Naturalistic Fallacy." *Mind* 48 (October):464-477. [Reprinted in several anthologies.]

1942   "Obligation and Value in the Ethics of G. E. Moore." Pp. 91-110 in P. A. Schilpp (ed.), *The Philosophy of G. E. Moore.* LaSalle, Ill.: Open Court Publishing Co.

1943   "Our Belief in Reason." *Papers of the Michigan Academy of Science, Arts and Letters* 19:571-586.

1948a   "Ewing's Case Against Naturalistic Theories of Value." *Philosophical Review* 57:481-492.

1948b   Review of A. C. Ewing, *The Definition of Good. Philosophical Review* 57/6 (November):605-607.

1949a   Review of Ray Lepley (ed.), *Value: A Cooperative Enquiry.* Philosophy and Phenomenological Research, 10:99-101.

1949b   Review of Stephen C. Pepper, *A Digest of Purposive Values. Philosophy and Phenomenological Research* 10/1 (September):130-132.

1950a   "Arguments for Non-Naturalism About Intrinsic Value." *Philosophical Studies* 1/4 (June):56-60.

1950b   "Obligation and Ability." Pp. 157-175 in Max Black (ed.), *Philosophical Analysis.* Ithaca, N. Y.: Cornell University Press.

1950c   Review of A. N. Prior, *Logic and the Basis of Ethics. Philosophical Review* 59/4 (October):554-556.

1951   "Moral Philosophy at Mid-Century." *Philosophical Review* 60/1 (January):44-55. [Reprinted in Rosalind Ekman (ed.), *Readings in the Problems of Ethics.*]

1952   "The Concept of Universal Human Rights." Pp. 189-207 in *Science, Language and Human Rights.* Volume I, Symposia, Eastern Division, American Philosophical Association.

1953   Review of E. W. Hall, *What is Value? Philosophy and Phenomenological Research* 14:253-258.

1954   "Sellars' Theory of Valuation." *Philosophy and Phenomenological Research* 15:65-81.

1955a   "Hutcheson's Moral Sense Theory." *Journal of the History of Ideas* 16/3 (June):356-375.

1955b   "Natural and Inalienable Rights." *Philosophical Review* 64/2 (April):212-232.

1956   "Towards a Philosophy of the Philosophy of Education." *Harvard Educational Review* 26:94-98.

1957a   "Ethical Naturalism Renovated." *Review of Metaphysics* 10/3 (March):457-473.

1957b   "Moral Philosophy in America." Pp. 348-360 in Vergilius Ferm (ed.), *Encyclopedia of Morals*. New York: Philosophical Library, Inc.

1957c   "Henry Sidgwick." Pp. 534-544 in Ferm (ed.), *Encyclopedia of Morals*.

1957d   "Sir (William) David Ross." Pp. 504-511 in Ferm (ed.), *Encyclopedia of Morals*.

1957e   Preface to D. H. Parker, *The Philosophy of Value*. Ann Arbor: University of Michigan Press.

1957f   Review of C. I. Lewis, *The Ground and Nature of the Right*. *Philosophical Review* 66/3 (July):398-402.

1958a   "Ethics, 1949-1955." Vol. III, pp. 42-77 in R. Klibansky (ed.), *Philosophy in the Mid-Century: A Survey*. Florence: Nuova Italia.

1958b   "MacIntyre on Defining Morality." *Philosophy* 33 (April):158-162.

1958c   "Obligation and Motivation in Recent Moral Philosophy." Pp. 40-81 in A. I. Melden (ed.), *Essays in Moral Philosophy*. Seattle: University of Washington Press.

1958d   "A Point of View for the Future." Pp. 295-309 in E. A. Walter (ed.), *Religion and the State University*. Ann Arbor: University of Michigan Press.

1958e   "Some Aspects of Language" and " 'Cognitive' and 'Non-Cognitive.' " Pp. 121-172 in Paul Henle (ed.), *Language, Thought and Culture*. Ann Arbor: University of Michigan Press.

1958f   "Toward a Philosophy of Moral Education." *Harvard Educational Review* 28:300-313. [Reprinted in several anthologies.]

1959a   "Broad's Analysis of Ethical Terms." Pp. 537-562 in P. A. Schilpp (ed.), *The Philosophy of C. D. Broad*. New York: Tudor Publishing Co.

1959b   "The Teaching of Religion: Some Guiding Principles." *Religious Education* 54/2 (March-April):108-109.

1959c   Review of C. A. Baylis, *Ethics*. *Harvard Educational Review* 29:251-253.

1960a   "Ethics in an Age of Science." Pp. 91-104 in *The Association of Princeton Alumni, Report of the Eighth Conference*.

1960b   Foreword in Jonathan Edwards, *On the Nature of True Virtue*. Ann Arbor Paperbacks. Ann Arbor: University of Michigan Press.

1961a   "Is the Philosophy of Education Intellectually Responsible?" *Proceedings of the Philosophy of Education Society* 17:36-45.

1961b   "Public Education and the Good Life." *Harvard Educational Review* 30 (Fall): 413-426. [Reprinted in several anthologies.]

1962a   "The Concept of Social Justice." Pp. 1-29 in R. B. Brandt (ed.), *Social Justice*. Englewood Cliffs, N.J.: Prentice-Hall, Inc.

1962b   Review of Carl Wellman, *The Language of Ethics*. *Journal of Philosophy* 59/11 (May 24):293-296.

1963a   *Ethics*. Englewood Cliffs, N.J.: Prentice-Hall, Inc.

1963b   "Lewis' Imperatives of Right." *Philosophical Studies* 14/1-2 (January-February):25-28.

1963c   "Recent Conceptions of Morality." Pp. 1-24 in H. N. Castaneda and G. Nakhnikian (eds.), *Morality and the Language of Conduct*. Detroit: Wayne State University Press.

1964a   "Decisionism and Separatism in Social Philosophy." Pp. 18-25 in C. J. Friedrich (ed.), *Nomos VII: Rational Decision*. New York: Atherton Press.

1964b   "Ethical Theory." Pp. 345-463 in R. Schlatter (ed.), *Philosophy*. Humanities Scholarship in America: The Princeton Studies. Englewood Cliffs, N.J.: Prentice-Hall Inc.

1964c   "C. I. Lewis on the Ground and Nature of the Right." *Journal of Philosophy* 61/17 (September 17):489-496.

1964d   "Love and Principle in Christian Ethics." Pp. 203-225 in Alvin Plantinga (ed.), *Faith and Philosophy*. Grand Rapids, Michigan: William B. Eerdmans Publishing Company.

1964e   "On Defining and Defending Natural Law." Pp. 200-209 in Sidney Hook (ed.), *Law and Philosophy*. New York: New York University Press.

1964f   "La philosophie moral contemporaine aux Etats-Unis." *Les Etudes Philosophiques* 2 (Avril-Juin):233-243.

1964g   "Three Comments on Lewis's Views on the Right and the Good." *Journal of Philosophy* 61/19 (October 15):567-570.

1965a   (Editor), *Philosophy of Education*. New York: Macmillan.

1965b   *Three Historical Philosophies of Education*. Chicago: Scott, Foresman.

1966a   "The Concept of Morality." *Journal of Philosophy* 63/21 (November 10): 688-696. [Reprinted in K. Pahel and M. Schiller (eds.), *Readings in Contemporary Ethical Theory*.]

1966b   "A Model for Analyzing a Philosophy of Education." *High School Journal* 2/1 (October): 8-13.

1966c   "On Saying the Ethical Thing." *Proceedings and Addresses of the American Philosophical Association* 39:21-42.

1966d   "Philosophical Enquiry." Pp. 243-265 (Chapter X) in John I. Goodlad (ed.), *The Changing American School*. The 65th Yearbook of the National Society for the Study of Education, Part II. Chicago: University of Chicago Press.

1966e   *Some Beliefs About Justice*. The Lindley Lecture, University of Kansas. (Delivered March 2.)

1966f   "G. H. von Wright on the Theory of Morals, Legislation and Value." *Ethics* 76/2 (January):131-136.

1966g   "J. D. Wild on Responsibility." *Philosophy and Phenomenological Research* 27/1 (September):90-96.

1966h   "Reply to Professor Wild." *Philosophy and Phenomenological Research* 27/1 (September):103.

1967a   "The Concept of Morality." *University of Colorado Studies in Philosophy* No. 3:1-22. [Reprinted in G. Wallace and A. Walker (eds.), *The Definition of Morality*. This is an earlier version of 1966a.]

1967b   "Frondizi on the Foundations of Moral Norms." Pp. 13-19 in *Proceedings of the Seventh Inter-American Congress of Philosophy*. Laval University Press.

1967c   "Value and Valuation." Vol. 8, pp. 229-232 in Paul Edwards (ed.), *The Encyclopedia of Philosophy*. New York: Macmillan and Free Press.

1968a   "Educational Values and Goals: Some Dispositions To Be Fostered." *Monist* 52 (January):1-10.

1968b   "Freedom: Responsibility and Decision." *Proceedings of the XIVth International Congress of Philosophy* 1:143-154.

1968c   "Two Notes on Representation." Pp. 49-51 in Roland Pennock (ed.), *Nomos X: Representation*. New York: Atherton Press.

1968d   "War and the New Morality." *Reformed Journal* 18:20-21.

1969a   (Ed. and Introduction, with Arnold S. Kaufman) Jonathan Edwards, *Freedom of the Will*. Library of Liberal Arts. Indianapolis and New York: Bobbs-Merrill Company, Inc.

1969b   "Ought and Is Once More." *Man and World* 2/4 (November):515-533.
1970a   "Educating for the Good Life." Pp. 17-42 in H. E. Kiefer and M. K. Munitz
         (eds.), *Perspectives in Education, Religion and the Arts*. Albany, N.Y.: State
         University of New York Press.
1970b   "A Model for Analyzing a Philosophy of Education." Pp. 15-22 in J. R.
         Martin (ed.), *Readings in the Philosophy of Education: A Study of the
         Curriculum*. Boston: Allyn and Bacon. [An expanded version of 1966b.]
1970c   "Prichard and the Ethics of Virtue." *Monist* 54/1 (January):1-17.
1970d   "The Principles and Categories of Morality." Pp. 93-106 in J. E. Smith (ed.),
         Contemporary American Philosophy, Second Series. London: Allen and
         Unwin.
1971a   "Moral Education." Vol. 6, pp. 394-398 in L. C. Deighton (ed.), *The
         Encyclopedia of Education*. New York: Macmillan and Free Press.
1971b   "Philosophy of Education." Vol. 7, pp. 101-104 in L. C. Deighton (ed.), *The
         Encyclopedia of Education*. New York: Macmillan and Free Press.
1973a   "The Concept of Education Today." Pp. 19-32 in J. F. Doyle (ed.), *Educa-
         tional Judgments*. London: Routledge and Kegan Paul.
1973b   "Education." Vol. 2, pp. 71-85 in P. P. Wiener (ed.), *Dictionary of the
         History of Ideas*. New York: Charles Scribner's Sons.
1973c   *Ethics*. Second edition. Englewood Cliffs, N.J.: Prentice-Hall, Inc.
1973d   "The Ethics of Love Conceived as an Ethics of Virtue." *Journal of Religious
         Ethics* 1 (Fall):21-36.
1973e   "Is Morality Logically Dependent on Religion?" Pp. 195-317 in Gene Outka
         and John P. Reeder (eds.), *Religion and Morality*. Garden City, N.Y.:
         Anchor Books.
1973f   "On Defining Moral Judgments, Principles, and Codes." *Etycka* 11:45-56
         [in Polish].
1973g   "The Principles of Morality." Pp. 43-76 in C. L. Carter (ed.), *Skepticism and
         Moral Principles*. Evanston, Illinois: New University Press.
1973h   "Under What Net?" *Philosophy* 48:319-326.
1974a   (Ed., with John T. Granrose), *Introductory Readings in Ethics*. Englewood
         Cliffs, N.J.: Prentice-Hall, Inc.
1974b   "The Philosopher's Attack on Morality." *Philosophy* 49:345-356.
1974c   "Sidgwick and the Dualism of Practical Reason." *Monist* 58:449-467.
1975a   "Spinoza's 'New Morality': Notes on Book IV." Pp. 85-100 in Eugene
         Freeman and Maurice Mandelbaum (eds.), *Spinoza; Essays and Interpreta-
         tion*. La Salle, Illinois: Open Court.
1975b   "Conversations with Carney and Hauerwas" *Journal of Religious Ethics*
         3/1: 45-62. Also includes complete bibliography of Frankena's writings.

                                   FORTHCOMING

a   "The Ethics of Respect for Life." Thalheimer Lecture, Johns Hopkins Uni-
         versity, 1975. To be published by the Johns Hopkins University Press.
b   "McCormick and the Traditional Distinction." To be published in Paul
         Ramsey (ed.), *Essays on Ambiguity in Moral Choice*.
c   *Three Questions about Morality*. The Carus Lectures for 1974. To be pub-
         lished by Open Court.
d   "G. H. von Wright on the Nature of Morality." To be published in P. A.
         Schilpp (ed.), *The Philosophy of G. H. von Wright*.

e   "Moral Philosophy and World Hunger." To appear in *World Hunger and Moral Obligation*, ed. by Will Aiken and Hugh LaFollette.

f   "Moral Authority, Moral Autonomy, and Moral Education." To appear in *Moral Education and Community Control*, ed. by Mark Sheldon.

Index

Abraham, L., 9
Agapism, 78 ff.; mixed, 84 f.; pure, 80 f.
Aiken, H. D., 58-59, 61, 119, 126, 143
   ff., 175-82
Alston, W. P., 173, 188
Antinomian. *See* Situationism
Aquinas, Saint Thomas, 87, 135, 137,
   145-46
Aristophanes, 163
Aristotle, 25, 50, 93, 95 f., 97 ff., 101,
   102, 128, 131, 149, 155-56, 159, 163,
   165
Arnold, M., 74
Attitudes: and beliefs, 118, 141; and
   judgments of obligation, 67, 116 ff.,
   120-24, 141, 145-46, 185; and value,
   15-23
Augustine, Saint, 81, 153, 155, 208
Austin, J. L., 112, 147, 171
Autonomy, 63, 163, 165
Ayer, A. J., viii, x, 37-38, 211

Baier, K., 126, 172, 174, 214, 216
Beneficence, principle of, 77, 93, 213
Benn, S., 103
Bentham, J., 106
Berdyaev, N., 38
Bergson, H., 84
Blake, R. M., 50, 59, 63
Blindness, moral or conceptual, 9-11
Brandt, R. B., ix, 176
Broad, C. D., 4, 26, 33-34, 36, 199 f.,
   209, 211
Brunner, E., 38, 81, 84, 87, 154, 155
Butler, J., 7, 57, 131, 151, 203, 206

Calvinism, 209
Campbell, C. A., 22, 209
Can Ideals and Norms Be Justified?
   (Garnett), 86
Carnap, R., 7
Carritt, E. F., 22, 35
Catholic philosophy and theology, 38
Chisholm, R., 117
Christian ethics, Ch. 7 *passim*; and virtue,
   155, 214, 216
Clarke, M. E., 2, 34-35
Clarke, S., 59, 84
Conscience, 68, 179 f.
Conscience and Christ (Rashdall), 80
Consciousness, moral, 72, 80
Cudworth, R., 168

Definism, 111-18, 138
Definist fallacy, 6 ff.
Definition of Good, The (Ewing), 24
Deontological views, 13, 77, 79, 85, 105,
   213
Descartes, R., 88
Descriptivist, 58
Dewar, L., 90
Dewey, J., 37, 39, 131, 133
Duty: ethics of, and virtue, Ch. 12 *passim;*
   prima facie, 14, 20-21; and self-
   interest, 195-207

Education, 212; methods, 166 f.; moral,
   161-67, 216
Egoism: ethical, 86, 129, 188, 195;
   psychological, 204; and utility and